MARKET
NEUTRAL

I N V E S T I N G

marketneutralstrategy. com

(P 247)

Advance Praise for *Market Neutral Investing*

A market neutral strategy can be a valuable tool for investors who want to shore up their portfolio's defenses. Market Neutral Investing *shows you how to build a hedged portfolio step by step. It's a good read for the do-it-yourself investor.*

—RUSS KINNEL
Director of Mutual Fund Research, Morningstar, Inc.

Writing in a clear, intelligent style so often lacking in investment primers, Mr. Stokes uses real-life examples to give readers the perspective to understand why market neutral investing can reduce risk and protect capital—in the face of the mainstream financial press that is eager to proclaim otherwise. Market Neutral Investing *provides the reader with a usable framework for stock picking and the tools to execute the strategy.*

—DANIEL T. HAYDEN
Managing Director, Client Advisory Group, Van Hedge Fund Advisors International, LLC

Market Neutral Investing *is essential reading for the individual investor and professional money manager alike. With this little known and often misunderstood approach, Eric Stokes provides a strong argument that anyone with funds to manage, on any level, can easily reduce risk and increase returns. Our own research efforts now include market neutral strategies, a direct result of Mr. Stokes' compelling research and presentation.*

—PAUL HENNEMAN
President of ValuEngine, Inc.

This is a strategy tailor-made for these interesting times we live in. Market neutral investing is probably the only proven approach to smooth over turbulent markets increasingly held to ransom by external, geopolitical events. For the small investor, Stokes brings clarity to a confusing and complex subject in an easy to read style.

—GEHAN TALWATTE
CEO, PowerInfo Ltd., London

Mr. Stokes provides great insight into the opportunities and risks of investing in today's sophisticated markets. This book is ideal for the investor looking to construct a portfolio that will perform in any market environment. Readers will learn from Mr. Stokes' well-supported ideas while enjoying his wit along the way.

—ANDREW J. PASSERI
Director, Citigroup Private Bank

MARKET NEUTRAL
INVESTING

ERIC STOKES

Dearborn™
Trade Publishing
A **Kaplan Professional** Company

This publication is designed to provide accurate and authoritative information in regard to the subject matter covered. It is sold with the understanding that the publisher is not engaged in rendering legal, accounting, or other professional service. If legal advice or other expert assistance is required, the services of a competent professional should be sought.

Vice President and Publisher: Cynthia A. Zigmund
Acquisitions Editor: Mary B. Good
Senior Project Editor: Trey Thoelcke
Interior Design: Lucy Jenkins
Cover Design: DePinto Design
Typesetting: the dotted i

Published by Dearborn Trade Publishing
A Kaplan Professional Company

Printed in the United States of America

04   05   06   10 9 8 7 6 5 4 3 2 1

Library of Congress Cataloging-in-Publication Data

Stokes, Eric, 1959-
    Market neutral investing : build consistent low-risk profits by creating your own hedged portfolio / Eric Stokes.
        p.   cm.
    Includes index.
    ISBN 0-7931-9414-8
    1. Portfolio management.   2. Hedge funds.   3. Investments.   I. Title.
HG4930.S76 2004
332.64'5—dc22

                                                                2004009568

Dearborn Trade books are available at special quantity discounts to use for sales promotions, employee premiums, or educational purposes. Please call our Special Sales Department to order or for more information at 800-621-9621, ext. 4444, e-mail trade@dearborn.com, or write to Dearborn Trade Publishing, 30 South Wacker Drive, Suite 2500, Chicago, IL 60606-7481.

Contents

1

THE CASE FOR MARKET NEUTRAL

From the time most of us were old enough to understand the word *invest,* we also began to receive a steady stream of advice about how to do it. Most people who have anything to say about the stock market can't help themselves from telling us *the* optimal way to invest our precious money.

In one sense, this book is no different because it too offers advice about investing. In another sense, this book is completely different, even radical to some readers, because its advice is so unique. In the pages that follow, you will learn about an investment approach that, while not new, has probably never been revealed to you.

Even more intriguing is the fact that some of the most successful and sophisticated money managers in the world have been using this approach for 40 years or more. Welcome to the world of equity market neutral investing.

The belief underlying market neutral investing for equities is that at any given time some stocks are priced too high and others are priced too low. Market neutral investing takes profitable advantage of this fact. Being market neutral means betting on the stocks that are priced too low by buying shares in them and, *at the same time,* betting against the stocks that are priced too high by selling their shares short. We will talk later about shorting stocks, but for now we simply note that borrowing shares and then returning them later at a lower price allows investors to profit from a decline in the price of a stock.

So while the vast majority of investment books are focused primarily on what stocks to buy, this book goes one step further. In it we develop a method for knowing what stocks are likely to rise in price and what stocks are likely to fall. Even more important, we show that by investing some money *long* and some money *short,* you can give yourself enormous advantages in the market.

If we know that at any given time some stocks are going to rise in price and others will fall, shouldn't we be able to capitalize on the fact that stock prices are constantly going in both directions? Why be limited to making a profit only when a stock goes up when everyone knows that at the same time, some other stocks will also go down? Why step into a boxing ring with one hand tied behind your back?

And as intuitive as that logic is, the best part about investing the market neutral way is that it lowers risk. For reasons that we will explore at great length, buying some shares and selling short others can make a powerful difference in how much risk investors are exposed to. Profitable investing with less risk is what most investors seek; market neutral investing holds the answer.

The Buy and Hold Theory

If you think back to your first lesson learned about investing, whether it was from your parents or a class in school, it probably went something like this: buy the stocks of large, well-known companies and hold on to them for a long time. The reason for this, and one not necessarily to be quibbled with, is that over the long haul, stocks go up. There are over 100 years of history demonstrating this fact. And if you buy stock in large, well-known companies, there's a good chance they will be around long enough for you to see the share price rise. (There may be some legitimate quibbling with that second part of the lesson.)

This buy-and-hold philosophy has continued to hold sway with at least two generations of investors. However, in the mid-1990s a new philosophy was born, and it took hold with a vengeance among a sizeable portion of the investing public.

The new way of thinking about the stock market compressed the time frame required to hold a stock and posited that the key to investment success was to buy stock in whatever company looked like it might be growing rapidly and be quick about it. What's more, don't worry about old-fashioned metrics of value; focus only on growth.

Even worse was the common practice of buying stocks that were not even growing but simply held out the promise of growth. Investors, egged on by the media and many brokerage analysts, were persuaded to buy stock in companies built on little more than an idea and a spreadsheet filled with financial projections.

Stories in the media about "day traders" began to appear, and investors who weren't buying technology stocks began to feel left behind. Millions of people began to shift their focus to this new paradigm. New measures of corporate success became the stuff of cocktail party chatter— "Did you see how many page views XYZ.com served up last month?" or "I just read an article about how SpeedNetworks Corp. is releasing a ten terabyte router that will set a new standard!" Traditional measures, like profits, or even sales, were largely ignored, dismissed as outdated and irrelevant in this new era.

Unfortunately, as we know now, the notion of investing on the basis of promised growth alone, without regard to other fundamental measures, such as cash flow or book value, proved to be woefully wrongheaded. Millions of people saw trillions of dollars evaporate after the party.

To be fair, losses stemming from the post-1990s bubble have not been as bad as many in the media now would have us believe. If you had invested $100,000 in the Nasdaq composite in January 1995, it would have been worth $266,000 by the end of 2003. That works out to a little better than 11 percent per year. So, investors who bought in to the technology craze early didn't suffer too badly (see Figure 1.1).

The reason there has been such a hue and cry about a "crash" is that from its peak, in February 2000, the Nasdaq composite index fell over 70 percent to its trough in the fall of 2002. So, the person with the worst possible timing would have seen $100,000 fall to $30,000 in the following 30 months. That works out to a loss rate of almost 30 percent per year when annualized. Imagine if the chart in Figure 1.2 reflected the value of your portfolio.

With that as the backdrop, many investors today aren't quite sure what to do. Many have returned to that earlier strategy of buy and hold.

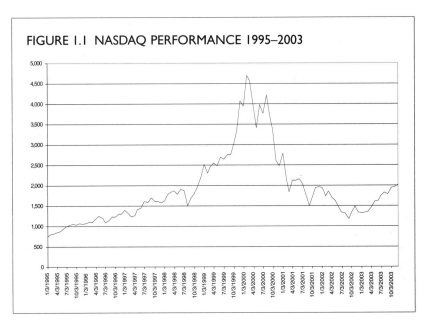

FIGURE 1.1 NASDAQ PERFORMANCE 1995–2003

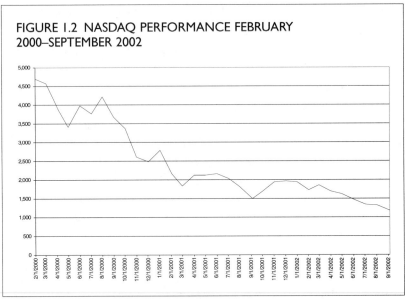

FIGURE 1.2 NASDAQ PERFORMANCE FEBRUARY
2000–SEPTEMBER 2002

And, historically, that is a pretty good prescription for success. Even including a dramatic downturn like that of 2000–2002, buying in 1995 and holding wouldn't have been so bad.

Does Buy and Hold Work?

Why have those early lessons we learned about buying stock in well-known, large companies stuck with us for so long and how useful are they? Does buy and hold really work?

The short answer is yes. Over time, the tendency of stocks is to go up. Just as the U.S. economy has steadily grown over the years, stocks of U.S. companies have grown in value. Ergo, if you own stock in companies that stay in business over a long period of time, there is a very good chance that you will make money. Pretty simple, isn't it?

Buy and hold has another advantage; it's not so much work. Whether it's implemented through owning individual stocks or through mutual funds, buy and hold is pretty low maintenance. An investor might check her portfolio every month and make minor adjustments every quarter or six months, but otherwise it doesn't require a great deal of effort.

Of course, that assumes the stocks or mutual funds being purchased have been thoroughly researched and indeed are positioned for success. Buy and hold wouldn't have worked so well if, for example, the shares being held were from a buggy whip manufacturer circa 1900. Not all companies are destined for long-term success.

Any portfolio has this potential problem associated with it: how to pick stocks that will live up to the happy scenario of a steady rise. If investors have learned anything in the past several years, it is that not all stocks rise in price—even the big, well-known companies that we have been taught to buy. In recent years, the financial headlines are filled with stories about firms that either collapsed completely, or whose stock fell so far as to be virtually irrecoverable.

Enron, Adelphia, Kmart, and Tyco were all "headline" stocks, the value of which evaporated, in some cases because of outright fraud and in other cases because of poor business practices. Buying and holding any of these stocks would have been a disastrous experience.

It used to be said that even widows and orphans could own utility stocks. They were considered a redoubtable safe haven, almost always paying a dividend, and they were the ultimate conservative investment. Not any more. For example, TXU Corp., one of the largest public utilities in the United States, lost 60 percent of its market value in 2002 . . . not much of a safe haven.

We could cite dozens of examples of large, well-known companies that lost significant market value in the last couple of years. That fact alone calls into question the buy and hold philosophy.

What's even more confusing, and indeed frightening, to investors is the idea that stock prices are sometimes pummeled for not very good reasons. A company might simply be doing business in an industry that has lost favor. If, in the collective judgment of a group of analysts, the widget sector doesn't look like it's going to outperform other sectors, it can be downgraded. When that happens, even a growing and profitable widget company will almost certainly see its stock price suffer.

A phenomenon that has occurred with some regularity in the past couple of years has been the way the broader market's decline has pulled down perfectly good stocks. Just as a rising tide lifts most boats, an ebbing tide pulls most boats down.

We'll explore both of these contextual elements in greater detail later. But for now, we merely wish to make the point that bad things *do* happen to good stocks. These broader factors can have negative consequences for the buy-and-hold approach.

But what about the earlier point that, in the long run, stocks tend to rise? Well, it's true. The question is how we define "the long run." If we define it as ten years, or longer, then yes, stocks will tend to rise. If it's one year or two, then maybe not. And we can't resist quoting John Maynard Keynes here, who famously said, "In the long run, we're all dead."

Some financial professionals will tell you that if your time horizon is "only" one or two years, you have no business investing in stocks. We disagree. Wanting to maximize returns in a one-year or two-year time frame seems like a perfectly reasonable goal.

So, to summarize the buy-and-hold philosophy, it is effective over the long run. And it is certainly more successful than the late 1990s strategy of chasing every new technology stock that managed to launch an initial public offering (IPO). However, it has two fundamental flaws.

1. It doesn't address the risks associated with a particular industry, or the potential downward movement of the broader market, unless...
2. The investor is able to focus only on a long time frame, of say, at least five years and preferably longer.

As seen above, buy and hold would have worked reasonably well from 1995 to 2003. It would have worked terribly from 2000 to 2002.

Passive Indexing or Market Neutral

There will, of course, always be ongoing debates among even the most astute financial experts about the best way to invest. At the most general level is the question of whether it is even possible to be effective at picking stocks or whether a better approach is to put money into an index fund and leave it alone. This latter view stems from the idea that it is impossible to pick individual stocks and beat the market over time. According to some experts, investors will achieve the best possible return in an index fund, which simply replicates what the broader market is doing. Their thinking suggests that "active management" of a portfolio is a waste of time.

This notion is advocated by believers in the Efficient Market Hypothesis, and frankly, it has a great deal going for it. The hypothesis states that all information about a stock is always, constantly, and completely incorporated into the price of that stock. Thus, no effort to pick stocks that are underpriced or overpriced can succeed, over time, because *there are no underpriced or overpriced stocks.* Instead, a stock's price is always exactly what it should be and reflects all that is known about the past record and future opportunities for the company.

The thinking is that millions of investors, who make billions of decisions to buy or sell stocks each day, are collectively 100 percent correct. Any news about a company, any success or failure of a firm's business plan, is instantly reflected in a stock's share price. This may be difficult for some to accept, but there is no denying that the stock market is enormously efficient.

The most well-known and articulate proponent of the efficient market hypothesis is Burton Malkiel, a professor at Princeton and the author of the popular book *A Random Walk Down Wall Street.* He acknowledges that there are some anomalies in the theory, such as the fact that low price/earnings (PE) stocks tend to outperform high PE stocks, but Malkiel insists that it is impossible to earn abnormally high returns over time. As evidence of this, he points to the fact that the average mutual fund manager is not able to achieve any sustainable higher return than a broad-based index fund. If presumably smart, well-informed mutual fund managers can only earn the same return as the market over time, the market must be unbeatable.

Whether the efficient market hypothesis is correct or not may not be knowable. Malkiel and others certainly put forth a powerful set of arguments in support of it. If they are correct, then investors have one clear choice as far as their own investment strategy. Use an index fund for that portion of their portfolio that is in equities. Period. Forget about any mutual fund that is actively managed, forget about investing in their own company's stock (unless it comes at a discount through a 401(k) or other company-sponsored investment plan), and forget about picking individual stocks based on any formula. Instead, use a passively managed index fund that tracks the S&P 500 or the even broader Wilshire 5000.

On the other hand, judging from real-life behavior, most investors do not accept the efficient market hypothesis. If they did accept it, the whole asset management industry would have been wiped out once the theory was promulgated in the 1970s. That investors aren't buying the hypothesis is evidenced by the existence of thousands of actively managed mutual funds, dozens of brokerage firms and their research teams, hundreds of newsletters, and scores of stock market news and data sources. None of those would be necessary in a world where investors "indexed" their equity investments.

Assuming that investors "vote" with their dollars, it is clear that they don't believe in the efficient market hypothesis. Instead, they believe it is possible to actively pick stocks that will outperform the overall market. How else to explain the fact that they spend billions of dollars on research and advice that is designed to generate returns in excess of "the market." So while Malkiel and others may have some good points, judging by investor's behavior, we know that they believe in something other than the efficient market hypothesis.

Given that investors embrace the idea that some stocks are better to buy than others, it must also be that investors believe some stocks are better *not* to own than others. After all, a decision to own some stocks but not others is another way for investors to say that they expect some stocks to go up and others not to go up.

This is a critical point. Based on the actions of investors, as a whole they expect some stocks to do better and other stocks to do worse than the overall market. And of course, that is an accurate statement. Every year some stocks *do* perform better and some stocks *do* perform worse than the overall market. What is self-evident from what each of us has observed is that some stocks will rise and some will fall in the future.

Because investors know this to be true, wouldn't it make sense for them to act in complete accord with the idea? Because they know that some stocks will underperform, shouldn't they invest some dollars in such a way as to benefit from that underperformance? Particularly when, by doing so, the amount of risk to their portfolio drops?

In the answer to those questions lies the most powerful argument in favor of market neutral investing. If investors believe that stocks can be successfully purchased outright, then those same investors would be logically inconsistent if they did not also sell short some other stocks. Moreover, by taking a market neutral approach, they have created a portfolio that is much less exposed to risk.

Anyone objecting to this argument must revert back to the point that it is difficult, or even impossible, to know which stocks will outperform and which will underperform. Fair enough. But if that is the reason to not use a market neutral strategy, it is also a reason not to actively pick stocks at all. For those who say, "I don't think I, or my financial advisors, can make a reasonable assessment about what to buy and what to sell short," then the answer is: use an index fund.

When put this way, the choice really becomes quite clear. Investors should either be active and use a market neutral strategy or be passive and use an index fund. The middle ground of only buying some stocks (and the approach actually used by most investors) is logically inconsistent. If investors know some stocks will fall *and* they believe there is some value in picking individual stocks, they should implement a strategy that includes both buying and selling short.

Finally, when considering the relative merits of market neutral investing and passive index investing, we must return to the question of time frame. If an investor's goal is to maximize returns over something less than five years or ten years, indexing can be less than adequate. It will probably be effective over the long haul, but it may not perform so well in the short run. Investors need only review what would have happened to a passive index investment between 2000 and 2002.

Improving the Odds

Just as there are advocates of market efficiency and passive index investing, there are others who believe the opposite—that because the market is not completely efficient, opportunities exist for making a profit by actively picking stocks. One such group includes the men and women who manage hedge funds. Hedge funds have long been reserved only for the wealthiest investors and institutions, making them appear secretive and, maybe, even a bit sinister. Despite that perception, there is no arguing about the fact that, overall, hedge funds have become one of the most successful investment vehicles around and are utilized by everyone from successful entrepreneurs to college endowments. One of the key methods employed by hedge funds is market neutral investing.

As we briefly stated on the first page of Chapter 1, market neutral investing entails buying shares of stock in one company and selling short shares in a different company at the same time. Investors and money managers do this when they believe that the stock of one company is likely to go up in price and the second company's shares are likely to fall in price.

For the uninitiated, when a stock is sold *short,* its shares are borrowed at today's price and then sold, to be returned at some future date. The borrower does this in the hopes that the stock price will fall and the shares can be returned at a lower price. The difference between today's price and the future, hopefully lower, price equals the profit. Thus, shorting a stock is synonymous with betting against it.

Hedge fund managers do this all the time, and thousands of funds with billions of dollars under management are engaged in the practice every day. They do it for a number of reasons, but two stand out: (1) because it reduces the risk level in their portfolio; (2) because they consider themselves excellent stock pickers and able to identify stocks that are headed for a fall just as they can select stocks that are going to rise.

On the latter point, it stands to reason that if a person is able to make very good stock selections, why limit themselves to profiting in only one direction? If, and this is a big if, a money manager can accurately predict the movement of individual stocks, wouldn't that manager be smart to place bets on stocks that are going up and also place bets on stocks that are going down? This would create twice the profit opportunity than a "long only" strategy does.

Of course, in what could be the understatement of the decade, not everyone has the ability to make such accurate predictions. And when that ability is lacking, being both long and short creates twice as many opportunities to *lose* money. So, the whole notion of market neutral investing is predicated on an investor's facility for selecting some stocks that are likely to go up and others that are likely to fall. To the extent that this can be accomplished, a neutral strategy will be very successful. Because it is so important, quite a bit of material in this book addresses stock selection.

There are countless methods used to pick stocks. Some rely on *technical analysis;* i.e., the study of stock price movements over time. Others use *fundamental analysis;* i.e., the study of underlying facts about a company. Our bias throughout this book is toward fundamental analysis, but it's worth noting that market neutral investing can work regardless of what method is used to pick stocks. It is easy to imagine a strategy of buying stocks that are in a technical uptrend and shorting stocks that are in a technical downtrend. The important point is that the selection method, whatever it is, must work.

In the case of fundamental analysis, the driving thesis is that there is some intrinsic value found in a company and that by looking at the facts related to a company's business, some assessment can be made about whether the company's stock price fairly reflects those facts. Many people believe that a stock price will often inaccurately reflect the intrinsic value of a company. The stock price may be too high or too low, but the thesis is that stocks can frequently be overpriced or underpriced relative to their business fundamentals.

As we discussed, a large group of intelligent investment professionals and finance professors believe that a stock price always perfectly reflects all of the known information about a company and its future prospects. If that is correct, it certainly puts a damper on any notion of identifying overvalued or undervalued stocks. However, we also know that, based on their actions, most market participants don't accept the efficient market hypothesis. So, let's assume for a moment that on any given day, some of the thousands of publicly traded companies in the United States are "mispriced." Some are too expensive; i.e., trading at a premium to their intrinsic value. Others are too cheap; i.e., trading at a discount.

If we accept this idea, then one very logical investment strategy would entail buying undervalued stocks and selling short overvalued stocks at the same time. This is the essence of market neutral investing. And not only does it allow the clever stock picker to profit in both directions, it reduces the risk that a negative move in the broad market will translate into a negative move for an investor's portfolio.

Market neutral investing provides some very real insulation against broad market swings. Of course, it most likely works as a brake when the market is heading down *and* when the market is moving up. It is not, after all, a one-way street. But when the market is heading down, generally speaking, a well-constructed market neutral portfolio will not show as much of a loss as the market indexes and, indeed, could show a gain. Conversely, when the market is moving up, a good market neutral portfolio should show a gain, but most likely not as much of one as the market indexes.

An Example of Market Neutral Investing

All of this may seem a little ethereal without an example to make it more concrete. So, in the interest of practicality, we offer up a sort of case study.

It would be difficult to find two companies whose fortunes are more inextricably linked to the broader economy than Ford Motor Company and General Motors Corporation (GM). These are cyclical companies whose results depend on consumer willingness to make a large purchase.

The two firms are by no means identical, but they have many shared characteristics in terms of how they make money and the markets in which they compete. So *if all things were equal,* we would expect their respective share prices to generally move together. Of course, all things are never equal.

A couple of factors might explain a difference in the future performance of Ford's stock versus GM's stock over a specific period of time. The first is what we might call an execution difference. That is, if Ford were to be more effective in gaining market share or keeping production costs lower than GM, then Ford's stock price would reflect this better execution.

The other factor that influences stock price performance is the starting valuation of each company's shares at the beginning of the period. In other words, the future performance of each company's stock is based in some measure on the relative starting points. If each company is valued differently to start with, based on fundamentals, and then each company subsequently executes their business plan equally well, over time the valuations will tend to converge. All other things being equal, there will be no reason for one stock to be valued at a premium or at a discount to the other.

Ford and GM *were* valued differently at the start of 2002. In order to better understand what the market thought about each company, it is necessary to review some common measures of value. Those measures, highlighted in Figure 1.3, consist of common ratios that are calculated by dividing each stock's current price per share by the following: (1) the amount of profit, or earnings per share (price-to-earnings ratio); (2) the amount of revenue, or sales per share (price-to-sales ratio); (3) the book value, or tangible assets of the company minus liabilities, per share (price-to-book ratio); and (4) the estimated future earnings per share (forward price-to-earnings ratio).

Ford's then-current PE ratio was 48 versus GM's 158, suggesting that based on current earnings, Ford was valued at much less than GM. Score one point for Ford as being "undervalued."

On the basis of price-to-sales (stock price divided by revenue per share) and price-to-book ratios (stock price divided by the assets of the company per share), Ford was a more expensive stock, although the difference in price-to-sales ratios was minimal. Score one and a half points for GM as being undervalued.

The past revenue growth of the companies was also quite similar. Comparing the then-current quarter with the prior year's quarter, sales were up slightly for each. Comparing the prior 12-month periods for each, sales were down slightly. On the question of whether one company or the other had better sales momentum than the other, it looks like a draw.

One remarkable divergence between the two lies in the future earnings estimates. We can see that analysts estimated that Ford would earn $0.34 per share on a pro forma basis in 2002 and GM would earn $1.88.

FIGURE 1.3 MEASURES OF VALUE FOR FORD AND GENERAL MOTORS

Statistic	Ford	GM
Price-to-earnings ratio	48	158
Price-to-sales ratio	0.18	0.15
Price-to-book ratio	2.16	0.94
Revenue growth: current quarter vs. prior year quarter	5.90%	4.60%
Revenue growth over trailing 12 months	−4.40%	−3.70%
2002 estimated earnings/share	$0.34	$1.88
Forward price-to-earnings ratio	47	26

Pro forma earnings do not conform to generally accepted accounting principles (GAAP), and often exclude certain items that the company believes might cloud the earnings picture. Examples might include the amortization of good will or the cost of stock-based compensation. Using the respective stock prices at the time to make the calculation, the future, or "forward" PEs of the companies were dramatically different. Based on anticipated earnings, Ford was quite a bit more expensive than GM. Score another point for GM as being undervalued.

Based on this quick and admittedly cursory analysis, we would probably conclude that GM was somewhat undervalued and Ford was a bit overvalued, relative to each other. A market neutral investor would take this information and implement an investment strategy designed to capture these differences in valuation and make a profit. The underlying premise would be that the respective stock valuations would converge toward each other over time.

That strategy, at its simplest level, would be to purchase shares of GM and sell short shares of Ford. We can see how this would have played out in Figure 1.4.

Clearly Ford's stock price underperformed GM in 2002. By the end of December 2002, Ford stock was down over 40 percent from the begin-

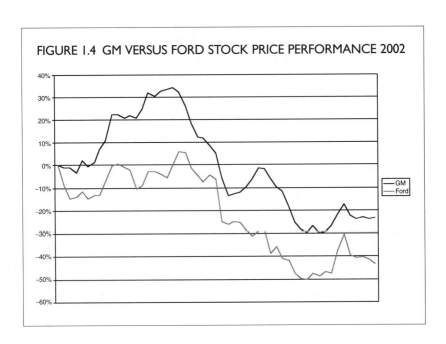

FIGURE 1.4 GM VERSUS FORD STOCK PRICE PERFORMANCE 2002

ning of the year. And while GM's price also fell, it fell much less drastically over the same time frame.

What that would have meant for our market neutral investor is this: buying $10,000 worth of GM stock in early January 2002 would have resulted in a loss of about $2,300 by the end of the year. Shorting $10,000 worth of Ford stock in early January 2002 would have resulted in a gain of approximately $4,300 by the end of the year.

Taking those two investments together, our hypothetical investor would have made $2,000 on a total investment of $20,000. This works out to be a gain of 10 percent in a year when the S&P 500 fell by over 20 percent. Our investor would undoubtedly be pleased with her analysis.

Was It the Performance or the Valuation?

And how well did Ford and GM perform, in terms of making and selling cars, in 2002? GM's sales were up slightly more than 5 percent in 2002 over 2001. In Ford's case, sales increased 1.2 percent. As for earnings, Ford actually earned more per share than had been estimated. Instead of earning $0.34 per share, the company earned $0.45 per share (again, on a pro forma basis). GM also did better than expected and went on to earn $6.54 per share instead of the estimated $1.88 per share.

Forgetting about stock prices, it seems fair to conclude that GM outperformed Ford "operationally" in 2002. Sales growth was better and GM's earnings exceeded expectations by a factor of 3. Ford's earnings were better than initially expected but not by such a large margin.

Unfortunately, that means we really aren't able to answer the question of whether it was GM's better execution or lower starting valuation that led to its better stock performance. Did GM's stock fall less because the company was better managed? Or was it because GM's stock was undervalued to start with? It is difficult to say which factor is responsible, or whether perhaps both factors were at work.

In order to shed some light on this question, we turn to a different example, one where two different companies start out the year with different valuations and perform in a similar manner. Like our Ford/GM example, this is anecdotal evidence, but it is instructive nonetheless.

At the beginning of 2002, WinTrust Financial and North Fork Bancorp were two of hundreds of U.S. regional banks. The stocks carried quite different valuations, (see Figure 1.5) even though they were in virtually the exact same business, albeit in different parts of the country.

Looking at this set of numbers, there were clearly some differences in how the two companies were being valued. Based on PE ratio, WinTrust and North Fork were almost identically valued, making that particular factor a tie.

Comparing how the firms were valued based on price-to-sales and price-to-book, however, WinTrust carried a much lower valuation than North Fork. Past sales growth was also much stronger at WinTrust, indicating that maybe the company had some strong sales momentum heading into 2002. Score points for WinTrust on all of these counts.

The two companies had forward PE ratios that, like the current PE, were identical. Another tie. Taken all together, an objective assessment would lead us to believe that WinTrust was at least somewhat undervalued relative to North Fork based on price-to-sales, price-to-book, and WinTrust's past strong sales performance.

What is particularly interesting about these two companies, and what couldn't have been known at the beginning of 2002, is that they subsequently turned in almost identical operational results that year. In 2002, earnings for both companies actually grew slightly more than 24 percent, and revenues grew between 7 percent and 9 percent. So, in terms of execution, we can observe that each company performed equally well.

Returning to our question of whether it is valuation or company performance that drives a company's stock price, this presents us with a case where the company performances are virtually equal. Based on the fact

---

FIGURE 1.5 MEASURES OF VALUE FOR WINTRUST AND NORTH FORK

Statistic	WinTrust Financial	North Fork Bancorp.
Price-to-earnings ratio	16.6	16.5
Price-to-sales ratio	1.79	4.69
Price-to-book ratio	2.18	3.66
Revenue growth: current quarter vs. prior year quarter	36%	15%
Revenue growth over trailing 12 months	22%	6%
Forward price-to-earnings ratio	14	14

that WinTrust was valued at a discount to North Fork at the beginning of the year, and achieved identical operational results, one would predict that WinTrust's stock price would perform better than North Fork's in 2002.

Indeed, that is precisely what proved to be the case, with WinTrust stock climbing almost 60 percent and North Fork stock up about 7 percent (see Figure 1.6). That each stock rose in a year when the market declined significantly is a tribute to each firm's strong operational results. That WinTrust rose so much more than North Fork appears to be a tribute to the initial discount the company carried at the beginning of the year compared to North Fork. Our hypothetical market neutral investor who noted the discrepancy in valuations and bought shares in WinTrust while selling short the same dollar value of North Fork shares, would have had a 20 percent return on the investment!

This example supports the idea that a company's valuation does play a role in how its stock performs. Again, while this is a single example, not a comprehensive analysis of the entire universe of stocks, it underscores the point that relative valuations can have an impact on relative stock price performance.

Imagine two runners at the starting line of a race. Each athlete is in exactly the same physical condition. Those two runners will probably cross

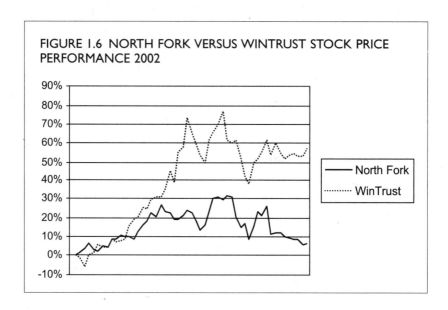

FIGURE 1.6 NORTH FORK VERSUS WINTRUST STOCK PRICE PERFORMANCE 2002

the finish line at the exact same time, if they truly are in identical shape. However, if one runner is forced to carry a ten pound weight, that runner is certainly going to finish behind the other. A company whose stock carries a premium valuation relative to a peer company, despite being in identical physical or operational condition, is like the runner forced to carry that weight. It will act as a drag on stock price performance.

The two examples cited, GM/Ford and WinTrust/North Fork, may give the impression that a market neutral strategy is simple to implement and will always work. Nothing could be further from the truth. Though much of the rest of this book will be devoted to how it can and should work, realize that some pretty smart people have failed in their efforts to make money using a market neutral approach. We will turn our attention to increasing the odds of success.

Bull? Bear? Don't Really Care

One of the attractive elements of market neutral investing is that it is not dependent for success on what the broader market is doing. Thus, it frees an investor from relying on something that can't be controlled. A "long only," or a buy-and-hold strategy relies to some significant extent on the upward movement of the broad market.

In the GM/Ford example, both companies turned in excellent performances in 2002. That did not offer much comfort to an investor who was long either of those stocks that year. Simply owning either of those stocks would have produced a loss of either 23 percent or 43 percent. Clearly the stock prices were impacted by a negative market environment. And this in a year when both companies were, forgive the pun, hitting on all cylinders! In contrast, a mini-market neutral portfolio comprised of a long/short position in GM/Ford produced gains independent of what was happening in the overall market.

To further illustrate, it is interesting to compare GM's 2003 operational and stock price performance with what occurred in 2002. In 2003, sales for GM rose 2.9 percent versus an increase of 5 percent in 2002. Earnings came in about where they were expected to be in 2003, at a little better than $5 per share, whereas in 2002 GM blew away initial estimates. It's clear that GM's operational performance was less impressive in 2003 than it was in 2002. So, it might be surprising that GM's shares were *up* almost 40 percent in 2003 instead of declining 23 percent as they did in 2002. This example serves as an excellent illustration of the impact market sentiment can have on an individual stock, regardless of operational performance.

A market neutral portfolio's independence from the market is probably the best reason to invest using this strategy, according to James Knowles, Director at York Hedge Fund Strategies, Inc.: "The reason to be market neutral is not to gain increased returns but to reduce volatility. The more predictable and reliable aspect of a market neutral portfolio is its greatest benefit."

On a practical level, there is something quite appealing about not having to worry about what "the market" is doing. Market neutral investors, presuming they have done their homework and chosen truly undervalued and overvalued stocks, can sleep more easily knowing that at least their market neutral portfolio is insulated from the vagaries of the broader indexes. Market neutral returns tend not to correlate very closely, if at all, to the overall stock market.

The good news for buy-and-hold investors is that equity markets tend to go up over time and thus benefit long-only portfolios. As pointed out earlier, in the long run it makes sense to buy equities because history tells us that there is a strong probability they will rise in value.

The bad news is that it can be a wild ride from start to finish. One attribute of a market neutral strategy is that it will tend to smooth out the bumps in the road, and, for some investors, this quality is very valuable.

The smooth ride occurs because the long and short offsetting positions found in a market neutral portfolio dampen the movement of the portfolio as a whole. So while the market is falling, the short positions in the portfolio should be falling just as much, and hopefully more. This makes up for the fact that the long positions are probably falling too. Taken together, these long and short positions effectively cancel out a great deal of the week-to-week ups and downs.

One final comment on terminology: technically speaking, market neutral investing refers to a perfectly balanced portfolio with the same amount of money invested long as is invested short. In contrast, there are also "long/short" portfolios that are not necessarily balanced. Instead, long/short is taken to mean that more money might be long or more money might be short. The distinction is worth noting, and, in Chapter 6 about balancing portfolios, the difference will become more apparent.

Summary

Market neutral investing can produce positive returns in any market environment, and it can reduce a portfolio's volatility dramatically. Using a market neutral approach is predicated on the belief that, at any given time, at least some stocks are incorrectly valued. It is a little-known strategy among individual investors, the success of which depends completely on the ability to correctly pick stocks that are overvalued and undervalued.

Perhaps the most compelling argument in favor of market neutral investing is that, as one expert put it, if you believe it is possible to actively manage a portfolio of stocks and beat the market, then doing so with a market neutral strategy is the most sensible way. Only *buying* stocks is a half-measure and not logically consistent. We'll talk about how investors and financial advisors can approach equity market neutral investing for themselves or their clients throughout the rest of this book.

2

ON RISK

Walk down the street and ask someone you see to define *risk,* and you will most likely hear them say, "It's the chance that something will go wrong." Walk down Wall Street, and you will most likely hear something entirely different and altogether more complicated.

The first response seems sensible. When evaluating risk, investors should think of it in terms of what might go wrong and what are the chances that it will. More important, risk should be considered in terms of what can be done about it.

To simplify and clarify our discussion of risk, let's start by making an analogy to real estate, a subject perhaps more familiar to many people than the stock market. Although there are some very real differences between buying a house and buying a stock, in some ways they are not so different. Both of them are assets that owners hope will appreciate in value over time. Both purchases carry some level of risk.

When you buy a house, you also buy insurance to protect yourself against the risk that something terrible could happen to that big investment. Whether it's from fire or natural disaster, you (and the bank that provided your mortgage) want some protection. The chances that something will destroy your home are relatively low, and thus the cost to insure it is relatively low.

Unfortunately there is no popular form of low-cost insurance to protect your investment in a stock. It may be surprising to some investors that you *can* purchase "insurance" for your stock at all, but indeed it can be done. Typically, though, that insurance comes at a fairly high price and is done through the purchase of equity options. We'll talk a little more about options in Chapter 7.

For now, let's just acknowledge that buying insurance on an individual stock, while possible, is generally too expensive for many investors to make it worthwhile. And the obvious reason is that the chances something will go wrong with a particular stock are actually quite high. Accordingly, the cost to "insure" a stock can also be relatively high.

So, while there are strong parallels between purchasing a home and purchasing a stock, there is this distinct difference when it comes to risk and insuring against catastrophic loss.

Another type of risk comes with buying a home. How many times have you heard the cliché that the three most important factors in valuing a house are "location, location, location?" Many real estate experts emphasize that the biggest influence on value is where the house is located.

But, what happens if the location of the home you purchase deteriorates? What if the neighborhood experiences a decline in economic status or sees a conversion to more rental properties? What if the city, county, or state decides to put a new highway very near your previously quiet front yard?

Such an occurrence will clearly have a negative impact on your investment. Interestingly, there is no homeowner's insurance available to protect against this sort of risk. The homeowner is on her own in assuming this second level of risk.

In addition, there is a third type of risk a homeowner takes on when a house is purchased: the risk that a broad economic downturn will reduce the demand for houses and thus have a depressing effect on prices. A good example of this occurred in the greater Silicon Valley region in 2000 to 2002 as jobs became more scarce and demand for houses and apartments waned.

Again, this broader, macroeconomic risk is something that homeowners bear alone. No insurance is available for purchase that would protect against a decline in home value. (Perhaps the creative underwriters at the leading insurers will take note of this deficiency.)

In any case, we can see that there are three levels of risk associated with owning a home:

1. The risk that some disaster will befall our specific house
2. The risk that our neighborhood will deteriorate
3. The risk that the economy (regional or national) will sour and put a damper on prices

Homeowners can, and almost always do, insure against the first one but never against the second and third.

Company Risk

Owning a stock carries the same three levels of risk. First, there is the risk that something bad will happen to a particular stock, and most of us are all too familiar with the many possibilities.

A company may see its products become less popular, or face new competition, cutting into profits and causing the price of its stock to fall. Or, the company could just begin to grow at a less rapid rate. Even though it is still making money, investors may turn away from a company that was growing at 20 percent per year but begins to grow at a good but less robust pace of 10 percent per year.

The most discouraging aspect of this risk is that it is present in the bluest of blue chip companies. A good example is what happened with General Electric (GE) in 2002. For the past decade, GE had been perhaps the most admired corporation in America. The management team was effective, and profits were growing at a fast clip. We choose GE as our example, not to pick on GE, but rather because if there ever was a stock loved even by widows and orphans, it was GE.

From the end of 1995 to the end of 2001, GE's revenues grew 13 percent per year, earnings per share grew 18 percent per year, and the stock price rose an average of 28 percent per year. In early 2002, Wall Street analysts still had an optimistic view; they were projecting earnings per share would grow 12 percent for the year and over 15 percent longer term.

Unfortunately for shareholders of GE stock, the reality of slowing growth became apparent as the year unfolded. By the end of the year, those same analysts had revised their thinking, estimating that GE's earnings would only grow 4 percent in 2002 and 13 percent in the longer term.

This reduced growth rate translated into a drastic decline in the company's stock price, as it tumbled almost 40 percent (see Figure 2.1), not quite twice as much as the broader market. And no one was saying that

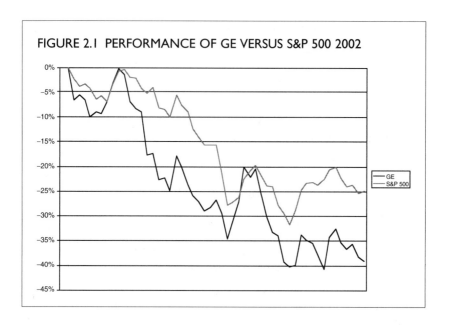

FIGURE 2.1 PERFORMANCE OF GE VERSUS S&P 500 2002

GE was suddenly a bad company. All it took was recognition that this successful firm would grow at a somewhat slower pace.

Clearly, there was a risk in owning GE stock. It was a risk specific to owning that particular stock at that particular time. And every stock we own as investors carries some risk that we are unable to insure against, at least practically speaking. Company-specific risk simply comes with the territory, and about the only action we can take to reduce that risk is to be diligent in our research. We may be able to avoid owning some stocks that are poised for a fall if we carefully investigate them ahead of time, but we really can't eliminate company risk through insurance.

Ironic, isn't it? Unlike home ownership, where all we *can* insure against is the risk that something bad will happen to our house, with stocks what we *can't* insure against is something bad happening to our particular company. We'll return to the subject of assessing company risk later in this chapter.

Sector Risk

But what about the other, broader risks of owning stock? Like real estate, are there "macro" risks? You bet there are. In fact, when we stop and think about all the risks, it's a wonder anyone owns a single share!

Just as we pointed out the "neighborhood" risk we have in real estate, there is a corollary "neighborhood" risk with stocks. Only in the stock market we call it "sector risk." *Sector risk* refers to the chance that something bad will happen to a particular industry or group of companies competing in the same business.

For example, it is not uncommon for a brokerage analyst to make pronouncements about the future prospects for a particular sector. Sectors get upgraded or downgraded all the time by someone or other. When that judgment occurs, many, if not all, stocks in that sector are rewarded or punished accordingly. Because we are focused here on risk, we'll confine ourselves to discussing downgrades.

Sector downgrades by analysts do serve a useful purpose. Because different businesses operate on different economic cycles, a sector downgrade may be appropriate. It's the analyst's job to warn investors when a particular sector might be facing a difficult period in the future.

Consider, for example, homebuilding stocks. When interest rates are low, more people are able to afford a mortgage, and the companies who build houses are likely to prosper in an abnormally robust way. Conversely, when interest rates begin to rise, homebuilding stocks may face a tougher operating environment. An analyst who foresees rising interest rates might decide to downgrade the homebuilding sector because he or she believes overall demand for houses will drop or at least level off.

As an investor, however, here's the problem. We may own stock in the very best homebuilding company in the United States. Let's say it's the number one homebuilder and a company that controls its costs and is better managed than any other competitor. What's more, let's say that the stock of this superstar company is already undervalued. It doesn't matter. Once that sector downgrade is issued, our superstar homebuilder stock is almost certainly going to fall along with the rest of the stocks in that sector.

It doesn't seem fair, does it? Why tar everyone with the same brush? Truth be told, it probably isn't completely fair, but as we pointed out, even the best homebuilder might face a slower growth rate if indeed interest rates go up. The problem is that in the short-to-intermediate term, the market isn't going to care that our undervalued company is still going to grow and prosper. Investors are constantly reallocating dollars, and a sector downgrade provides a good reason to move their money from one sector to another. What's more, moving money from one stock or one sector to another has become more frenetic in recent years as transaction costs (i.e., commissions) have dropped.

A more interesting question is what can we do about it? Is there a way to protect ourselves from sector risk? Is there some "insurance" we can buy? Indirectly, there is. When we initially buy shares in our undervalued homebuilder, we can simultaneously short the shares of another, lower quality company whose shares are overvalued.

Remember, when we short shares of stock, we make money if the price of the stock goes down. So, if we have a long position and a short position in each of two stocks in the same sector, we effectively protect ourselves against a sector downgrade. If both stocks' prices fall, we can make up for our loss in the shares we own outright with a profit in the shares we sell short. Indeed, if we choose our two stocks carefully, we can actually turn a profit. This will occur if the stock we sell short falls further than the stock we purchase.

We can illustrate this with a real example. By the end of 2002, many observers were beginning to believe that mortgage rates were probably not going to fall much further than they already had. A lot of talk began to surface about a "housing bubble," and analysts became much more negative about the prospects for homebuilding stocks. Let's take a look at what happened to two different stocks in that sector over the next few months.

In late December of 2002, of all the major homebuilders, Beazer Homes (BZH) had the lowest forward PE ratio (stock price divided by the coming year's expected earnings per share) at 4.5 and the second best sales growth rate. Palm Harbor Homes (PHHM) had the highest forward PE ratio at 35.5 and the next to worst sales growth rate. The chart in Figure 2.2 illustrates what happened to their respective stock prices in 2003.

The divergence of the two stocks could not be more apparent. BZH shares rose 60 percent and PHHM shares hovered around the unchanged mark for most of the year. As a point of comparison, the S&P 500 was somewhere in the middle, up about 26 percent. An equal long/short investment in BZH/PHHM would have yielded a return of 31 percent, even better than an investment in a S&P 500 index fund. But the most important point is that the investment in Beazer carried no sector risk because it was "hedged" away by the short position in Palm Harbor.

Selling short PHHM was a little like buying some insurance against the risk that the homebuilding sector would be downgraded or just perform poorly as a whole. Indeed, sector risk stems from more than just

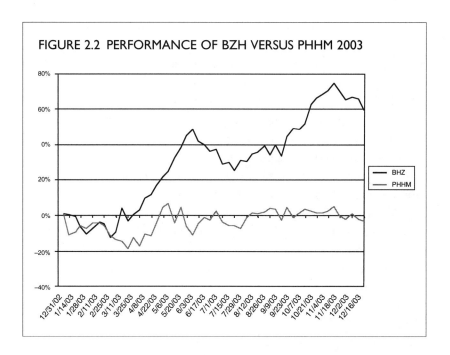

FIGURE 2.2 PERFORMANCE OF BZH VERSUS PHHM 2003

analyst downgrades. In industries where there is one dominant company, bad news for that company often translates into bad news for the entire industry. In semiconductors, for example, Intel is such a preeminent company that if it misses earnings estimates or warns about upcoming results, other chip companies often suffer. When Intel sneezes, it's common for its competitors to catch a cold.

Sector risk is probably one of the most misunderstood and unacknowledged dangers to owning stocks. Insuring against it is one of the smartest steps an investor can take.

Market Risk

Another element of risk to owning stocks is the corollary to the macroeconomic risk of owning a home. We are referring to the risk that the entire stock market will fall and thus carry our individual stocks down with it. Anyone who was invested in the stock market between March 2000 and the end of 2002 is familiar with this market risk and the havoc it can wreak on even the best individual stocks.

Just as a rising tide tends to lift all boats, a falling tide tends to pull all boats down. Market risk refers to the chance that something bad will happen to the entire market and a falling tide will ensue.

These bear markets have historically been relatively infrequent, and thus the degree of risk is somewhat lower than it is for individual companies or sectors. It is, nonetheless, a very real risk, and it can be very damaging to a long-only portfolio.

Let's look at what happened over the last ten years to one of the safest and most mundane stocks available to investors. What could be more boring and more predictable than a water utility company?

California Water Services (CWT) provides water to the western United States, nothing more complicated or fancy than that. It is a regulated utility with a solid dividend. And yet we can see what the broader market's impact was on even this most stolid of companies during the period from 1992 to 2002.

From 1992 to 2000, CWT stock returned an average of 5.8 percent per year, not adjusted for dividends. That's about what we might expect from a company operating in a regulated environment without many external threats to its business. During that same period the S&P 500 climbed an average of 15.8 percent per year, evidence that those eight years were very broadly bullish. We can see a comparison of the two in Figure 2.3.

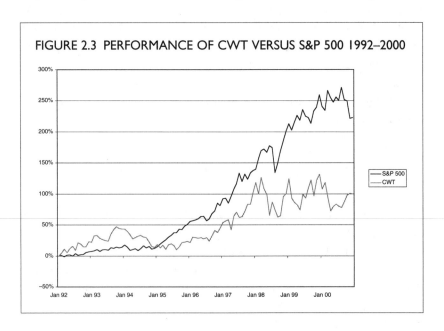

FIGURE 2.3 PERFORMANCE OF CWT VERSUS S&P 500 1992–2000

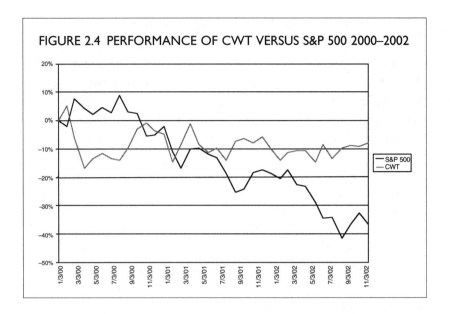

FIGURE 2.4 PERFORMANCE OF CWT VERSUS S&P 500 2000–2002

But from 2000 to 2002 we see a different picture (see Figure 2.4). CWT stock actually fell during that three-year period, right along with the S&P 500. It didn't fall nearly as far, but it fell nonetheless. CWT didn't suddenly change its strategy or become involved in a new type of business. It simply was a victim of market risk.

Even though CWT was still earning money and still paying a dividend, a falling tide pulled the boat down. It was a well-constructed boat and remained so during the bear market, but it couldn't resist the gravitational pull of the broader market's decline.

Much like the remedy available to us for sector risk, there is also a remedy for market risk. We can "buy insurance" in the form of shorting other stocks, or even selling short the broader market. We will cover some techniques for doing this in Chapter 7. For now we simply want to make the point that all stocks carry some level of market risk, no matter how seemingly safe they may be.

That does not mean that all stocks will fall during a market downturn. There will always be stocks that move independently—rising in falling markets or falling in rising markets. However, the odds are that individual stocks will be heavily influenced by broad market trends.

Measuring and Responding to Company Risk

At the beginning of Chapter 2, we alluded to the fact that many people on Wall Street have a definition of risk that is a good deal more complicated than what we have explained here. A lot has been written about company risk and how to evaluate the risk level of a particular stock. In fact, it's almost a cottage industry among professors of finance and market pundits.

The traditional thinking about measuring how risky an investment in one company boils down to this: how much does a stock price move relative to the collective movement of all stocks taken together? If a stock moves a lot relative to all other stocks, then it is considered more risky. Most often, the S&P 500 index is used as a proxy for "all other stocks."

Put another way, if we look at the past price movement of a company's shares and they have gone up further than the S&P 500 when the S&P 500 is going up, or have fallen further than the index when it is falling, conventional wisdom tells this is a risky stock.

We illustrate this in the chart in Figure 2.5, where the graph depicts the movement of one company's stock price and the movement of a hypothetical broad market index. We can see that Stock A's price moves a great deal more, from one week to the next, than the index does. Because of this greater movement, or volatility, many experts will tell you that Stock A is riskier than other stocks.

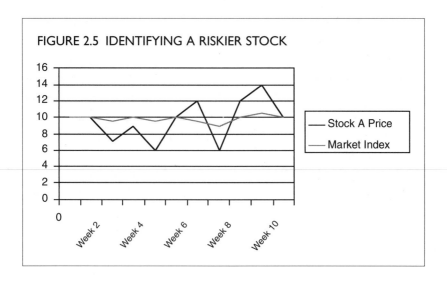

FIGURE 2.5 IDENTIFYING A RISKIER STOCK

Note that Stock A's price and the market index end up at the same place. There is no gain and no loss after ten weeks. Nonetheless, conventional wisdom dictates that Stock A carries a relatively high level of risk.

A mathematical computation has been developed to quantify this measure of risk in a single number. That number is called *beta,* and it is a statistical measure of how volatile a single stock is relative to a broad index. The beta for Stock A in this example would be 4.3. If Stock A moved in the same direction and to the same degree as the index, its beta would 1.0.

Let's look at another example, where a stock is *less* volatile than the index (see Figure 2.6).

The beta in this example is a very low 0.10, meaning that Stock B moves quite a bit less dramatically than the index as a whole. Again, if Stock B moved in exactly the same direction and to the same degree as the index, it would have a beta of 1.0. Instead, we can see that the price movement of Stock B is gradual and does not perfectly follow the contours of the index.

So, based on our hypothetical examples and the conventional view of company risk, Stock A is more risky than Stock B. But wait a minute. Looking at those charts more carefully, we see that Stock A didn't lose any ground and Stock B lost value. So how can Stock B be less risky?

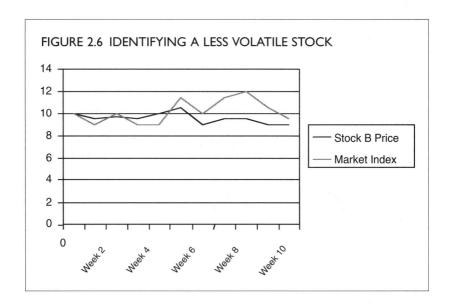

FIGURE 2.6 IDENTIFYING A LESS VOLATILE STOCK

Good question. And it's a question that highlights the shortcomings of how company risk is typically measured. Just because a stock is volatile (i.e., it has a high beta) doesn't really mean that it is more likely to fall in price than any other stock. Nor is a stock with low volatility *less* likely to fall in price than any other stock.

Volatility is just that: volatility. It is not a useful gauge of whether a stock will be a good investment or not. There are countless examples of low volatility stocks that have lost money and an equally countless number of examples of high volatility stocks that have made investors a pile of money.

And yet, to the uninformed investor, who hasn't gone through the above exercise, there is likely to be a misconception about volatility. High beta stocks are not necessarily bad, nor are low beta stocks necessarily good. *The problem arises when there is the perception that beta is something more than a statistical measure of volatility.*

One of the more high profile corporate failures in the last several years was Kmart's. In order to illustrate our point, we reviewed the volatility of Kmart's stock prior to the initial speculation that the company might have to file for bankruptcy. The first public hint about this possibility began to surface in January 2002.

Prior to that, in December 2001, the beta of Kmart was 0.98. That tells us that by the traditional measure of risk, Kmart was fairly "typical." Its stock tended to move up when the S&P 500 index moved up and down when the index moved down. But what we really know now is that just because Kmart's stock price didn't move much differently than the broader market, it didn't mean the stock would be a successful investment, nor that it would be a stock with "average" risk, as most of us think of risk.

Now, to be fair, the measure of a stock's volatility does have great utility, particularly when applied to the analysis of a group of stocks. For example, knowing individual stock volatility is helpful when trying to assemble a portfolio of stocks that complement each other. But as a tool to measure how great the chance is that a particular stock will be a profitable investment, beta is really not much help at all.

So the obvious question is, how *does* one determine the risk level of a particular company? Unfortunately, there are no easy answers to this question. Thorough research of the company's past track record, its current valuation, and a comparison of that valuation with industry norms is the best way to mitigate company risk.

Measuring and Responding to Sector Risk

There is also a body of conventional wisdom on the subject of "sector risk" and how to deal with it. As even the most casual investor knows, one of the first lessons we are taught is to diversify our investments. "Don't put all your eggs in one basket" is a bit of common sense we learn at a young age.

The idea behind diversification is a sound one, and it does serve as a partial antidote to sector risk. By spreading investments out among a variety of stocks, which are *in different industries,* an investor does create a safer portfolio. There is less likelihood of something bad happening to a wide range of stocks than something happening to just one.

It is important to underscore the point that for diversification to be effective at all, investments must be placed across different sectors. Owing different stocks does not, by itself, reduce sector risk. If an investor tries to achieve diversity by buying ten different stocks, all in, say, the semi-conductor industry, that investor will have failed in her or his effort. True diversification only occurs if it is across industries.

Is cross-industry diversification effective? Yes, but only to a point. While it spreads the risk, it doesn't counteract risk. No matter how many stocks an investor owns in a wide range of industries, there is still a reasonable chance that a loss will be incurred in at least some of those investments.

Returning to our real estate example, diversification is comparable to a homeowner protecting against "neighborhood risk" by buying homes in multiple locations. A chance still exists that one neighborhood might deteriorate, but it's unlikely to happen in all of them at one time. Having multiple homes is better than taking no action at all, but it doesn't really protect against a loss.

As a practical matter, there is a disadvantage to diversification. As James Cloonan wrote in a November 2002 *AAII Journal* article, "If you didn't care about risk, you would put all of your assets into the single investment you thought had the likelihood of the greatest gain. But in order to diversify, you must put some assets in investments that you expect will have less potential returns."

In other words, diversification necessarily forces us to invest in what we believe are suboptimum choices. No less an investment sage than Warren Buffett once said that diversification is for people who don't know what they are doing. His point being that if an investment is really understood and made with complete confidence, there is no need to diversify against risk.

While we don't completely agree with Buffett on this subject, we appreciate his point. Diversification is, at best, an imperfect method of dampening sector risk. What's more, because of its standing as unassailable investment wisdom, there is a danger that investors will conclude that by diversifying they have done everything they can to reduce their risk. The table in Figure 2.7 summarizes the three types of risk and their respective magnitude.

The Long/Short Solution to Managing Risk

As discussed above, another way of dealing with risk is to use a market neutral investment approach. This has a number of advantages and some disadvantages too.

Using a long/short strategy is, theoretically at least, a surer way of reducing sector risk than diversifying. As we pointed out, diversification distributes risk but it doesn't really mitigate it. An investor might own stocks in six different sectors, but a downturn or a downgrade in any single sector will still most likely result in a loss for the stock held in that sector.

Instead of relying on diversification, an investor can use a long/short strategy by being long one stock and short a different stock in the same sector. While a negative development for that sector will translate into a

---

FIGURE 2.7 THREE RISKS AND THEIR SERIOUSNESS

Type of Risk	Degree of Risk
Company Risk	High
Sector Risk	Moderate
Market Risk	Low

loss for the long position, it will likely create a corollary gain for the short position. Being long and short really does act as a sort of insurance.

Another advantage market neutral investing offers is that it reduces the need to make the suboptimum investments that are required in a diversification strategy. By choosing the most undervalued stock in a sector to buy and the most overvalued stock in a sector to short, the investor has created a lower risk environment without having to settle for a "second best" idea.

Also, being market neutral protects against both sector risk and market risk at the same time. As we pointed out, market risk is the threat we are least concerned about, but it is still a genuine threat. In the event of a broad-based bear market, a market neutral strategy can still be profitable because of the gains generated by a portfolio's short positions.

Finally, market neutral investing allows an investor's stock picking skills to really shine. Because sector risk and market risk are effectively filtered out of the equation, a market neutral portfolio will truly reflect the accuracy of an investor's analysis. A typical long-only portfolio will have its performance at least partially masked by what occurs in various sectors or the broader market.

If beta is a measure of how volatile a stock, or a group of stocks, is when compared to the market as a whole, *alpha* is the measure of the excess movement of a stock's price, *independent of the market*. A market neutral portfolio can be successful only if the alpha is high. With both long and short holdings, beta is largely cancelled out and what we are left with is alpha. Through careful stock selection, a market neutral portfolio's long selections should rise higher (or fall less) than the broader market, and short selections should fall further (or rise less) than the broader market. When that happens, it means the alpha is high, and it is a necessary condition for a profitable market neutral portfolio.

Suppose that in a given year the overall market rises 15 percent. To the extent that an investor's long stock picks rise even further, we can say the portfolio has a strong alpha. Or, if the investor has some short holdings, and those stocks don't rise when the overall market rises 15 percent, again the investor's portfolio has a positive alpha. We can think of alpha as "excess return."

Remember the efficient market hypothesis from Chapter 1? There is no room for alpha in that theory because, according to its adherents, any relative out-performance is either temporary or random luck or both.

Even though most investors disagree with this thinking, they should acknowledge that picking the right stocks is hard work.

Disadvantages of Relying on Alpha

The alpha element of a market neutral strategy is a double-edged sword. If an investor or money manager is a lousy stock picker, it will be very painfully clear. The vagaries of the broader market cannot be blamed for poor performance, nor will a generally rising market cover up mistakes. If there is one reason not to utilize a market neutral strategy, it is this: alpha is hard to come by.

How do we know this? In the evidentiary lineup, Exhibit A is the fact that the majority of mutual fund managers do not exceed the broad market's returns. Put another way, most (but not all) mutual funds do not demonstrate alpha. Instead, their results can largely be explained by what occurs in the overall market.

And because alpha is not commonly found, it makes market neutral investing seem intimidating. Compared to a more traditional buy-and-hold approach to investing, a market neutral strategy is doubly unforgiving of errors. An investor can be wrong two ways instead of just one, buying a stock that loses value *and* selling short a stock that increases in value. Buy-and-hold investing, for all of its flaws and risks, requires only one type of decision making: which stocks look undervalued.

What's more, over the long term, we know that stocks tend to rise in value. Thus, a long-only portfolio will, eventually, probably return a profit. It's just that the profit can be a long time in coming, and it comes with more risk than an investor may want.

Another disadvantage is that a do-it-yourself market neutral strategy can't be implemented in a tax-deferred retirement account. Shorting stocks, as we will see later, is not permitted without a margin account. The irony is that the rules governing retirement accounts were established to protect investors from loss of capital. Selling stocks short is not compatible with that goal in the eyes of the regulators. The good news is that using a market neutral *mutual fund* is permitted in tax-deferred accounts and, in fact, is the best place for such a mutual fund because of the short-term capital gains that can be thrown off. Chapter 9 contains a full discussion of this special category of mutual fund.

Finally, it's very important to note that even a well-crafted market neutral portfolio is likely to produce relatively lower returns during a bull market. That's not to say it won't, or can't, show a profit, but rather that it will probably return less of a profit than a long-only portfolio. In effect, this relatively lower return is like paying an insurance premium. In order to receive some protection against a downturn, investors will give up something in return. However, instead of writing a check to the insurance company, the "cost" comes in the form of opportunity cost rather than an outright expense.

Market Neutral Portfolio Example

Let's take a look at how this might work in a hypothetical portfolio. In the simple example that follows, we will examine a market neutral portfolio and its performance in two different broader market scenarios, one bullish and one bearish.

The portfolio in Figure 2.8 is a market neutral portfolio of approximately $10,000, with an almost perfectly equal dollar amount long and

FIGURE 2.8 MARKET NEUTRAL PORTFOLIO—BEGINNING

Stock	Initial Share Price	Share Number	Initial Value
Long Positions			
Alpha Manufacturing	$13	77	$1,001
New Semiconductor Inc.	$21	48	$1,008
First Pulp and Paper Co.	$40	25	$1,000
Healthy Hospitals Inc.	$33	30	$ 990
Pizzazz Retail Corp.	$10	100	$1,000
Subtotal			**$4,999**
Short Positions			
Beta Manufacturing	$15	−67	−$1,005
Obsolete Semiconductor Inc.	$17	−59	−$1,003
Second Pulp and Paper Co.	$45	−22	−$ 990
Pallid Hospitals Inc.	$27	−37	−$ 999
Plodder Retail Corp.	$ 8	−125	−$1,000
Subtotal			**−$4,997**

short. Note that the short positions are represented by a negative number of shares.

We can see that this portfolio appears to be perfectly market neutral because all of the stocks on the long side are in industries that match up with those on the short side. There are two manufacturing firms, two semiconductor firms, etc. This provides the insurance against industry risk that was discussed above. It is also a portfolio with a broad representation of different industries, which is not a requirement for a market neutral portfolio, but it is not a bad idea.

What's more, with an equal amount of money divided between longs and shorts, this portfolio has a reduced level of market risk. Regardless of whether the broad market crashes lower or explodes higher, this portfolio will be insulated from that movement. The theoretical beta of this collection of stocks should be close to 0, with little or no correlation to what the overall market does.

Now let's see what might happen to this portfolio during a three-month period when the broad market enjoys an impressive 10 percent gain. We're going to assume that the hypothetical investor who put this portfolio together is a pretty good stock picker. Put another way, we will assume the portfolio demonstrates a moderately strong alpha. We are further going to assume that because the investor is pretty good, but not perfect, the long selections perform as well as the broader market and the short selections also go up, but only by half as much as the broader market (see Figure 2.9).

This assumed performance yields a net positive return of $252. The long side of the portfolio goes up $499, the short side goes down $247, and the net rate of return, given the $10,000 invested, is 2.5 percent. That is a far cry from the 10 percent return the investor would have received if he had simply put the money in an index fund. It is easy to understand from this example how a market neutral portfolio might lag the broader market in a bullish time period. The cost of the insurance comes in the form of lower returns when the market is rising.

Now we'll see what would have happened to that same portfolio during a period when the bears held sway and the broader market declined 10 percent (see Figure 2.10). Once again we will make some reasonable assumptions about how skilled the investor is; good but not perfect. Our calculation will suppose that the short positions decline 10 percent, just

FIGURE 2.9 MARKET NEUTRAL PORTFOLIO—BULL MARKET

Stock	New Share Price	Share Number	Current Value
Long Positions			
Alpha Manufacturing	$14.30	77	$1,101.10
New Semiconductor Inc.	$23.10	48	$1,108.80
First Pulp and Paper Co.	$44.00	25	$1,100.00
Healthy Hospitals Inc.	$36.30	30	$1,089.00
Pizzazz Retail Corp.	$11.00	100	$1,100.00
Subtotal			**+$ 498.90**
Short Positions			
Beta Manufacturing	$15.75	−67	−$1,055.25
Obsolete Semiconductor Inc.	$17.85	−59	−$1,053.15
Second Pulp and Paper Co.	$47.25	−22	−$1,039.50
Pallid Hospitals Inc.	$28.35	−37	−$1,048.95
Plodder Retail Corp.	$ 8.40	−125	−$1,050.00
Subtotal			−$ 246.85
Net Total after 3 months			**$ 252.05**

FIGURE 2.10 MARKET NEUTRAL PORTFOLIO—BEAR MARKET

Stock	New Share Price	Share Number	Current Value
Long Positions			
Alpha Manufacturing	$12.35	77	$ 950.95
New Semiconductor Inc.	$19.95	48	$ 957.60
First Pulp and Paper Co.	$38.00	25	$ 950.00
Healthy Hospitals Inc.	$31.35	30	$ 940.50
Pizzazz Retail Corp.	$ 9.50	100	$ 950.00
Subtotal			$4,749.05
Short Positions			
Beta Manufacturing	$13.50	−67	−$ 904.50
Obsolete Semiconductor Inc.	$15.30	−59	−$ 902.70
Second Pulp and Paper Co.	$40.50	−22	−$ 891.00
Pallid Hospitals Inc.	$24.30	−37	−$ 899.10
Plodder Retail Corp.	$ 7.20	−125	−$ 900.00
Subtotal			−$4,497.30
Net Total after 3 months			**$ 251.75**

like the indexes, and the long positions also decline, but only at half the rate, or by 5 percent.

Once again, given the simplistic and uniform assumptions we made, the portfolio returned 2.5 percent. The long positions would be down $251 and the short positions would be up $503. This portfolio performance makes for a much happier investor than one who would have lost 10 percent by being long-only during this period.

Each of these examples, though simplified, is a reasonable scenario that might well be played out in a real market neutral portfolio. A well-constructed long/short mix, with a good alpha, can show a gain no matter what the broader market does. However, it is likely to lag the market during a period of strong gains.

We can take this simple analysis a step further and see what would have happened if these two scenarios had played out over two successive quarters. A long-only portfolio that behaved like the broader market would have been down by 1 percent after six months. The initial $10,000 after the first quarter would have become $11,000 but after a loss of 10 percent in the second quarter, it would only be worth $9,900. In contrast, the market neutral portfolio would have risen from $10,000 at the beginning of the first quarter to $10,250 and then climbed again to $10,500 in the second quarter. The total gain after two quarters would have been 5 percent.

Now, to be fair, this little two-quarter scenario is not the long term. Over the long term, the stock market tends to rise rather than advance and decline by the same amount in two consecutive periods. But there are a couple of questions that investors or financial planners must answer:

1. "What *do* I do about the short term?"
2. "Am I willing to accept potentially smaller returns over the long term in exchange for lower risk?"

Each of us might answer those questions differently. For those who are concerned about the short term and don't want to rely only on a long-term market rise, a market neutral, or similar type of hedged portfolio, may be the answer. That will be especially true if the answer to the second question is yes. In the next couple of chapters we will take a look at some possible ways of improving alpha so that good returns are generated and risk is lowered.

Summary

Conventional ideas about risk, and risk management, may not be as useful as many Wall Street mavens would have us believe. This becomes more apparent when risk is defined as the likelihood that an investment, or a portfolio, will lose money. Beta, a perfectly correct measure of how volatile a stock is, doesn't really tell us anything about the chances a stock will fall. Diversification is a fine way to spread risk, but it doesn't reduce the risk of a loss.

Market neutral investing does indeed reduce risk, specifically sector and market risk. It serves as a form of insurance protection against sector downgrades, investor rotation out of particular sectors, and broad bear markets.

Its greatest disadvantages are: (1) that it heightens the importance of careful analysis of specific stocks, and (2) that it will likely underperform during a bull market. Even with these drawbacks, the fact that market neutral investing serves as a form of insurance makes it a very appealing strategy.

3

BUILDING BLOCKS

If we can agree that at any given time some stocks are overvalued and others are undervalued, we are then faced with the daunting challenge of figuring out which is which. It is neither easy nor obvious. Of course, the idea is to buy shares in undervalued stocks with the expectation that the price will rise to fully reflect fair value, while selling short shares in overvalued stocks whose price will someday fall to fair value.

But that task is made difficult by the somewhat subjective nature of valuation. If deciding a stock's fair value was completely straightforward, there would be no instances of "misvaluation," now would there? We set for ourselves an undertaking that, by its very nature, will lead to a conclusion not shared by everyone else. That can be uncomfortable and intimidating, but there is no other way. If we are to independently identify stocks that are not correctly valued, we will by definition be going against the conventional wisdom that assigned those values incorrectly in the first place.

This effort to select undervalued and overvalued stocks is not for the faint of heart, but there are some measures we can take that will help. Ideally, we would like to develop a *methodology* for deciding which stocks are cheaper than they deserve to be and which are unjustifiably expensive. Then, it will be necessary to apply that methodology with consistency and discipline in order to overcome our tendency to go along with "the crowd." If we base our decisions on numbers, we have a reasonable chance of success. However, drawing conclusions about value based on instinct, or intuition, will not work. It is all too easy to be swayed or subsequently question our original thesis. The only way to engender confidence is to *quantify* the characteristics of stocks that are likely to rise in price and those that are likely to fall in price.

Relatively Speaking

The best way of taking a stab at valuation is to compare how one company is priced relative to how other, similar companies are priced. If a company is trading at a premium or a discount compared to its peers, then we may have a case of misvaluation. However, it is pretty important that our comparisons are valid. One of the simplest rules to follow is to always compare apples with apples, or in this case, widget-making companies with other widget makers. Because every industry has its own set of unique operating norms, we must make sure that our comparisons reflect those norms.

For example, if you were told only that Company A has a PE ratio of 20 and Company B has a PE ratio of 30, would it be fair to conclude that Company A is undervalued and Company B is overvalued? After all, Company A is earning more money per dollar of share price.

What if you learned that Company A is a steel producer, in an industry where the average PE ratio at the beginning of 2004 was 19? Hmmm. Maybe Company A is not so undervalued but slightly overvalued! And what if you learned that Company B is a semiconductor company, where the industry average PE ratio at the beginning of 2004 was 60? Company B doesn't look quite so expensive now, does it?

The importance of relative valuation can't be underestimated. *Maybe no other concept in this chapter is more important.* A judgment about valuation can't really be made at all unless we know something about the dynamics of the industry we are talking about and, more important, how our specimen company compares to the industry norms.

Another, related, rule is to make certain the company in question is classified in the right industry. This can be a challenge because different data sources occasionally place a company in one industry when, in fact, its business more correctly belongs somewhere else. We will spend some time on the subject of fundamental data sources in the Appendix, but there are not always easy answers.

As one example, a popular Internet data service, with a reputation as a high-quality supplier of fundamental data, had some unusual classifications related to what would seem like a mundane and uncomplicated industry: Crops. Most of us would think of companies producing crops as easily defined. They grow things that we eat.

This data source, however, included a winery in their "Crops" classification. OK, maybe it can be included based on the fact that the company does grow grapes. But there is another classification titled "Beverages—Alcoholic" and a competing winery was placed in this latter group. Clearly such variances in data can lead to erroneous conclusions. The business of making and selling wine is quite different from growing table grapes because the wine producer will enjoy much higher gross profit margins but also higher regulatory costs. The point is that it would be a mistake to try and place a fair value on a winery by comparing its ratios to a grower of grapes.

Here is another example of how data can be misleading: *not* included in that same Crops classification was well-known banana grower, Chiquita Brands. Instead, Chiquita was listed as a "Food Processor," even though 75 percent of the company's business is growing and selling unprocessed fruit. Fresh Del Monte Produce, a direct Chiquita competitor, *was* classified under Crops.

Confusing? Yes, indeed. Not unworkable, but it points up the importance of double-checking any companies that come to our attention as potential candidates to buy or sell short. Is the company classified correctly?

And then there are the companies that defy classification. The online auction company eBay is a perfect example of this. Yes, the company is a retailer, and it utilizes sophisticated software technology in order to facilitate transactions. But eBay isn't really a software company. Is it a retailer? Well, sort of. While eBay sells retail merchandise, because it carries no inventory, its business dynamics are quite different from most retailers.

Almost no other company does what eBay does, connecting buyers and sellers at the retail level. It may not be a monopoly but it's darn close, and thus there is no basis upon which to decide if eBay is overvalued or undervalued. There is no valuation "baseline." It would not have been smart to conclude that because eBay carried a PE ratio of 101 at the end of 2002—and retailers on average had a PE ratio of 16—that eBay was overvalued. The company is so unique that it is impossible to decide what value is fair. In statistics, these sorts of phenomena are called "outliers," and they are discarded from the analysis.

As an aside on eBay's valuation, some critics would simply observe that no company deserves to be valued at 100 times last year's earnings. However, that is more of a visceral reaction and not a very helpful analysis in the development of our methodology. Those same critics would surely have thought eBay overvalued at the beginning of 2002 when the stock had a PE ratio of over 200! They would have been wrong. As it turns out, the stock price actually went up ever-so-slightly in 2002. The PE ratio fell from 200 to 100 because earnings improved, not because the stock price fell. What's more, eBay again had a PE ratio of about 100 at the end of 2003—altogether the stock price rose almost 100 percent those two years. What a great illustration of how important it is to look at valuation ratios in context.

The idea that we should "comparison shop" among stocks is not very revolutionary in some sense. If a consumer is considering the purchase of a used car, it would be most unusual if she did not compare prices among similar makes and models offered from different dealers or individuals. This is no different than making comparisons among stocks. In the case of a car, we look at mileage, service record, and the general condition of the vehicle. In the case of a stock, we look at PE ratio, past sales, expected earnings growth, and some other factors.

The process is quite intuitive in the case of a car, and it should be no less so with stocks. The valuation process is just comparison shopping. We can also further extend our analogy if we think of a company like eBay as an extremely rare or unusual car. It is much more difficult to figure out the fair price of a 1927 Nash as opposed to a 2000 Honda.

What to Look For in Earnings

Volumes have been written about what factors should be considered when assessing the value of a stock. This chapter will focus on a manageable number of primarily fundamental, as opposed to technical, elements. Our goal will be to weave a mosaic that ultimately gives us a rich picture of how a company is being valued. Because no one figure can do an effective job of that, we focus on a handful of measures of earnings and sales.

First, let's examine the most commonly used appraisal of valuation, the price-to-earnings ratio. Again, this number is calculated by dividing the price of a share of stock by the earnings per share. PE ratios are probably used more often than any other single factor but suffer from at least three drawbacks.

First, a PE ratio is a backward-looking measure. PE ratios use earnings from the previous 12-month period, and so a it is necessarily a look at the past, not the future. It doesn't tell us what we might expect in the quarters or years ahead.

Second, it is a snapshot. It tells us nothing about whether earnings are increasing or shrinking. Ideally, we would like a dynamic view of earnings, but a PE ratio by itself is static.

Third, earnings are very much subject to manipulation, at least in the short run. One-time events, say a plant closing, can be charged off without affecting earnings, making them a less-than-perfect reflection of a company's real results. For these reasons, earnings are not a great summary of company health.

With that said, a PE ratio is useful, so long as its shortcomings are recognized and it forms just one data point among several in our analysis. Generally, lower PE ratios reflect lower valuation, and higher PE ratios higher valuation. A negative PE should be viewed in a negative light—it depicts a company that has been losing money. That doesn't mean we can't find companies worth buying that have a negative PE, but it may make the case for buying shares less compelling.

Again, a PE must be viewed in the context of a company's particular industry. As discussed earlier, a company PE of 20 might be relatively high or low, depending on the norms for its industry. As a point of reference, the table in Figure 3.1 lists average PE ratios for a number of industries at the end of 2003.

As can be seen, there is wide variation among industry groups. At the extremes, Airlines traded at only 15.9 times their trailing earnings, while semiconductor companies traded at 58.6 times earnings. Thus, the average airline was valued at a little more than one-fourth the average semiconductor company. To think of it another way, if the average airline produced $1 per share in earnings, an investor would pay $15.90 for a share of that stock. To own that same $1 per share in earning power,

FIGURE 3.1 PE RATIOS FOR SELECT INDUSTRIES

Industry	Average PE Ratio 12/31/03
Airlines	15.9
Biotechnology and Drugs	28.7
Casinos/Gaming	18.4
Chemical Manufacturing	21.7
Electric Utilities	16.2
Hotels	30.3
Paper Products	19.9
Retail–Apparel	19.1
Savings Banks and Thrifts	17.1
Schools	39.3
Software	36.7
Semiconductors	58.6
Trucking	22.9

an investor would have paid $58.60 for a share in a semiconductor company.

That may seem odd, but it has everything to do with the expectations, and the hopes, for earnings growth. The market rewards growth and clearly the market expects semiconductor companies to grow earnings in a much more robust fashion than airlines. To gain a better understanding of what growth factor is at work, we can look at what is often called the "forward PE."

The *forward PE,* as its name suggests, is calculated by dividing the current price of a share of stock by the expected *future* earnings per share of the company. Obviously, in order to come up with this number, we need to have some clue about what those future earnings are going to be. For this information, we can turn to the brokerage community that routinely makes predictions about future earnings.

Because brokerage estimates are generated for only some companies, we necessarily reduce the universe of stocks that can be evaluated on a forward PE basis. That's not all bad. With so many thousands of publicly traded companies in the United States, using forward PE in our analysis will immediately shrink our workload. For example, in one database of 8,600 public companies, only 3,700 carried earnings estimates. The disadvantage is that we may miss out on some opportunities among companies that are not covered, but the value of using a forward PE out-weighs this disadvantage.

Forward PEs are often lower than current PEs because earnings (the "E" in the calculation) are often projected to be higher than they were in the prior year because earnings do tend to grow over time and be-cause Wall Street estimates are often thought to carry an optimistic bias. Simple arithmetic tells us that if a company's share price is $25 and earn-ings last year were $1 per share, the current PE is 25. If earnings for next year are expected to be $1.25, the forward PE is 20.

The table in Figure 3.2 provides a summary of a few industry for-ward PEs as of the end of 2003.

One insight this gives us is the degree of optimism or pessimism that existed about each of these industries heading into 2004. We can make this determination by juxtaposing current PE ratios next to forward PEs. If we divide the current PE by the forward PE ratio, we end up with the industry's expected earnings growth rate for 2004.

For example, Wall Street was feeling very good about the Schools in-dustry, expecting earnings to rise by almost 50 percent. We conclude this because at the time the current PE ratio was 39.3, as seen in Figure 3.1, but the *forward* PE ratio in Figure 3.2 was only 26.6. Because the average share price was the same in each case, we can calculate that earnings

FIGURE 3.2 FORWARD PE RATIOS FOR SELECT INDUSTRIES

Industry	Average Forward PE Ratio 12/31/03
Airlines	13.8
Biotechnology and Drugs	24.7
Casinos/Gaming	16.0
Chemical Manufacturing	16.1
Electric Utilities	14.0
Hotels	20.8
Paper Products	17.1
Retail–Apparel	17.7
Savings Banks and Thrifts	14.3
Schools	26.6
Software	37.9
Semiconductors	54.9
Trucking	16.4

(the denominator) must be going up 47.7 percent. The outlook for Hotels was also extremely positive, predictions being that earnings would rise by 45 percent. In the "less-than-rosy outlook" category, earnings for the Software industry were actually expected to shrink by 3 percent.

The more important consideration is not what industry has the best or worst outlook, but rather that our analysis should take in to account a company's forward PE in relation to its industry forward PE. Generally speaking, undervalued stocks will tend to have lower-than-average forward PE ratios, and overvalued stocks will tend to have higher-than-average forward PE ratios. While there may be extenuating circumstances, *if all else was equal*, we would tend to think of an airline stock with a forward PE of 10 as undervalued and one with a forward PE of 18 as overvalued.

All That Static

As important and useful as PE ratios are, particularly when we look at both current and forward PEs, they do not by themselves give us a perfectly clear picture of earnings. As we mentioned, both ratios, taken separately, are static numbers. Because the market rewards earnings growth and punishes earnings declines, we need to know what direction earnings are going and at what pace. Otherwise, we might be fooled into thinking that because a company carries a low PE ratio it is a bargain, when instead it might be legitimately discounted because of a low earnings trajectory.

There is a way to get around this shortcoming by calculating a different number called the PEG ratio. PEG stands for Price/Earnings/Growth, and it is calculated by taking a company's PE ratio and dividing by its expected earnings growth rate. The higher the resulting ratio, the more overvalued the company, and vice versa.

For example, a company with a PE ratio of 20 that is expected to have earnings growth of 5 percent has a PEG ratio of 4, which is pretty high. A more reasonable valuation would be found in a company with a PE ratio of 20 and expected earnings growth of 25 percent. The PEG ratio in such a case would be 0.80.

The PEG ratio is handy because it combines a backward look (past earnings), a current look (the current price), and a forward look (earnings growth) into one simple number. Typically, a PEG ratio of 1 has been viewed as "fair value." In other words, many experts suggest that stocks with PEG ratios of less than 1 are undervalued and those greater than 1 are overvalued. In fact, at the end of 2001, the median PEG ratio was about 1.4. At the end of 2002, the median had fallen to about 1.3. At the end of 2003, the median PEG ratio had risen again to slightly more than 1.4.

It's interesting to note that the drop in the median PEG ratio from 2001 to 2002 was the result of higher PE ratios combined with heightened expectations for earnings growth. At the end of 2001, a typical company carried a PE of 15 and was expected to grow earnings by a bit more than 10 percent. At the end of 2002, median PEs were 16 and 12 percent growth was expected. At the end of 2003, it was more of the same, but PE ratios had climbed quite a bit higher than growth expectations, causing the median PEG ratio to tick up (see Figure 3.3). Looking at this "big picture," the fall in overall PEG ratios would suggest that the market was more fairly valued at the end of 2002 than it was at the end of 2001 or 2003.

In any case, the lower the PEG ratio, the more likely that a group of stocks, or an individual stock, is undervalued. A high PEG ratio suggests that the price of a stock is trading at a premium relative to its future growth prospects. One problem with PEG ratios, as they are normally calculated and published by the available data services, is that the growth rate used is for the next five years. Projections extending out this far are of questionable validity—ask any frontline manager to predict sales and profits much beyond the next few *quarters* and a blank look will most likely ensue. Consequently, PEG ratios use an earnings growth rate that is almost certainly off the mark. However, it is possible to calculate a PEG ratio yourself using just next year's growth rate, as was done in Figure 3.3.

In some ways it doesn't matter how it is done as long as the calculation is uniformly made because it facilitates an apples-to-apples comparison. If the five-year estimates are wildly optimistic for one company, they are probably equally optimistic for another, and that allows PEG ratios to retain some utility. Perhaps we should say they facilitate a spoiled-apples-to-spoiled-apples comparison.

FIGURE 3.3 STOCK VALUATION AND THE PEG RATIO

Year	Median PE Ratio	Median Growth Rate	PEG Ratio
2001	14.6	10.5%	1.39
2002	16.0	12.0%	1.33
2003	20.2	14.0%	1.44

FIGURE 3.4 HIGH AND LOW PEG STOCK PERFORMANCE

Year	High PEG Stocks	Low PEG Stocks	S&P 500
2002	−31%	−22%	−24%
2003	+15%	+79%	+22%

As an example of how PEG ratios can be put to use, Figure 3.4 shows the results from two searches for high PEG and low PEG stocks using data from late 2001 and then late 2002. In the following calendar years high PEG stocks performed worse than the S&P 500 and low PEG stocks performed better than the S&P 500.

As the table in Figure 3.4 illustrates, both categories fell in 2002 along with the broader market, but high PEG stocks fell further and low PEG stocks fell slightly less. In 2003, both high and low PEG stocks rose, but low PEG stocks dramatically outperformed the market and the high PEG stocks underperformed to some extent.

What are the implications for a market neutral strategy? Let's assume that an investor bought $50,000 worth of the low PEG stocks and sold short $50,000 worth of the high PEG stocks. The net return in 2002 would have been $4,500 or 4.5 percent. The net return in 2003 would have been $32,000, or 32 percent.

Those are impressive returns, especially when we consider a comparable $100,000 investment in an index fund. The index fund investment would still be in the red after two years, while the market neutral investment would be up $36,500. And, at the same time, the market neutral approach hedged away a great deal of risk!

Sales Ratios

Another fundamental data point that is extremely useful relates to company revenues and valuation. Particularly important is the price-to-sales (PS) ratio, a number calculated by taking the price of a share of stock and dividing it by the company's revenue per share of stock. Another way to think of PS ratio is if we could sell a company to some buyer for the same amount of money that the company generates in sales, the PS ratio would equal 1.

This ratio is considered by many to be even more helpful in valuing a company than a PE ratio. While earnings come in different stripes, pro forma versus GAAP, for example, there can't be much debate about what is, or is not, revenue. PS ratios avoid the many points of view surrounding earnings: should options expenses be included? Are one-time charges important to the bottom line? Do we really need to consider taxes and depreciation?

Of course, in cases of outright fraud, sales can be inflated. But generally, a dollar of revenue is a dollar of revenue, making the PS ratio a somewhat more reliable valuation tool than earnings-based ratios. In his seminal book *What Works on Wall Street* (2nd Edition, 1998, McGraw Hill), O'Shaughnessy concludes that of all the numbers used to predict a stock's future performance, the PS ratio is the single most effective one.

As with PE ratios, undervalued stocks tend to have low PS ratios and overvalued stocks high PS ratios. However, once again, the key is to evaluate a PS ratio relative to the company's industry peers. There will be wide variations among industries, and the absolute number is not as important as the relative number.

Similar to the list of selected PE ratios, the table in Figure 3.5 lists the median PS ratio for a cross section of different industry groups, as of the beginning of 2004.

FIGURE 3.5 SELECT INDUSTRY PS RATIOS 2004

Industry	Median PS Ratio 1/1/04
Airlines	0.3
Biotechnology and Drugs	6.3
Casinos/Gaming	0.9
Chemical Manufacturing	0.9
Electric Utilities	0.9
Hotels	1.3
Paper Products	0.7
Retail–Apparel	0.6
Savings Banks and Thrifts	2.8
Schools	2.4
Software	2.1
Semiconductors	3.3
Trucking	0.5

We can see a wide variation among these ratios, with one industry selling, on average, for over six times revenue and others selling for just one-third of revenues. The disparity can be attributed to the perceived opportunity for growth, much as it was with the variability among PE ratios. Intuitively, we recognize that the trucking industry, as a whole, is not going to see spectacular increases in revenue, or earnings. Biotech companies, on the other hand, do have the potential for new blockbuster drugs and explosive growth. The market is pricing those industries accordingly. What's more, many biotech companies are in the development stage, where they have very little revenue, and the PS ratio will be skewed higher. By the way, the median PS ratio for all publicly traded companies at the time was 1.54.

We would like to use relatively low or high PS ratios to help identify undervalued or overvalued individual companies. So, for example, if we could find a semiconductor company with a PS ratio of "only" 2.0, it might well be undervalued. Or, if we found a trucking company with a PS ratio of 1.0, it may be overvalued.

Using data from 2002 and 2003, a small experiment yielded promising results. A search for companies that traded at 40 times or more their industry median PS ratio produced 28 firms at the beginning of 2002. Those stocks fell during the year an average of 53 percent, more than twice as much as the S&P 500 fell over the same time period. Conversely, a group of 27 companies that were trading at only one-tenth of their industry median PS ratio fell 23 percent in 2002, about the same as the market.

The same parameters in 2003 generated a smaller list of stocks, but with similarly good results. The low PS ratio stocks rose a remarkable 68 percent, and the high PS ratio stocks were up about 22 percent, much like the overall market (see Figure 3.6).

For at least those two years, a high relative PS ratio did indeed seem to harbinger poor or average stock performance while low relative PS

FIGURE 3.6 HIGH AND LOW PS STOCK PERFORMANCE

Year	High PS Stocks	Low PS Stocks	S&P 500
2002	−53%	−23%	−24%
2003	+22%	+68%	+22%

ratio companies performed as well, or better than the broader market. To be sure, there were a few good stock performances among the overvalued group and a number of poor performers in the undervalued group. On balance, though, it was a very good way of separating the winners from the losers and supports O'Shaughnessy's contention that PS ratios are good predictors of future price performance.

Creating a market neutral portfolio with these sets of stocks would have produced an excellent return each year. In 2002 the net gain would have been 15 percent and in 2003 it would have been 23 percent.

One caution about using super-high or super-low PS ratios as identifiers of short or long candidates: there will inevitably be some companies in each list that really deserve the ratio they carry. In 2002, for example, 3 of the 27 companies on the "undervalued list" declared bankruptcy. In those cases, the low PS ratio was not a sign of being undervalued, but it was, instead, telegraphing that all was not well. No doubt an investor using this method would have had some stomach-churning experiences, despite it being a profitable strategy.

Wind in the Sails

Having looked at three different sets of fundamental factors—earnings ratios, earnings growth, and sales ratios—we will now examine two more elements that are useful in finding undervalued and overvalued companies. One of these elements is another fundamental factor; the other is a technical indicator. Both serve as a measure of whether there might be some wind in the sails of the companies we are examining.

First, when evaluating a company, we want to consider past revenue growth. This is a common-sense sort of criteria based on the idea that companies with strong sales growth have a certain level of momentum. If sales are up in the past 12 months over the prior 12 months, there is some reason to believe the trend will continue. A company may have developed better products or better distribution, or it may have been able to raise prices without hurting volumes. Whatever the reason, strong sales growth is clearly a positive sign for the health of a business.

Of course, sales trends sometimes reverse themselves too. Obviously, companies don't enjoy perpetual revenue growth. Consequently, there is some risk that at any point in time a company's sales may be leveling off or beginning to head in the other direction. When we find a company with strong revenue growth, there is no guarantee that the growth will continue, but it is an encouraging development. Conversely, shrinking sales are a warning flag and may indicate further trouble ahead. Also, don't be fooled by increases in sales that are solely attributable to acquisitions. Acquisition-based revenue growth isn't bad, but it isn't as bullish as "organic," or internally driven growth. Purchasing another company or outside product line costs money and may or may not ultimately increase profits.

As with all fundamental analysis, sales growth or decline should be viewed in the context of industry norms. If we find a company that grew sales by 10 percent over the past year, but is in an industry with particularly favorable conditions, where the average industry growth was, say, 15 percent, we may not be terribly impressed. Or we might find a company with a sales decrease of 1 percent in an industry where, on the whole, revenues were down 10 percent. The latter case suggests that a company is weathering an industry storm better than its competitors and could continue to outperform when the climate improves.

The relative sales performance is more important than the absolute performance. In our quest for stocks to buy, we should consider more favorably those firms that have demonstrated better-than-industry average sales. Likewise, those with sales lagging the industry average will be more likely to end up on the list of stocks to sell short. As a point of reference, Figure 3.7 contains sales growth rates for a few select industry groups.

In assessing a specific airline stock, for example, we should consider whether sales are stronger or weaker than the 8 percent industry average gain. By itself, past sales data is a relatively poor indicator of future stock price performance and says nothing about how a stock is being valued. But it does give us a more complete picture of a company's health.

Finally, we want to consider a technical factor called the "relative strength index," or RSI. It is a very common technical tool that measures how much momentum a particular stock has based on its own past price movements. More specifically, a *relative strength index* is a calculation that compares how much a stock moved up on an up day with how much it moved down on a down day. That calculation will oscillate between 0 and 100, with lower numbers indicating negative momentum and higher numbers positive momentum.

FIGURE 3.7 SELECT INDUSTRY SALES GROWTH RATES

Industry	Percent Sales Growth in 2003
Airlines	8.0
Biotechnology and Drugs	16.9
Casinos/Gaming	3.8
Chemical Manufacturing	4.4
Electric Utilities	9.1
Hotels	1.9
Paper Products	1.7
Retail–Apparel	4.2
Savings Banks and Thrifts	−7.3
Schools	16.4
Software	1.8
Semiconductors	5.8
Trucking	8.7

A number of investors reject the whole notion of technical analysis, and this book is oriented much more toward fundamental analysis. But there is data that supports the use of technical studies. For example, there is some credible evidence that stocks moving higher tend to continue that path and those moving lower have a propensity to move lower still, regardless of underlying fundamentals.

With that in mind, we want to incorporate a simple technical momentum factor into our methodology—not by itself, but as an adjunct to the fundamental analysis. We can think of it as an overlay to the fundamentals. If, for example, we can identify a stock that is undervalued based on its price relative to earnings, its price relative to earnings growth, its price relative to sales, past sales growth, *and* that has some upward momentum behind it, we will have found a stock that is probably worth buying.

Off Limits

One cautionary restriction must be added to all of the foregoing. A category of stocks exists for which it is dangerous to apply the type of analysis just described. It is biotechnology stocks.

The reason for this is that biotech stocks tend to trade on factors not captured by fundamentals. A true biotech firm that is engaged in research on a new compound, or a new drug, carries a level of complexity that is not reflected in standard valuation ratios. What tends to drive the prices of biotech stocks are the actions of the Food and Drug Administration (FDA) and/or clinical research results, whether favorable or unfavorable. If approval for a drug is forthcoming or if test results are negative, a biotech stock will react to that information in a significant manner. There is no way that even a painstakingly careful fundamental analysis is able to assess what might or might not happen in the lab or in the halls of the FDA.

This is not true of major pharmaceutical firms, which have a more stable and predictable pipeline of new drugs as well as a cadre of established medications. While certainly impacted by research and development results, major pharmaceutical companies are less likely to be dramatically impacted by a single new study or FDA decision.

For that matter, *all* companies are impacted by singular events. No review of financial numbers can allow us to predict a host of externalities that might impact a particular firm. Whether it be legislation, litigation, natural disaster, a breakthrough in the lab, or countless other influences, we cannot predict new developments. Fundamental valuation analysis is effective, however, in informing us whether a company's prospects are generally good, bad, or indifferent, and whether its stock price correctly reflects those prospects.

We make an exception for biotechnology companies because their share prices are almost completely determined by medical research results. Because there is no way for most of us to draw valid conclusions about those results before the fact, the prudent course of action is to exclude those companies from our analysis.

In Chapter 4, all of these elements: PE ratios, PEG ratios, PS ratios, past revenue growth, and relative strength will be assembled in such a way that a quantitative model emerges. By using a multifactor approach, the model we build will not rely on any single set of numbers but will seek confirmation of valuation in several ways.

Perhaps more important is the fact that the logic behind each criterion is intuitive. Most investors can easily grasp the idea that a company with a relatively high PE ratio and relatively high PEG ratio might very well be overvalued. Or that a company with a relatively low PS ratio and strong revenue growth may be undervalued.

Summary

Establishing a long/short or market neutral portfolio is appealing from a conceptual point of view, but as a practical matter, it requires some reliable method of selecting undervalued and overvalued stocks. Investors can choose from any number of criteria, but the emphasis here is on several important types of fundamental data. With a slight nod to technical analysis, one momentum-type indicator is also highlighted. This list is far from exhaustive and indeed was selected because it represents a manageable number of criteria. Figure 3.8 summarizes what to look for among this handful of factors.

FIGURE 3.8 SUMMARY OF MANAGEABLE VALUATION FACTORS

Factor	Undervalued	Overvalued
PE Ratio	Low	High
PEG Ratio	Low	High
PS Ratio	Low	High
Revenue Growth	High	Low
RSI	High	Low

4

ASSEMBLING THE BLOCKS

In Chapter 3 we outlined a set of criteria that have potential merit in helping an investor decide if a stock is undervalued or overvalued. None of the ideas presented is radical; indeed, they follow fairly conventional thinking about stock valuation. They are predicated on the belief that an individual stock should be valued based on its price relative to past earnings, expected earnings growth, sales, and sales growth. What's more, each stock must be assessed relative to how it compares to its industry peer group. Our next step is to use all of these "building blocks" to see what kinds of stocks, and portfolios of stocks, they might identify. At the same time, we will move beyond the hypothetical and use real companies and real data.

Undervalued Model

Putting multiple factors all together is often times referred to as a building a "model." Our model will use the criteria outlined in the previous chapter, and also add an additional requirement: we will screen out very small companies by requiring a market capitalization of greater than $100 million. While a $100 million market cap does not represent a particularly large company, adding that minimum requirement does help eliminate some of the many penny stocks that abound. The original database used for this work contained a universe of approximately 8,600 companies. When we eliminated companies with a market cap less than $100 million we were left with less than half, about 3,800 in all.

Also, using a forward PE as part of the selection criteria (meaning a company for which there are earnings estimates) tends to raise the bar in terms of company size because only reasonably large companies receive analyst coverage. Using data from both 2002 and 2003, a search was conducted for undervalued companies, firms with the following characteristics:

- A market capitalization greater than $100 million
- A PE ratio lower than its respective industry average
- A forward PE ratio lower than its expected earnings growth rate
- A PS ratio lower than its respective industry average
- Sales growth over the past 12 months that was better than its industry average
- Relative strength greater than 50 over the prior 12 months

Firms meeting these criteria would seem like strong candidates for a rise in stock price. Relative to both past and expected earnings, they will be priced lower than their industry peers. The stock will also be priced low relative to past sales. Sales growth will be better than competitors. And the stock price will have some momentum behind it. If the theory is correct, we would expect companies like this to outperform the broader market during the subsequent 12 months. In fact, in both 2002 and 2003 they did.

The top 25 companies meeting these criteria in late 2001 had an average price increase of 10 percent in 2002. That's not bad in any environment, but it is particularly impressive in a year when the S&P 500 fell 24 percent. Using similar criteria, a different list of undervalued stocks was generated at the end of 2002. Again selecting the top 25 companies, the results were quite good. The full list of undervalued companies can be found at the end of this chapter in Figures 4.7 and 4.8. In 2003, the average gain among the stocks was 49 percent. That works out to be almost twice as much as the S&P 500's rise of 26 percent (see Figure 4.1).

We used results from 2002 and 2003 because they give us two very different market environments—one that was excessively bearish and

FIGURE 4.1 UNDERVALUED VERSUS S&P 500 STOCKS 2002–2003

Year	Undervalued Model	S&P 500
2002	+9.9%	−23.4%
2003	+48.8%	+26.4%

another that was equally bullish. A model should have the ability to work in all types of situations, and the two years we examined were about as different as they could be in terms of market sentiment. However, it would also be unfair to assume that because this model worked quite well in two different years it will work in subsequent years. About the most we can say is that it looks very promising.

To further quantify the performance of these stocks, we can calculate what would have occurred with a hypothetical portfolio (see Figure 4.2). If an investor had plunked down $1,000 in each stock, or a total of $25,000 at the end of 2001, he or she would have had $27,500 one year later. That same $25,000 invested in an S&P 500 index fund would have dwindled to $19,000. In 2003, an investor would have ended the year with $37,250 by buying the undervalued stocks and $31,500 by buying an S&P 500 index fund.

One characteristic of the stocks that turned up in the model is that they represent a diverse group. Because relative valuations were used, we did not end up with a list of "undervalued" companies all from the same two or three industries. Were we to have used absolute valuations, we would probably have had a highly concentrated list of stocks from sectors that were slow growing. For example, if the criteria stipulated all stocks that had the lowest PE ratios and the lowest PS ratios without regard to

FIGURE 4.2 UNDERVALUED VERSUS S&P 500 STOCKS 2002–2003

	Initial Investment	Ending Value
2002 Undervalued Stocks	$25,000	$27,475
2002 S&P 500	$25,000	$19,150
2003 Undervalued Stocks	$25,000	$37,200
2003 S&P 500	$25,000	$31,600

industry, the list would have been dominated by mining and chemical companies, which have historically carried low ratios.

Instead, there was actually quite a broad cross section of industries represented, everything from banks to semiconductor companies. Clearly there proved to be some clunkers mixed in with the very solid performers. As noted in Chapter 1, the starting valuation of a company is only part of the subsequent story. Actual business execution will also have a critical impact on stock price. But investors can give themselves an advantage by paying close attention to the valuation assigned to a stock at the beginning of any period.

To be sure, there were a few clunkers, particularly in 2002. One stock, Spartan Stores, lost almost 90 percent of its value, and in hindsight it is clear that the stock deserved the low valuation it had at the outset. On the other hand, another 2002 stock, Old Dominion Freight Lines, more than doubled, and clearly the winners outnumbered the losers.

Overvalued Model

We now have the beginnings of a market neutral portfolio, but the next step requires finding some overvalued stocks to combine with the undervalued group. The most obvious way of doing this would be to simply reverse the criteria and look for stocks with the following characteristics:

- A market capitalization greater than $100 million
- A PE ratio *higher* than its respective industry average
- A forward PE ratio *higher* than its expected earnings growth rate average
- A PS ratio *higher* than its respective industry average
- Sales growth over the past 12 months that was *worse* than its industry average

This model would seem likely to produce stocks that are destined to fall in price. Compared to other companies in the same industry, the price of these stocks will be high relative to both past and expected earnings. A high PS ratio also suggests that the company's valuation is high because it is generating less revenue per dollar of share price than is typical. What's more, sales for these firms were either declining at a faster rate or growing less quickly than competitor's sales. We did not include a negative price momentum factor in our otherwise mirror image simply because in testing possible outcomes, it did not benefit the model's results. See Figures 4.9 and 4.10 for the complete list of overvalued stocks.

Based on this reverse logic, we would expect stocks conforming to these specifications to decline, or at least underperform the overall market. Again, in 2002 and 2003 they did, although not to the remarkable degree that the undervalued stocks outperformed. Recalling our earlier discussion of alpha, based on the results obtained, we can say that the undervalued model has a high alpha and the overvalued model has a low alpha.

That's because the overvalued stocks declined only slightly more than the broad market in 2002 and gained just a bit less than the market did in 2003 (see Figure 4.3). It is surprising, frankly, that these stocks held up as well as they did. If they were so overvalued then our expectation would be for them to fall quite a bit further or rise significantly less than the general stock market. Instead, the top 20 overvalued stocks identified at the beginning of 2002 fell 27 percent on average. In 2003 the top 22 overvalued stocks gained an average of 25.1 percent.

There is certainly nothing to be ashamed of with this performance. Anytime a model lives up to its mandate by even a small degree, in this case underperforming the market, there is cause for satisfaction. Had these stocks gone *up* in price in 2002, for example, then we would know our model was a failure.

Once again a mix of stocks turned up in the lists. There were a few companies represented from the energy sector, consumer products, telecommunications, semiconductors, etc. This broad diversity is a positive attribute because it helps avoid overexposure to any one sector. In

FIGURE 4.3 OVERVALUED VERSUS S&P 500 STOCKS 2002–2003

Year	Overvalued Model	S&P 500
2002	−27.0%	−23.4%
2003	+25.1%	+26.4%

Chapter 6 we will discuss the implications of matching up undervalued companies with overvalued companies according to sector such that complete balance is achieved.

Selling short the 20 stocks in 2002, again assuming a $25,000 total investment, would have yielded a profit of $6,750 at the end of the year. In 2003, shorting the overvalued stocks would have resulted in a loss of $6,275 (see Figure 4.4).

Total Return

Our two lists of undervalued and overvalued stocks both behaved reasonably well, vis-à-vis our hopes and expectations. Taken together, they would have formed a fine market neutral portfolio in both 2002 and 2003. The first year's return would have been $9,225, or 18.4 percent. The second year the return would have been less impressive, with profits of $5,925 or 11.8 percent (see Figure 4.5).

The return on investment is obvious, but what is not so easy to see is the reduced risk that this portfolio carried in both years. Because there was

FIGURE 4.4 SHORT SALE OF OVERVALUED STOCKS 2002–2003

	Initial Investment	Ending Value
2002 Overvalued Stocks	$25,000	$31,750
2002 S&P 500	$25,000	$19,150
2003 Overvalued Stocks	$25,000	$18,725
2003 S&P 500	$25,000	$31,600

FIGURE 4.5 MARKET NEUTRAL PORTFOLIO RESULTS 2002–2003

	2002 Performance	2003 Performance
Long Portfolio of Undervalued Stocks	9.9%	48.8%
Short Portfolio of Overvalued Stocks	−27.0%	25.1%
Combined Long/Short Result	18.4%	11.8%
S&P 500	−23.4%	26.4%

an equal amount of investment long and short, the market risk was considerably less than with an all-long or, for that matter, an all-short portfolio.

As it turned out, 2002 was a punk year for stocks, and the hedged portfolio was insulated from the downturn. Conversely, in 2003, with the market roaring ahead, our hypothetical portfolio would have lagged considerably. This is not a surprising result, but it is helpful to underscore the idea with some real numbers. The important question is whether an investor would have been more or less satisfied with the hypothetical portfolio instead of an investment in an index fund over those two years.

We can calculate the total return over both years as if an investor had put $50,000 in a long/short portfolio at the beginning of 2002. With compounding, by the end of 2003 there would have been a 32.3 percent return. Compare that to an index fund investment that would have declined by 3.2 percent at the end of those two years. A rational investor would definitely choose the market neutral investment.

However, there are likely to be more years when the market is up than years when the market is down. Meaning that a long/short or market neutral portfolio is likely to lag by some degree more often than not. In the above example the deck is stacked because, historically, we have not often experienced big declines like we did in 2002. Instead, over time we are more likely to see the market make moderate gains.

Therein lies the real disadvantage of long/short or market neutral investing. While it can look very attractive when the market is languishing, it can be discouraging when the market is racing ahead. As has been mentioned before, this is clearly a trade-off that market neutral investors need to accept. But while it's easy to observe the returns generated by either a long-only portfolio versus a market neutral portfolio, what is not as obvious is the reduced level or risk.

Most investors had a real roller-coaster ride in 2002 and 2003. The big slide in 2002 caused a great deal of concern for many, and then the meteoric rise in 2003 made them nervously giddy. Many investors would prefer a more temperate, less volatile return and would gladly accept a little less performance in exchange for a little more moderation.

Let's assume that the three years following 2003 follow the pattern below. Ask yourself whether you would prefer Scenario A or B outlined in Figure 4.6.

How you answer the question says something about your tolerance for roller coasters and how you might trade-off return and volatility. In

FIGURE 4.6 TWO INVESTMENT STRATEGY RESULTS OVER TIME
2003–2006

	2003 Performance	Estimated 2004 Performance	Estimated 2005 Performance	Estimated 2006 Performance
Scenario A	+26%	+15%	−10%	+15%
Scenario B	+12%	+10%	+5%	+10%

Scenario A, the return after four years is a gain of about 50 percent. In Scenario B, the return is considerably less at 42 percent. But Scenario B has the advantage of having a moderate gain each year and no down years. This would be typical of a good long/short portfolio—no outsize gains but no disasters either.

Growth Investing versus Value Investing

Returning to our model, some may wonder how it fits into the on-going debate about growth investing versus value investing. Much has been written and said about these two different investment schools of thought. The conventional wisdom is that investing in growth stocks is very different from investing in value stocks and that the two styles are mutually exclusive.

A *growth investment strategy* is defined as buying stock in companies that are rapidly expanding sales and earnings, almost without regard to the valuation assigned to the company's stock. The general theory is that almost any premium is worth paying, so long as that company is growing, and growing rapidly.

A *value investment strategy* is defined as buying stock in companies that may not be growing rapidly but are being valued at a substantial discount in the market. For whatever reason, the market has so marked down the price of the stock that it becomes an attractive buy. Generally, value investors are attracted to stocks for which they believe there is little downside.

One of the advantages of the market neutral methodology is that it largely sidesteps this debate. The undervalued stocks were discounted, as evidenced by low PE ratios and low PS ratios and thus appeal to value investors. However, it is also true that sales were better at these firms than at their competitors. On average, at the beginning of 2003, sales were up for the undervalued group by 16 percent. The median for all companies was −1 percent. And there was decent earnings growth among the undervalued. The average expected earnings growth for the 2003 list was 13.3 percent, slightly below the median for all companies. These companies can be fairly described as growing *and* priced at a discount.

The overvalued stocks were growing less rapidly, averaging 13.1 percent in expected earnings growth at the beginning of 2003. Sales results were even worse, with the average 2003 overvalued firm having experienced a drop in sales of 2 percent in the prior year. Thus, the group can't exactly lay claim to being hot growth companies when sales are shrinking and expected earnings growth is average. But despite those uninspiring statistics, the shares of the overvalued companies were marked up at a big premium.

Thus, the growth investing versus value investing debate becomes an almost moot point, derailed by the identification of low-valued good-growth and high-valued low-growth companies from a wide range of industries. It is one of the many reasons the market neutral stock selection method is attractive. In Chapter 5 we will examine, in greater detail, what happened with some of the companies that showed up on our lists.

Summary

There is something innately satisfying about assembling a group of stocks that we hypothesize will behave in one particular way and then going on to discover that they largely lived up to our expectations. The model described produced undervalued stocks that outperformed the broad market and overvalued stocks that underperformed, albeit in the latter case only slightly. As a result, a market neutral portfolio containing those stocks would have produced a good return in both 2002 and 2003.

Because 2002 was an unusually bad year for the stock market, it is unfair to conclude, based on the two years of data used, that a market neutral portfolio will outperform the market as a whole. Indeed, it is more likely to underperform based on the fact that the overall market tends to rise. That underperformance, however, comes with a sop. A market neutral portfolio will be much less likely to experience a disastrous year and investors must weigh that trade-off.

FIGURE 4.7 UNDERVALUED STOCKS 2002

Company	Symbol	Industry	Percent Price Change 2002
Aviall, Incorporated	AVL	Aerospace and Defense	6.8
BEI Technologies, Inc.	BEIQ	Scientific & Technical Instruments	−32.6
Brown Shoe Company, Inc.	BWS	Footwear	40.1
Building Materials Hldg.	BMHC	Retail (Home Improvement)	31.2
Capitol Bancorp Limited	CBCL	Regional Banks	71.9
Constellation Brands Inc.	STZ	Beverages (Alcoholic)	23.7
Del Monte Foods Company	DLM	Food Processing	−11.2
EMS Technologies, Inc.	ELMG	Communications Equipment	−2.7
Flagstar Bancorp, Inc.	FBC	Savings Banks and Thrifts	63.4
Group I Automotive, Inc.	GPI	Retail (Specialty Nonapparel)	−16.3
Lithia Motors, Inc.	LAD	Retail (Specialty Nonapparel)	−22
MCSi, Inc.	MCSI	Computer Peripherals	−76.9
Moog Inc.	MOG.A	Scientific & Technical Instruments	40.1
Norsk Hydro ASA	NHY	Oil & Gas—Integrated	5.7
Nortek Incorporated	NTK	Miscellaneous Capital Goods	69.4
Old Dominion Freight Line	ODFL	Trucking	128.1
PacifiCare Health Systems	PHSY	Insurance (Accident & Health)	74.3
ScanSource, Inc.	SCSC	Computer Peripherals	4
Shoe Carnival, Inc.	SCVL	Retail (Apparel)	4.2
Smithfield Foods, Inc.	SFD	Food Processing	−11.9
Spartan Stores, Inc.	SPTN	Retail (Grocery)	−87.6
SRI/Surgical Express Inc.	STRC	Medical Equipment & Supplies	−66.4
Standard Commercial Corp	STW	Tobacco	6.4
TETRA Technologies, Inc.	TTI	Oil Well Services & Equipment	−6.4
Westcorp	WES	Savings Banks and Thrifts	12.9
Average Price Change			**9.9%**

FIGURE 4.8 UNDERVALUED STOCKS 2003

Company	Symbol	Industry	Percent Price Change 2003
Acuity Brands, Inc.	AYI	Electronic Instruments & Controls	96.9
Advanced Marketing Services	MKT	Printing & Publishing	–23.8
Bancolombia S.A. (ADR)	CIB	Regional Banks	148.4
Bunge Limited	BG	Food Processing	45.2
Cash America International	PWN	Miscellaneous Financial Services	12.6
CSS Industries, Inc.	CSS	Printing & Publishing	37.8
First American Corp.	FAF	Insurance (Property & Casualty)	35.6
Gart Sports Company	GRTS	Retail (Specialty Nonapparel)	46.4
Group 1 Automotive, Inc.	GPI	Retail (Specialty Nonapparel)	52.1
GTSI Corp.	GTSI	Computer Hardware	3.5
Hughes Supply, Inc.	HUG	Miscellaneous Capital Goods	83.6
LandAmerica Financial Group	LFG	Insurance (Property & Casualty)	43.2
Moog Inc.	MOG.A	Scientific & Technical Instruments	62.8
Pittston Company	PZB	Security Systems & Services	22.2
Pomeroy Computer Resource	PMRY	Computer Hardware	23.2
Rock-Tenn Company	RKT	Paper & Paper Products	30.2
ScanSource, Inc.	SCSC	Computer Peripherals	85.1
Stewart Information Services	STC	Insurance (Property & Casualty)	96.7
Tyson Foods, Inc.	TSN	Food Processing	18.2
U.S. Concrete, Inc.	RMIX	Construction—Raw Materials	16.0
Unilever PLC (ADR)	UL	Personal & Household Products	2.2
Universal Forest Products	UFPI	Forestry & Wood Products	53.5
Vitro S.A. (ADR)	VTO	Containers & Packaging	26.1
W.R. Grace & Co.	GRA	Chemical Manufacturing	27.9
WESCO International, Inc.	WCC	Electronic Instruments & Controls	62.4
Average Price Change			**48.8%**

FIGURE 4.9 OVERVALUED STOCKS 2002

Company	Symbol	Industry	Percent Price Change 2002
Altera Corp.	ALTR	Semiconductors	−45.0
BG Group PLC	BRG	Natural Gas Utilities	4.7
Coca-Cola Company	KO	Beverages (Nonalcoholic)	−7.1
E.I. DuPont de Nemours	DD	Chemicals—Plastics & Rubbers	−0.6
E.W. Scripps Company	SSP	Printing & Publishing	13.6
Enbridge Energy Partners,	EEP	Oil Well Services & Equipment	0.0
Entercom Communications	ETM	Broadcasting & Cable TV	−5.3
Exar Corporation	EXAR	Semiconductors	−43.2
Gillette Company	G	Personal & Household Products	−9.5
Medtronic, Inc.	MDT	Medical Equipment & Supplies	−11.0
Micrel, Inc.	MCRL	Semiconductors	−67.1
Molex, Inc.	MOLX	Electronic Instruments & Controls	−26.6
PanAmSat Corporation	SPOT	Communications Services	−34.5
Procter & Gamble Co.	PG	Personal & Household Products	8.3
Semtech Corporation	SMTC	Semiconductors	−70.5
Sun Microsystems, Inc.	SUNW	Computer Hardware	−75.3
Tellabs	TLAB	Communications Equipment	−54.0
Univision Communications	UVN	Broadcasting & Cable TV	−40.1
Vicor Corporation	VICR	Electronic Instruments & Controls	−51.4
Westwood One, Inc.	WON	Broadcasting & Cable TV	−25.0
Average Price Change			**−27.0%**

FIGURE 4.10 OVERVALUED STOCKS 2003

Company	Symbol	Industry	Percent Price Change 2003
Autonomy Corporation plc	AUTN	Computer Services	47.3
Bandag, Inc.	BDG	Tires	4.4
BellSouth Corporation	BLS	Communications Services	8.2
Boca Resorts, Inc.	RST	Hotels & Motels	40.2
Brookline Bancorp, Inc.	BRKL	Savings Banks and Thrifts	27.0
Campbell Soup Company	CPB	Food Processing	15.7
Cincinnati Financial	CINF	Insurance (Property & Casualty)	11.0
Dover Motorsports, Inc.	DVD	Recreational Activities	–20.5
Electro Rent Corporation	ELRC	Rental & Leasing	5.9
EOG Resources, Inc.	EOG	Oil & Gas Operations	15.1
Inet Technologies	INTI	Communications Equipment	98.3
Municipal Mortgage & Equity	MMA	Consumer Financial Services	–1.7
Novellus Systems, Inc.	NVLS	Semiconductors	47.0
PanAmSat Corporation	SPOT	Communications Services	49.0
Patterson-UTI Energy, Inc.	PTEN	Oil Well Services & Equipment	7.5
Robert Half International	RHI	Business Services	48.8
Rowan Companies, Inc.	RDC	Oil Well Services & Equipment	0.6
Tollgrade Communications,	TLGD	Communications Equipment	44.3
Tom Brown, Inc.	TBI	Oil & Gas Operations	25.9
Topps Company, Inc.	TOPP	Food Processing	18.6
Verizon Communications	VZ	Communications Services	–9.8
WMS Industries Inc.	WMS	Casinos & Gaming	69.0
Average Price Change			**25.1%**

A CLOSER EXAMINATION

The model outlined in Chapter 4 was successful in identifying undervalued and overvalued stocks for the two years it was tested. Now, to add some color to the picture, it is worthwhile examining what exactly transpired in 2002 and 2003 with a few specific stocks. Doing so will give us a better idea of what was going on "behind the scenes" and a better understanding of the market neutral model's inner workings.

Two stocks surfaced in the 2002 lists that were in the Communications Equipment classification. Recall that the model's method of stock selection called for companies that had the following traits:

- Were priced below (for undervalued) or above (for overvalued) the average industry PE ratio
- Carried a forward PE below (for undervalued) or above (for overvalued) the 2002 estimated earnings growth rate
- Were priced below (for undervalued) or above (for overvalued) the average industry PS ratio
- Had, in the past 12 months, experienced sales growth above (for undervalued) or below (for overvalued) the industry average
- Had a relative strength index rating of greater than 50 (for undervalued)

On the long side was EMS Technologies (ELMG) and on the short side was Tellabs (TLAB). Both stocks behaved as the fundamentals would have predicted: the undervalued stock fell less than the broad market, and the overvalued stock fell further. Let's see if we can understand why. For their respective statistics at the beginning of the year, see Figure 5.1.

ELMG provides a wide range of communications gear for both satellite and other wireless applications. At the end of 2001, estimates were that ELMG would earn about $0.98 per share in 2002, a big jump over 2001. What's more, longer term ELMG was looking forward to an average annual increase of 24 percent. At $16 per share, the forward PE was 16.3. Thus, relative to such robust expected growth, the price of the stock seemed quite reasonable. And the stock also seemed reasonably priced on the basis of past sales, trading at just 0.57 times revenue. We know this because the industry average was 1.3 times revenue.

During the course of the year, earnings estimates held steady up until late in September 2002, when the company announced it was reducing its forecast for the then-current quarter. Estimates dropped to $0.80 per share for the full year, which in fact is what the company did earn.

As might be expected, the share price plunged along with the forecasted earnings. From mid-September to late September, the stock fell from about $22 per share to a little over $10 per share (see the weekly closing price in Figure 5.2). Investors were clearly disappointed at the turn of events. By year's end, the share price had recovered to about $15.50.

By late 2002, then, the share price was down about 3 percent from where it started the year. Not good, but not so terrible either, particularly in light of the S&P 500's 24 percent drop. One might have expected the

---

FIGURE 5.1 ELMG AND TLAB VALUATION CRITERIA 2001

	ELMG	**TLAB**	**Industry Average**
PE Ratio 12/2001	28.6	35.1	29.8
Forward PE	16.3	65.8	31.4
Expected Earnings Growth			
(5 Year)	24%	21%	25%
PS Ratio 12/2001	0.57	2.24	1.30
Sales Growth in 2001	0.0%	−1.9%	−0.1%
Relative Strength	77	NA	NA

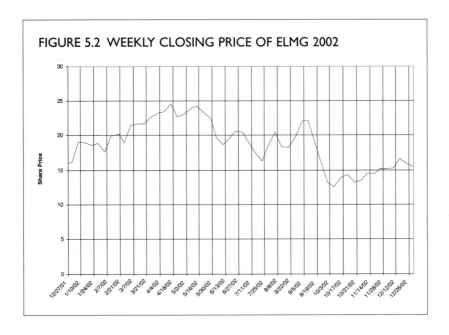

FIGURE 5.2 WEEKLY CLOSING PRICE OF ELMG 2002

stock price to fall at least as much as the earnings estimates, which were lowered by 18 percent. And not only were earnings going to be less, but suddenly the *rate* of growth was much lower. We have to conclude that while ELMG disappointed investors and analysts alike, the effect on the stock price by year-end was less dramatic than it might have been.

This raises the obvious question, "why?" It seems quite likely the reason for the somewhat benign reaction to a big reduction in earnings, vis-à-vis expectations, has everything to do with the discount the stock carried going into 2002. Because ELMG was already priced at less than the going rate for similar stocks, it had a sort of cushion in the event of disappointment. This is the essence of why undervalued stocks can be such a good investment. The company still increased earnings over the prior year, unlike many other companies in 2002. ELMG just didn't perform quite as well as was initially expected.

Tellabs (TLAB) tells quite a different story when we take a closer look at what happened with the company in 2002. It too is a maker of telecommunications gear, with a slightly different focus than ELMG. Much more of TLAB's business is centered on switching gears used by the traditional telephone companies, while ELMG has a greater emphasis on satellite applications. So, while the companies don't compete head on, there is no denying that they both draw their revenues from hardware that facilitates telecommunication.

At the end of 2001, TLAB was expected to earn $0.24 per share in 2002 and the stock was trading at a little under $16 per share. Right from the start, then, the market was placing a much higher valuation on TLAB than ELMG. For an investor to attain roughly equal amounts of earning power the investor could own *four shares of TLAB* and expect to see $0.96 in earnings or *one share of ELMG* which was expected to generate $0.98 in earnings.

As 2002 unfolded, the TLAB story became an unhappy one almost right away. By the end of March, earnings estimates for the year had fallen from $0.24 per share to $0.15. By the beginning of May, they were down to $0.13 per share. In October, analysts suggested that TLAB was actually going to lose $0.06 per share. Later, the estimates ticked up to a loss of $0.05.

The chart in Figure 5.3 tracks the earnings per share (EPS) estimates and TLAB's stock price throughout the year, with the bars representing estimates.

As the chart makes obvious, TLAB's stock price tracked closely with estimates until the last quarter of the year. Estimates were raised ever-so-slightly by November, and the stock price jumped considerably. Aside

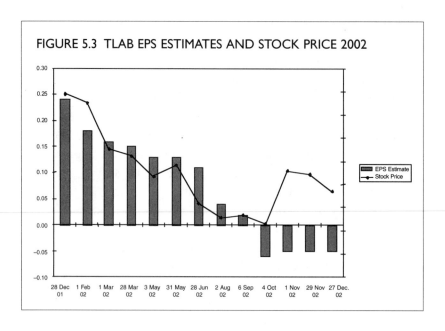

FIGURE 5.3 TLAB EPS ESTIMATES AND STOCK PRICE 2002

from the faintly improved outlook, there are two other possible reasons for the outsized share price increase in the last three months of the year. First, the broad market rallied strongly in October, and that rally may have helped lift TLAB. Second, at some point on the calendar, attention shifts more to *next* year's expectations rather than the current year. This may have begun to occur with TLAB by October.

The bigger question is how to evaluate TLAB's performance as a company and as a stock. Clearly, the company did not carry out its business plan in such a way that it achieved its goals. When TLAB fell so far short of delivering promised results, investors dumped the stock, driving prices down 53 percent by year-end. So, in this case, we cannot conclude that TLAB shares underperformed the market because it was overvalued to begin with. Instead, the decline in price probably needs to be attributed to a dismal operational record in 2002.

Would the stock have fallen less if the initial valuation had not been so high? Unfortunately there is no way to know. The situation is reminiscent of the Ford/GM example cited in Chapter 1; the long/short strategy worked, but we can't know for sure whether it was the operational difference or the initial valuation difference, or both. Sounds like the old Miller beer commercials: "Tastes Great" or "Less Filling."

When the News Diverges

Another example may shed more light. In 2003 the model found several companies in the Food Processing industry. While far from being direct competitors, both Campbell Soup (CPB) from the overvalued list and Bunge (BG) from the undervalued list have exposure to some of the same economic factors, including consumer demand for food products, transportation costs, pricing power, etc. Valuation metrics for each, as of the end of 2002, are shown in Figure 5.4.

BG is perhaps the world's largest producer of soybeans and soy-related products but has operations that extend all the way into the retail environment, selling flour, margarine, shortening, etc. CPB is probably more familiar to most investors, with its eponymous soups as well as pasta sauce, beverages, and Pepperidge Farm frozen bakery products. We can see from Figure 5.4 that even though BG had a better recent sales track record and reasonably good growth prospects, CPB shares were selling

FIGURE 5.4 BUNGE AND CAMPBELL SOUP VALUATION FACTORS

	BG	**CPB**	**Industry Average**
PE Ratio 12/2002	9.3	17.6	16.8
Forward PE	8.5	15.3	14.7
Expected Earnings Growth			
(5 Year)	8.9%	6.3%	10%
PS Ratio 12/2002	0.18	1.56	0.50
Sales Growth in 2002	14%	3%	8%
Relative Strength	66	NA	NA

at a relative premium. For example, CPB had a lower expected earnings growth rate but a higher forward PE. Sales in the prior year at CPB were up slightly but lagged both the industry average and BG.

What happened with each of these stocks in 2003 speaks to the question of operational performance versus initial valuation factors on stock prices. Neither BG nor CPB turned in remarkable numbers in 2003 relative to expectations. At the beginning of the year, BG was expected to earn $2.68 per share, and CPB was pegged to earn $1.57 per share. (Because CPB's fiscal year ends in July and BG's ends in December, we use CPB's 2004 estimates.)

Three months later, those estimates were holding steady, with a tiny reduction for CPB of one-half of 1 percent. By the end of June, estimates for both had been raised slightly: 1.5 percent for BG and 2 percent for CPB. However, the difference in stock price half way through the year was quite significant. BG's price was up 27 percent from where it was at the beginning of the year and CPB's price was up only 5 percent. Even though the outlook had become relatively more positive for CPB, investors were not rewarding the company by buying up the stock.

At the end of December 2003, by which time both firms' estimates had become more reliable, BG's estimates had actually fallen. Instead of earning $2.68 per share, EPS was anticipated to be $2.48. Conversely, CPB's EPS estimates were up fractionally to $1.58. But what about the stocks' prices? BG shares were up 45 percent and CPB shares were up 16 percent for the year (see Figure 5.5).

This is a counterintuitive result on the face of it. If we accept that there is some relationship between expected earnings and share price,

FIGURE 5.5 BUNGE AND CAMPBELL SOUP STOCK
PERFORMANCE 2003

	BG	CPB
Change in 2003 or 2004 Earnings Estimates	−7%	+0.5%
Change in 2003 Stock Price	+45%	+16%

then the decline in BG's estimates and accompanying rise in share price don't make much sense. At the same time, CPB's estimates went up, albeit slightly, and the share price went up, but not as much as the broader market did. We might have expected CPB shares to rise at least as much as the S&P 500 with the market's rising tide lifting all boats, particularly those with improved outlooks. Recall that the S&P 500 was up 26 percent in 2003.

How to explain this seemingly aberrant stock price/earnings estimate behavior? It was generally agreed that CPB was performing better at the end of 2003 than anyone had thought at the beginning of the year. BG's earnings performance was going to be less than the analysts had thought. So, what could cause BG's stock price to rise almost twice as much as the market and CPB shares to go up only a little more than half as much? There could be other explanations, but the most obvious one is that BG started out the year with an undeservedly low valuation and CPB with one that was too high.

In Chapter 1 an analogy was made between stocks and runners. If two runners are in the exact same condition and have the exact same physical attributes, they will cross the finish line at virtually the same time. Saddle one of those runners with a ten pound weight and she or he will certainly finish last. In this case, CPB was actually a slightly faster runner, in an operational sense, but the company was saddled with the burden of a high valuation going into the race. Thus, BG won the competition.

An Imperfect Solution

Before leaving this subject, another example is worth studying, one where the results were not what we would have wanted. Returning to late

2001, two companies in the Medical Equipment industry looked like great candidates for the undervalued and overvalued lists.

SRI/Surgical Express (STRC) provides daily delivery of medical supplies—gowns, towels, instruments—to hospitals. At the end of 2001, STRC was coming off a good year and was expected to earn $1.05 in 2002. Just as important, the company was trading at a significant discount to the industry average in terms of current PE, forward PE and PS ratio.

Medtronic (MDT) is also a medical equipment company, known primarily for developing implantable devices that assist in managing pain, heart disease, diabetes, etc. Unlike STRC, shares of MDT at the end of 2001 were commanding a high premium, making the stock appear overvalued. Growth prospects were good but below the industry average. Figure 5.6 provides a snapshot of what valuations looked like at the end of 2001.

What happened with these two companies in 2002 serves as a cautionary tale and underscores the fact that initial valuations may be important but they are not everything. As the year unfolded, STRC began to revise its earnings outlook, at first suggesting that earnings per share would be $0.64 rather than the original estimate of $1.05. By December that number had come down even further to $0.38 per share, a 64 percent drop.

Investors' reaction to this bad news was understandable. They dumped the stock, and by the end of 2002 shares were down 66 percent. Even a low starting valuation could not save STRC from being soundly punished in the marketplace for a poor performance. MDT's estimates held almost perfectly steady throughout the year, going from $1.42 at the beginning of the year to $1.41 by the end. Despite that solid accomplishment MDT's shares fell 11 percent during the year (see Figure 5.7).

FIGURE 5.6 SRI/SURGICAL AND MEDTRONIC VALUATION FACTORS

	STRC	MDT	Industry Average
PE Ratio 12/2001	17.4	75.3	28.4
Forward PE	16.1	36.1	24.4
Expected Earnings Growth (5 Year)	25%	17%	23%
PS Ratio 12/2001	1.2	10.3	2.4
Sales Growth in 2001	15%	10%	10%
Relative Strength	63	NA	NA

FIGURE 5.7 SRI/SURGICAL AND MEDTRONIC STOCK PERFORMANCE 2002

	STRC	MDT
Change in 2002 Earnings Estimates	−64%	−0.5%
Change in 2002 Stock Price	−66%	−11%

The important point is that poor operational results cannot be salvaged by an initial low stock valuation. STRC stock was a big loser in 2002, and it deserved to be, even though shares appeared to be discounted at the beginning of the year. That does not mean the model is a failure, just that it will not pick winners and losers with 100 percent accuracy. No methodology will be able to correctly predict changes in a company's ability to carry out its business plan. Instead, the model serves to put the odds in investors' favor by highlighting stocks that seem to be unfairly discounted or marked up at a premium.

Timing Trade-Offs

Of course, it's important to remember that what is undervalued today may be fairly valued tomorrow. Every time a stock price changes, the ratios used to help us place a value on the stock change too. A PS ratio of 0.8 today (say, for example a stock price of $20 and revenue per share of $25) will become a PS ratio of 1.0 if the share price moves from $20 to $25 next week. Even as sales and earnings grow, if the price of a stock rises even more rapidly, at some point the stock reaches "fair value" and no longer seems as attractive as an investment.

If valuations change every day, should portfolios change every day? Of course not. But a periodic review of both long and short holdings is necessary. For many investors that review might occur every calendar quarter, but a case could be made for a review as often as every month or as infrequently as every year. The decision is a personal one and trade-offs are to be expected.

A more frequent review of valuations can bring to light quickly any big changes in company fundamentals. But the subsequent realignment of holdings will result in a high-turnover portfolio. Portfolio turnover is a lot of work, and trading costs can be high. Examining valuations less often may mean that a company's business has changed dramatically long before an investor spots it.

We tracked the results of our model based on a one-year holding period, not because it was the ideal period of time but because it was simple. For those investors who want to keep their time commitment to a minimum, that might be about right. For investors who prefer to take a more active role in managing their portfolio, waiting a whole year will seem like an eternity.

On Being Systematic

Whether an investor identifies undervalued and overvalued stocks using criteria like those outlined in Chapter 4 or develops her or his own, a consistent application is important. Screening tools, where fundamental criteria are stipulated and then stocks with those characteristics are filtered out, have become widely available. This allows investors to crunch through an enormous amount of data in seconds. Several such screening tools are available for free on the Internet. See the Appendix for more information.

Such screening tools have the advantage of enforcing a level of discipline that is important. But, no mechanical system is sufficient by itself. All long or short candidates need to be researched and vetted individually. There is no substitute for reading about a company, verifying its fundamentals, and getting to know something about its business.

An investor might also use an outside stock rating service, like Value-Line, Morningstar, or lesser-known Camelback Research (available through Microsoft Money Central at http://www.moneycentral.msn.com, or direct from http://www.camelbackresearch.com). These services all use some ranking system to grade stocks from poor to excellent. A market neutral strategy using these services would entail buying the highest rated stocks and selling short the lowest rated stocks. Charles Schwab also has developed a proprietary stock ranking system and gone one step further in creating a market neutral mutual fund that incorporates those rankings.

For those who prefer technical analysis, another perfectly viable market neutral approach can be developed using technical indicators. Long candidates could be high-momentum, strong trendline stocks; short candidates could be low-momentum, weak trendline stocks.

Another idea is using short interest in a stock as an indicator. Short interest is calculated monthly and provides a measure of how much money is being bet against a stock. The higher the short interest, the more market participants are anticipating a decline in the stock. Some experts contend that stocks with a very high short interest are actually good candidates to rise in price. All those borrowed shares must be returned at some point in the future, and short-covering can really fuel a rally if the shares turn up. Thus, according to some pundits, a high short interest is a contrarian indicator that suggests a likely advance in stock price.

However, some academic research on short interest suggests just the opposite. In an October 2002 paper by Desai, et al., published in the *Journal of Finance,* the authors found that a high level of short interest correlates with subsequent abnormally high negative returns. Their conclusion is that when companies have a large short interest, it is a signal that negative information and results are likely to lie ahead. We touch on this subject again in Chapter 8. If these research studies are correct, investors could develop a market neutral strategy that calls for selling short stocks that already carry a relatively high short interest and buying stocks in competing companies that have little or no short interest.

Whatever methodology an investor chooses, whether it is based on fundamentals, outside research, technical indicators, short interest, or some combination of all of those, it has to be tested over time and shown to work. Remember though, in a sense, the methodology is secondary to the idea that being both long and short at the same time is a way to reduce risk.

As we discussed in Chapter 1, if an investor believes that it is possible to pick stocks that will outperform the broad market, then that same investor also must believe it is possible to pick stocks that will underperform. Consequently, there is no reason to take on the risk of picking individual stocks without some insurance, or hedge, in the form of short sales. And if an investor doesn't believe individual stock selection can work as a way to "beat the market," then the only sensible approach is to put money into an index fund and be done with it.

Industry Exposure

One of the pitfalls that comes from using a model like the one we constructed in Chapter 4 is that it can result in lists of stocks that are unbalanced in terms of industry exposure. The subject of building a balanced portfolio will receive treatment in Chapter 6, but examining the specifics of the model's performances is not complete without a look at industry exposure.

Fortunately, in the examples given, both the 2002 and 2003 portfolios were reasonably balanced. Each of the undervalued and overvalued lists of stocks had fairly broad representation across industries. If the model had produced too many stocks in one industry, it should have set off an alarm bell. That is because of the external factors that can impact a particular industry group, and there are two examples where industry representation *was* a little too heavy.

The year 2002 was a very good year for banks and thrifts. Mortgage refinancing was rampant, and profits at many financial institutions soared. Results varied in different parts of the country, but regional banks generally did well. A stock index of thrifts operating across the nation was up 17 percent in 2002. That worked in our model's favor because there were three banks/thrifts on the undervalued list and none on the overvalued list.

However, that is less than ideal portfolio construction because 2002 might have turned out to be a poor year for banking and our portfolio would have suffered. Something similar occurred in 2003, again to our model's advantage, when three property/casualty insurance firms showed up on the undervalued list. Closer examination reveals that these companies all sell title insurance, which benefited from the continuation of heavy mortgage refinancing.

Creating a market neutral portfolio is intended to reduce risk and generate positive returns. To the extent that there is a great deal of exposure to a single industry, the portfolio is not doing as good a job of reducing risk as it could. In the above examples, it all worked out OK, but it could just as easily have not. The composition of a market neutral portfolio involves more than just determining which stocks are undervalued and which are overvalued. It has to account for industry exposure and industry risk.

Market Cap and Beta

Finally, we will take a quick look at what our model turned up in terms of market capitalization and beta. These two elements can be important in understanding performance and, as we will see in Chapter 6, can play a role in establishing the proper balance of a portfolio.

The undervalued stocks in both 2002 and 2003 were, on average, much smaller companies with lower volatility than the overvalued stocks. In 2002 the average undervalued company on our list was only $870 million in market cap and the average beta was 0.66. In 2003 the average size doubled to $1.69 billion and the beta was about the same at 0.64.

Contrast that with the overvalued stocks, which were gargantuan in size relative to the undervalued group: average market cap in 2002 was $23.2 billion and $9.0 billion in 2003 (see Figure 5.8). The beta was also quite a bit higher for the overvalued stocks, averaging 1.20 in 2002 and 1.13 in 2003.

What is the significance of these statistics? We can make a couple of observations. First, it is clear that our model did not produce a very balanced portfolio. The overvalued stocks were both larger and more volatile, and that sort of imbalance is something to avoid. Generally we would prefer a portfolio that had stocks of roughly equal size and volatility on the long side and the short side of the portfolio. There have been periods of time, for example, when large-cap stocks have outperformed small-cap stocks, or vice versa, and ideally we would want our market neutral portfolio to avoid any bias in either direction.

Which brings us to our second point: the difference in company size may explain the difference in performance over those two years. That is possible because in both years small-cap companies handily outperformed

---

FIGURE 5.8 MARKET NEUTRAL STOCK'S MARKET CAP AND BETA 2002–2003

	Average Market Cap	Average Beta
Undervalued Stocks in 2002	$0.87 B	0.66
Undervalued Stocks in 2003	$1.69 B	0.64
Overvalued Stocks in 2002	$23.2 B	1.20
Overvalued Stock in 2003	$9.0 B	1.13

large-cap companies, particularly in 2003. The Frank Russell company tracks the share performance of thousands of U.S. companies and has two indexes that nicely represent both large-cap and small-cap companies. The Russell 3000 index is made up of the 3,000 largest publicly traded firms and is further divided into the largest 1,000 and the smallest 2,000. In mid-2003 the average market cap of the largest 1,000 was $10.2 billion and the average of the smallest 2,000 was $0.4 billion.

In 2002 the Russell 1000 (larger companies) fell 21.3 percent, and the Russell 2000 (smaller companies) fell slightly less at 20.5 percent. In 2003 the difference was very dramatic: the Russell 1000 was up 27.3 percent and the Russell 2000 was up 46 percent! For whatever reason, investors showed a marked preference for shares of smaller sized firms. Because our model was biased toward being long on small caps and short on large caps, it could be that the model's strong performance can be attributed to that difference. While we might be pleased with the result, we have to be concerned about what might happen in the future if that trend reversed, with large caps outperforming small caps.

We can speculate that the model was simply showing us the way—that small cap stocks tended to be more undervalued in 2002 and 2003, and they subsequently outperformed large-cap stocks, both in our model and in the world at large. Or was the model just lucky? Unfortunately, that answer is "unknowable." What we do know is that because an unbalanced portfolio carries some additional risk, we might take some steps to avoid it. We turn to that topic next.

Summary

By exploring what specifically occurred with several of the stocks found by our model, we gain a bit more insight into what is driving the returns. We saw that in the case of Bunge and Campbell Soup, the share price of the undervalued company, Bunge, fared much better, even though its results were more disappointing relative to expectations. We also observed that a low starting valuation won't always save the day if operating results are poor, as they were in the case of SRI/Surgical Express.

While the model developed in Chapter 4 was successful in the years 2002 and 2003, it is not necessarily *the* model to emulate. There are an almost infinite combination of methods that can successfully select under-valued and overvalued stocks. Indeed, important considerations for any portfolio being assembled, no matter how it was derived, are whether it has balance in terms of industry exposure, market capitalization, and beta.

6

LOOKING FOR BALANCE

Developing a market neutral portfolio is a balancing act. By correctly balancing long and short positions, an investor can wring some of the risk out of his or her portfolio. There are several ways to achieve balance, and we will review some of those methods here. But first, it is worth observing that sometimes absolutely perfect balance can quickly get a portfolio nowhere.

After all, a *perfectly* balanced portfolio could consist of a long and short position in the same instrument. The balance might be great, but the profits would be nonexistent. Indeed, with some transaction cost, the profits would be negative. To take an absurd example, one could buy shares in IBM and, at the same time, sell IBM short. Such a ploy would have the virtue of being balanced. Unfortunately, the investor would be getting no risk *and* no reward.

Striving for balance is important, but perfect balance is impossible and may not even be desirable. In this chapter we will look at different ways of deciding how to best construct a portfolio so that it reduces the risk but keeps the potential for reward.

Market Neutral versus Long/Short

The term *market neutral,* as defined by the hedge fund industry, may mean several things, but it certainly means dollar neutral. A market neutral hedge fund will have the same amount of money in long positions as it has in short positions. Using the hypothetical stocks from Chapter 2, Figure 6.1 shows an example of a market neutral portfolio.

Note that there are $4,999 worth of long positions and $4,997 worth of short positions, making this a perfectly neutral portfolio. (Obviously, the $2 difference is immaterial given the size of the portfolio.)

A long/short hedge fund, in contrast, is likely to have more money committed to short positions than long positions, or vice versa, at any given time. It will, by definition, be less balanced. There may be times when a long/short portfolio is exactly neutral, but more often, when the dollars are netted against each other, there is a long or short bias. Figure 6.2 shows an example of a long/short portfolio because there are more dollars long than short.

Observe the difference between this long/short portfolio and the market neutral portfolio. In this hypothetical example, the investor has

---

FIGURE 6.1 EXAMPLE OF A BALANCED MARKET NEUTRAL PORTFOLIO

Stock	Initial Share Price	Share Number	Initial Value
Long Positions			
Alpha Manufacturing	$13	77	$1,001
New Semiconductor Inc.	$21	48	$1,008
First Pulp and Paper Co.	$40	25	$1,000
Healthy Hospitals Inc.	$33	30	$990
Pizzazz Retail Corp.	$10	100	$1,000
Subtotal			**$4,999**
Short Positions			
Beta Manufacturing	$15	−67	−$1,005
Obsolete Semiconductor Inc.	$17	−59	−$1,003
Second Pulp and Paper Co.	$45	−22	−$990
Pallid Hospitals Inc.	$27	−37	−$999
Plodder Retail Corp.	$ 8	−125	−$1,000
Subtotal			**−$4,997**

FIGURE 6.2 EXAMPLE OF A LONG/SHORT PORTFOLIO

Stock	Initial Share Price	Share Number	Initial Value
Long Positions			
Alpha Manufacturing	$13	77	$1,001
New Semiconductor Inc.	$21	48	$1,008
First Pulp and Paper Co.	$40	25	$1,000
Healthy Hospitals Inc.	$33	60	$1,980
Pizzazz Retail Corp.	$10	100	$1,000
Subtotal			**$5,989**
Short Positions			
Beta Manufacturing	$15	−67	−$1,005
Obsolete Semiconductor Inc.	$17	−59	−$1,003
Second Pulp and Paper Co.	$45	−22	−$990
Pallid Hospitals Inc.	$27	−19	−$513
Plodder Retail Corp.	$ 8	−125	−$1,000
Subtotal			**−$4,511**

a bullish view of the hospital sector overall. Accordingly, she creates a relatively heavy concentration in Healthy Hospitals, Inc. (HH) by doubling the amount of money invested. Then she lightens up her exposure in the corollary short position in Pallid Hospitals, Inc. (PH). This results in a portfolio that is net long; i.e., 57 percent of the funds are long and 43 percent are short.

Now, let's suppose that the hospital sector does indeed make a big upward move, perhaps because of some positive changes to Medicaid policy, and the whole sector rises 10 percent over the next several months. Furthermore, let's suppose HH was indeed undervalued to begin with, and PH was overvalued. It is most likely that in a hospital sector rally, HH will gain disproportionately, say 20 percent. And PH, though overvalued at the outset, is likely to increase in price too, as the rising hospital sector tide lifts all boats. Accordingly, it might not climb as much as HH, but instead see a 5 percent increase in share price. Under this scenario (a 20 percent rise in the price of HH and a 5 percent rise in the price of PH), the investor would gain $396 in HH and lose $26 in PH. The net gain for the two holdings together would be $370, or almost 15 percent (see Figure 6.3).

FIGURE 6.3 HEALTHY HOSPITALS AND PALLID HOSPITALS
LONG/SHORT PORTFOLIO RESULTS

Long/Short	Initial Price	Ending Price	Share Number	Gain/Loss
Healthy Hospitals Inc.	$33.00	$39.60	60	$396.00
Pallid Hospitals Inc.	$27.00	$28.35	−19	−$26.00

What if, on the other hand, the portfolio was completely balanced, as shown in the market neutral example? That is, what if the same amount of money was invested in each stock instead of having more long and less short. If the same scenario unfolded (HH up 20 percent and PH up 5 percent) but there was exactly the same amount of money in both hospital stocks, the result would be quite different. The return would still be good, but not as good. HH would have a profit of $198 (30 shares times $6.60 of profit per share) and PH would post a loss of $50 (37 shares times a loss of $1.35 per share), making the net gain $148, or a little more than 7 percent (see Figure 6.4).

Being long/short instead of market neutral had the effect of increasing returns because the investor made a bet on the hospital sector that turned out to be correct. Had the prediction been incorrect, had those Medicaid policy changes been negative for hospitals, then the long/short portfolio would have had *lower* returns than the perfectly balanced market neutral portfolio. Any long/short approach tends to introduce some additional risk by weighting stocks differently and magnifying net gains or losses. If the underlying premise is correct, returns will be disproportionately good; if it is incorrect, the returns will be disproportionately poor.

FIGURE 6.4 HEALTHY HOSPITALS AND PALLID HOSPITALS
BALANCED PORTFOLIO RESULTS

Market Neutral	Initial Price	Ending Price	Share Number	Gain/Loss
Healthy Hospitals Inc.	$33.00	$39.60	30	$198.00
Pallid Hospitals Inc.	$27.00	$28.35	−37	−$50.00

What would happen if the news out of the hospital sector *was* bad and our investor's prediction turned out to be incorrect? Most likely, even the undervalued shares of Healthy Hospitals would fall, but perhaps not so far as the overvalued shares of Pallid Hospitals. For illustration, let's assume a 5 percent decline in HH and a 20 percent decline in PH. If that had happened, there would be virtually no gain in the unbalanced long/short pair. The big gain resulting from PH's drop in price is blunted by having sold short only a few shares. Under this "bad news" scenario, when the investor was expecting "good news," the profit and loss cancel each other out as seen in Figure 6.5.

We can see that our hypothetical investor was partly correct and accurately assessed the relative valuation of the two stocks. After all, HH dropped much less than PH when bad news arrived. But, by weighting the shares differently and making a separate and incorrect bet on the prospects of hospitals overall, our investor eliminated her profit.

Conversely, a bad hospital news scenario (HH down 5 percent and PH down 20 percent) in the market neutral portfolio, where equal amounts of dollars are both long and short, would have produced a solid gain of $150, or 7.5 percent, as seen in Figure 6.6.

FIGURE 6.5 HEALTHY HOSPITALS AND PALLID HOSPITALS LONG/SHORT STRATEGY IN "BAD NEWS" MARKET

Long/Short	Initial Price	Ending Price	Share Number	Gain/Loss
Healthy Hospitals Inc.	$33.00	$31.35	60	−$99.00
Pallid Hospitals Inc.	$27.00	$21.60	−19	$103.00

FIGURE 6.6 HEALTHY HOSPITALS AND PALLID HOSPITALS MARKET NEUTRAL STRATEGY IN "BAD NEWS" MARKET

Market Neutral	Initial Price	Ending Price	Share Number	Gain/Loss
Healthy Hospitals Inc.	$33.00	$31.35	30	−$50.00
Pallid Hospitals Inc.	$27.00	$21.60	−37	$200.00

The point is that having an unbalanced portfolio can create the opportunity for greater returns but will also carry some higher level of risk. Being market neutral will keep the risk level lower and may dampen returns slightly. One approach is not necessarily better than the other. All things being equal, long/short portfolios will tend to be more volatile than market neutral portfolios and may offer opportunity for greater returns. It's important to remember that both approaches carry less risk than a long-only portfolio.

From the Top Down

The difference between market neutral and long/short performance can also be seen in the hedge fund results tracked by HedgeIndex.com, a joint venture of CSFB and Tremont Advisors. HedgeIndex.com collects, aggregates, and categorizes performance statistics for hedge funds with over $10 million in assets. Over the five years ending in December 2003, the market neutral and long/short indexes created by HedgeIndex.com show marked differences (see Figure 6.7).

For example, out of the 60 months, the index of market neutral hedge funds experienced a decline in only 5 months. In contrast, the long/short hedge fund index had declines in 23 out of 60 months. On that basis, the market neutral funds were certainly more consistent performers overall.

Total returns were quite good for both types of funds over those same five years. But a quick glance at the table in Figure 6.7 highlights how much more volatile the long/short funds were versus the market neutral

FIGURE 6.7 AVERAGE MARKET NEUTRAL AND LONG/SHORT FUND PERFORMANCE

Year	Market Neutral Average Fund Performance	Long/Short Average Fund Performance
2003	7%	17%
2002	7%	–2%
2001	9%	–4%
2000	15%	2%
1999	15%	47%

funds. Again, these are averages, and many individual hedge funds would have had a very different performance record.

This data supports the conclusion that a market neutral portfolio will experience fewer ups and downs than a long/short portfolio. A long/ short portfolio, by definition, is adding some layer of risk not found in a market neutral approach. But that additional risk may bring increased returns. Again, don't lose sight of the fact that *both* types of portfolio will have lower risk than the more ubiquitous long-only portfolio.

In Practice

To show how this works in practice, recall the portfolio we constructed in Chapter 4. In order to keep the number of stocks manageable, we focused on the top 20 to 25 stocks, wanting to keep the numbers of long and short candidates roughly equal. By tightening and/or loosening the criteria, the model was made to generate the 25 *most* undervalued stocks and a similar, but smaller number of overvalued stocks. Without that alteration and in its "raw form," the model produced a larger number of stocks. At the end of 2001, it generated 35 undervalued and 38 overvalued stocks. Using the exact same criteria 12 months later, in late December 2002, the model uncovered more undervalued stocks and far fewer overvalued stocks (see Figure 6.8).

Because the criteria were identical, what could explain this difference? Most likely it was that overall valuations in the stock market had fallen by the end of 2002 creating more undervalued and fewer overvalued opportunities.

During the calendar year 2002, the S&P 500 index was down about 23 percent. Because the model relies heavily on price-to-sales, price-to-

---

FIGURE 6.8 MARKET NEUTRAL STRATEGY STOCK RESULTS 2001–2002

	Undervalued Stock Number	Overvalued Stock Number
December 28, 2001	35	38
December 27, 2002	46	22

earnings, and earnings growth projections, if prices were down while sales, earnings, and earnings growth were higher, the number of stocks fitting our definition of "undervalued" would be fewer.

In any case, confronted with this fact, an investor establishing or rebalancing our model portfolio in late 2003 had four choices: he or she could

1. take a long/short approach, leave the criteria alone, and invest an equal amount of money in each stock, accepting that the resulting portfolio will be skewed net long; or
2. alter the model by loosening the criteria on one side or tightening it on the other, or both, in such a way that it mechanically produces the same, or almost the same, number of stocks for each side of the portfolio (as was done in Chapter 4); or
3. leave the criteria alone but divide the amount of money equally between the undervalued stocks and overvalued stocks, thus creating for 2003 a "dollar neutral" portfolio but with 46 long holdings and 22 short positions; or
4. hand select stocks from the original lists, with an eye toward maintaining balance in terms of industry exposure as well as dollars.

The decision about what to do is dependent on risk tolerance and whether the investor wants to allow the model some freedom to range beyond perfect balance. As we have seen, being long/short instead of market neutral is somewhat riskier. Investors who are particularly risk-averse will want to keep the amount of money equally divided among longs and shorts, using either option #2, #3, or #4. (Option #3 is actually a sort of hybrid solution that takes the lower risk, neutral approach but does not require any adjustment to the model.)

If, on the other hand, the investor is less risk-averse, option #1 may be a better choice. Like the hypothetical investor above who believed good things were in store for the hospital sector, option #1 would be a way to take a more bullish stance on the market as a whole. If, at the end of 2002, an investor had a positive view of the stock market, and that outlook proved correct, the long/short approach in this case would produce returns that were almost certainly better than a strictly neutral approach.

To keep a bit of perspective on the subject, bear in mind that a long/short portfolio is never as bullish as holding only long positions. If investors were really completely certain that the broad market was going to rise, they would be smart to abandon their long/short or market neutral portfolio and just buy stocks. Of course, investors are never really completely certain the market is headed up. Our only point is that a long/short, or imbalanced, portfolio can be either bullish or bearish, while a neutral portfolio leans in neither direction.

Option 1—The Long/Short Approach

Using the full set of data from the end of 2002, we examine what each of the three options would have yielded in terms of portfolio results. We already know that the 22 overvalued stocks rose, on average, 25 percent. The larger set of undervalued stocks, 46 in all, was up 46 percent (just fractionally less than the smaller set) as seen in Figure 6.9.

A long/short portfolio would have experienced an excellent return. Assuming a $1,000 investment in each stock, the initial investment would have been $68,000—$46,000 committed to long holdings and $22,000 to short holdings. After 12 months, those holdings taken together would have been worth $83,660, or about a 23 percent gain. The same $68,000 invested in an index fund would have been worth $85,680. Figure 6.10 summarizes these results.

FIGURE 6.9 LONG/SHORT APPROACH PERFORMANCE 2002–2003

March 29, 2002–March 28, 2003

Undervalued Stocks	+46%
Overvalued Stocks	+25%
S&P 500	+26%

FIGURE 6.10 LONG/SHORT APPROACH AND INDEX FUND PERFORMANCE 2002–2003

Long/Short Approach	Average Performance	Initial Value	Ending Value
Undervalued Stocks	+46%	$46,000	$67,160
Overvalued Stocks	+25%	$22,000	$16,500
Combined Results	**+23%**	**$68,000**	**$83,660**
S&P 500	+26%	$68,000	$85,680

While not quite as good as a long-only portfolio, this long/short approach worked out very well because the bias was in the right direction. A heavy weighting on the long side paid off when the overall market went up so much. Of course, if the model had produced more short selections than longs, the long/short portfolio would have performed poorly.

Option 2—The Market Neutral Approach

We already know that a market neutral approach, with the model altered to produce roughly the same number of long selections as short selections, would have done fine but not as well as the long/short. By tightening the criteria to produce fewer undervalued stocks, we were able to bring the numbers to being almost aligned: 25 undervalued and 22 overvalued. A $47,000 portfolio would have gained 14 percent, becoming $53,750, as summarized in Figure 6.11.

Option 3—The Hybrid Market Neutral Approach

The third approach would have been the worst with this particular set of data and timetable. Using the original 46 long selections and the 22 short selections but dividing the money equally between the long and short sides of the portfolio would have returned 4 percent. The hybrid method suffered a bit because of the slightly worse average performance of the 46 stocks versus the smaller group of 25 stocks (see Figure 6.12).

FIGURE 6.11 MARKET NEUTRAL APPROACH AND INDEX FUND PERFORMANCE 2002–2003

Market Neutral Approach	Average Performance	Initial Value	Ending Value
Undervalued Stocks	+49%	$25,000	$37,250
Overvalued Stocks	+25%	$22,000	$16,500
Combined Results	**+14%**	**$47,000**	**$53,750**
S&P 500	+26%	$47,000	$59,220

FIGURE 6.12 HYBRID MARKET APPROACH PERFORMANCE 2002–2003

Hybrid Approach	Average Performance	Initial Value	Ending Value
Undervalued Stocks	+46%	$25,000	$36,500
Overvalued Stocks	−25%	$25,000	$18,750
Combined Results	**+10%**	**$50,000**	**$55,250**
S&P 500	+26%	$50,000	$63,000

So, three different ways of creating a portfolio and three different sets of results. To review, the long/short approach performed the best, with a gain of 23 percent. Second best was the market neutral portfolio with a gain of 14 percent. Worst of all was the hybrid version with a gain of 10 percent. The latter two methods share one key element: the same amount of money is long as short, making those portfolios "dollar neutral." Obviously, all three underperformed the S&P 500's 26 percent gain. We will turn to Option 4 shortly.

Using 2003 data and the model developed in Chapter 4, we found considerably more undervalued than overvalued stocks and the broad market rose over the next 12 months. This is only one instance, but it will be interesting for investors who develop their own models to see whether they can be used as the basis for conclusions about where the overall stock market might be headed.

Industry Exposure

Aside from the question of being market neutral or long/short, there are some other elements that should be considered when assembling a portfolio. Probably the most important among them is industry, or sector, exposure. (We will use the terms *industry* and *sector* interchangeably here, although many data services make a distinction.)

Just as a rising or falling market tends to carry the prices of individual stocks along with it, the same is true for industry groups. If a particular industry is in especially high or low favor, the individual companies in the industry will be impacted positively or negatively. In order to reduce risk, some attention must be paid to keeping the industry exposure balanced on both the long and short side of a portfolio. For example, a "market neutral" portfolio that has ten semiconductor stocks on the long side and ten trucking stocks on the short side is far from "neutral," nor is it low risk.

A handful of factors have some bearing on an industry's prospects and outlook. Business cycles are one. Different industries will experience peaks and valleys depending on their respective normal business cycle. A classic example is the home-building industry that tends to do well when interest rates are low. Between 2001 and 2003, as the Federal Reserve lowered interest rates, the home-building companies enjoyed a boom period. Lower mortgage rates make housing more affordable to more people, creating stronger demand for houses.

As another example, during periods when the stock market itself has boomed, the brokerage and asset management industries have enjoyed favorable conditions. As the value of stocks goes up, more trading takes place, more initial public offerings are made, and the value of assets under management rises. As this occurs, more profits are earned by brokerages and money managers, boosting their share prices. Conversely, when the stock market contracts, these same companies suffer disproportionately. Many sectors have their own unique business cycle and a good market neutral portfolio will invest across multiple industries in order to counteract this cyclicality.

Commodity prices, especially oil and natural gas, can have an enormous impact on particular industries. Oil prices, in turn, are often driven by very unpredictable geopolitical events or by macroeconomic conditions. Higher oil prices, for example, can dramatically eat into profits for transportation companies, be they airlines, truckers, or railroads. Of course, the companies try to pass along the higher costs to consumers, but even so, profits tend to suffer.

The impact of oil prices points out a subtle complexity in building a neutral portfolio. Higher oil prices might be bad for truckers but good for oil producers. That inverse relationship could spell disaster for an investor who had some trucking companies on the long side of a portfolio and some oil producers on the short side. If the price of oil surged, the portfolio would get hurt on both sides at the same time. Looking for this sort of not-so-obvious relationship is important.

Aside from real, tangible macroeconomic factors impacting specific industries, there are ethereal factors as well. For any number of reasons, some valid, some not, there is a tendency for members of an industry group to move together. Market sentiment is often the culprit, and whether the sentiment is well-grounded or not, it *will* move stocks.

The primary source of sentiment is the brokerage community that often makes prognostications about the outlook for particular industries. Whether its Merrill Lynch saying things look good (or bad) for automakers or Lehman Brothers opining about improved technology spending and what it will do for software firms, brokerages have a substantial impact on entire sectors.

Financial journalists, television commentators, newsletter writers, all can shape the prevailing sentiment about a sector of the stock market. Sometimes the logic or rationale is weak, other times it is well-reasoned. In most cases it does not matter. A neutral portfolio needs to be prepared for shifting views about an industry's outlook. That preparation means the portfolio cannot have too much exposure to a single industry unless that industry is also equally, or almost equally, represented on the opposite side of the portfolio.

An outgrowth of sentiment is a phenomenon known as *sector rotation*. After a period of sustained favorable conditions, it is not uncommon for investors to rotate funds out of a particular sector, perhaps because the fundamentals have changed or because of a belief that nothing lasts forever. Sector rotation can have a powerful effect on groups of stocks.

Diversification is a concept that was discussed in Chapter 2. As was pointed out then, diversifying across industries is healthy and spreads risk out, but it does not reduce risk. That is why market neutral investing is so important; it actually does reduce risk. Market risk is reduced by having some money long and some money short. Sector risk is reduced by making certain that a portfolio contains companies from a number of different industry groups with no heavy concentration in one industry.

How to Balance Industry Exposure

As a practical matter, investors must answer the question of how much representation from one industry to allow. Is it OK to have five software stocks sold short or is that too many? The best answer will result from considering the overall size of the portfolio and something we will call net exposure.

Net exposure refers to the degree that one industry is over-represented on one side of a neutral portfolio. For example, if there are five software companies among the short holdings in a portfolio and three other software companies on the long side, the net exposure is –2. Generally, the closer the net exposure is to 0, the better.

Taking this one step further, what we really care about is the dollar amount of exposure, not simply the number of stocks. If there was $1,000 invested in each of the five shorted software stocks and $1,000 invested in each of the three long software stocks, the net exposure is –$2,000. The dollar exposure in a particular industry is what matters the most. A portfolio that is somewhat imbalanced is illustrated in Figure 6.13.

Again, the closer industry net exposure is to $0, the better. But is –$2,000 of net exposure too much? That depends on the size of the portfolio. If the above example is the full extent of the portfolio, then –$2,000 net exposure is too much. (Not to mention the fact that a portfolio made up of only software companies has other problems.) But net exposure has to be weighed in the context of the size of the entire portfolio.

A –$2,000 net exposure in a $1 million portfolio is certainly reasonable. Or, if the above software companies represent only a small subset

---

FIGURE 6.13 IMBALANCED SOFTWARE STOCK PORTFOLIO

Stock	Industry	Initial Value
Long Positions		
Whizzy Software	Software/Programming	$1,000
Bang Tech.	Software/Programming	$1,000
Webby Development	Software/Programming	$1,000
Subtotal		**$3,000**
Short Positions		
Crash Tech.	Software/Programming	–$1,000
Whoopsy Development	Software/Programming	–$1,000
Bugged Engineering	Software/Programming	–$1,000
Reboot, Inc.	Software/Programming	–$1,000
Blue Screen Mediasoft	Software/Programming	–$1,000
Subtotal		**–$5,000**
Net Exposure		**–$2,000**

of stocks in a portfolio valued at $100,000, then the net industry exposure for software stocks is reasonable. If the software stocks are part of a portfolio fully valued at $30,000, then the net exposure is too high. The rules are not set in stone, but avoiding net exposure of greater than 5 percent of the total portfolio is a good rule of thumb. In a $30,000 neutral portfolio, there probably should be less than $1,500 of net long or net short exposure to one industry.

Recall the hypothetical portfolio from earlier in the chapter where the investor had a bullish bent for hospitals (see Figure 6.14).

The net exposure for hospital stocks is +$1,467 ($1,980 long in Healthy Hospitals minus $513 short in Pallid Hospitals equals $1,467). That represents almost 14 percent of the total portfolio value of $10,500 and heightens the risk to this portfolio considerably. The closer to 0 the better, but it is prudent to keep net exposure below 5 percent of the portfolio value. Implementing that rule would require holding fewer shares of Healthy Hospitals or selling short more shares of Pallid Hospitals such that the net industry exposure is no greater than +/− $525.00 for a small portfolio like this.

FIGURE 6.14 IMBALANCED HOSPITAL STOCK PORTFOLIO

Stock	Initial Share Price	Share Number	Initial Value
Long Positions			
Alpha Manufacturing	$13	77	$1,001
New Semiconductor Inc.	$21	48	$1,008
First Pulp and Paper Co.	$40	25	$1,000
Healthy Hospitals Inc.	$33	60	$1,980
Pizzazz Retail Corp.	$10	100	$1,000
Subtotal			**$5,989**
Short Positions			
Beta Manufacturing	$15	−67	−$1,005
Obsolete Semiconductor Inc.	$17	−59	−$1,003
Second Pulp and Paper Co.	$45	−22	−$990
Pallid Hospitals Inc.	$27	−19	−$513
Plodder Retail Corp.	$8	−125	−$1,000
Subtotal			**−$4,511**

Market Cap and Beta

Of less importance but worth discussing are market capitalization and beta as elements that should be balanced. Market cap, or company size, is considered important by some market neutral hedge fund or mutual fund managers. At issue is whether small cap stocks will underperform or outperform large cap stocks over some finite period of time. To the extent that small company stock prices behave differently than large company stock prices, as they have over the last few years, a neutral portfolio should have an equal balance of big and small companies among long and short selections.

While it is worth considering, market cap is less critical to achieving good balance than industry exposure. There *are* periods when small caps will perform better or worse than large caps. And a neutral portfolio should not have all small caps on the long side or all large caps on the short side, as our Chapter 4 portfolios did. But for investors assembling a neutral portfolio some broad guidelines should suffice. For example, setting a requirement that all companies have a capitalization of between $1 billion and $5 billion should be sufficient, or checking to see that the average market cap for each side of the portfolio is not way out of whack.

Recall that beta measures how volatile a stock is relative to the overall market. Stocks that rise or fall dramatically from one day to the next tend to have high betas. Some market neutral money managers will insist on a portfolio being "beta neutral." When they construct a portfolio, they will require that stocks on both the long and short sides pair up reasonably well on measures of beta. The idea is that the portfolio should not have a group of wildly volatile stocks on one side and a group of staid, slow-moving stocks on the other.

This is a sensible requirement but it probably takes care of itself to a large extent so long as industry exposure is carefully monitored. After all, software stocks will tend to share some of the same volatility characteristics. Most members of most industry groups will have similar volatility profiles. Thus, if industry exposure is balanced, betas will tend to be balanced. As an example, the table in Figure 6.15 highlights betas for the seven largest appliance/tool companies at the end of 2003.

With a range of 0.31 to 1.74, clearly there is some variability, but their beta is clustered within 0.20 of each other.

FIGURE 6.15 BETA FOR SEVEN APPLIANCE/TOOL COMPANIES

Company	Beta
Black and Decker	1.17
Electrolux AB	0.97
Makita	0.31
Maytag	1.74
Snap-On	1.06
Stanley Works	0.80
Whirlpool	1.01
Average	**1.01**
Median	**1.01**

The chances are slim that a neutral portfolio with multiindustry representation and low net industry exposure will end up with a large percentage of mismatched betas. With smaller portfolios, it will be difficult enough to find undervalued and overvalued companies and then make sure that the industry net exposure is appropriate. Balancing market cap and beta on top of that may add a level of complexity not justified by the benefit.

Finally, the total number of stocks held in a portfolio does matter. The conventional wisdom for some time has been that a portfolio of 20 to 30 stocks creates enough diversification to broadly distribute risk. Some studies show that individual stocks have become more volatile over the last few years and so the minimum number of stocks held should probably be raised. However, if the number grows too large, most investors have trouble keeping abreast of all the developments surrounding all of the companies. As with much of investing, a balance has to be struck, but a portfolio of at least 30 stocks is a good idea.

An Example of Option 4

Using actual data from late 2003, we will go through the process of developing a market neutral portfolio from scratch and "by hand." In its raw form, the model initially produced a total of 25 undervalued stocks and 20 overvalued stocks. Ideally, the closer the number of undervalued stocks equals the number of overvalued stocks the better, although it may not be practical to make the numbers identical. As we review the stocks further, we will look for opportunities to remove a couple of undervalued entries. Alternatively, we could loosen up the criteria for "overvalued" and generate some more prospects. In Figures 6.16 and 6.17 are the 45 companies, arranged by industry group.

We will start by assuming a portfolio comprised of these stocks and an investment of $1,000 in each or $45,000 total. Two readily apparent observations about these lists of stocks: the average market cap of the

FIGURE 6.16 TWENTY-FIVE UNDERVALUED COMPANY STOCKS

Undervalued Company	Symbol	Industry	Market Cap (in millions)
Kellwood Co.	KWD	Apparel/Accessories	1,106
ArvinMeritor	ARM	Auto & Truck Parts	1,163
Constellation Brands	STZ	Beverages (Alcoholic)	3,459
Stet Hellas Telecom.	STHLY	Communications Services	1,110
Beazer Homes	BZH	Construction Services	1,331
Chiquita Brands	CQB	Food Processing	922
Univeral Forest Products	UFPI	Forestry & Wood Products	564
America Service Group	ASGR	Healthcare Facilities	210
Amerigroup	AGP	Insurance (Accident & Health)	1,047
Fidelity National Financial	FNF	Insurance (Property & Casualty)	5,708
First America Corp.	FAF	Insurance (Property & Casualty)	2,370
DHB Industries	DHB	Medical Equipment & Supplies	282
PolyMedica Corp.	PLMD	Medical Equipment & Supplies	682
RailAmerica	RRA	Railroads	380
Blockbuster	BBI	Recreational Activities	3,183
Fremont General	FMT	Regional Banks	1,253
ITLA Capital	ITLA	Regional Banks	305
PC Mall	MALL	Retail (Catalog & Mail Order)	181
Sonic Automotive	SAH	Retail (Specialty Nonapparel)	926
United Auto Group	UAG	Retail (Specialty Nonapparel)	1,273
First Mutual Bancshares	FMSB	Savings Banks and Thrifts	115
Hawthorne Financial	HTHR	Savings Banks and Thrifts	323
Sterling Financial	STSA	Savings Banks and Thrifts	517
WestCorp.	WES	Savings Banks and Thrifts	1,623
Navarre Corp.	NAVR	Software & Programming	132
Average Market Cap			**1,207**

FIGURE 6.17 TWENTY OVERVALUED COMPANY STOCKS

Overvalued Company	Symbol	Industry	Market Cap (in millions)
Radio One	ROIAK	Broadcasting & Cable TV	2,037
PanAmSat	SPOT	Communications Services	3,257
Telstra Corp.	TLS	Communications Services	47,478
Autonomy	AUTN	Computer Services	471
Emerson Electric	EMR	Conglomerates	27,276
General Electric	GE	Conglomerates	312,471
Tektronix	TEK	Electronic Instruments & Controls	2,736
Tredegar Corp.	TG	Fabricated Plastics & Rubber	605
Topps Company	TOPP	Food Processing	418
Gabelli Asset Management	GBL	Investment Services	1,223
Pixar	PIXR	Motion Pictures	3,819
Global Sante Fe	GSF	Oil Well Services & Equipment	5,803
Hong Kong Land Holdings	HKHGY	Real Estate Operations	3,717
May Department Stores	MAY	Retail (Department & Discount)	8,181
Wild Oats Markets	OATS	Retail (Grocery)	386
Capitol Federal Financial	CFFN	Savings Banks and Thrifts	2,639
Westfield Financial	WFD	Savings Banks and Thrifts	246
ARM Holdings	ARMHY	Semiconductors	2,376
Tibco Software	TIBX	Software & Programming	1,472
Swedish Match	WSMAY	Tobacco	3,424
Average Market Cap			**21,502**

undervalued stocks is far, far lower than that of the overvalued stocks; and there is too much Insurance and Banking/Thrift net industry exposure in the undervalued list.

With six firms operating as either Regional Banks or Thrifts on the undervalued list and only two on the overvalued list, we should eliminate two from the undervalued group. That will leave a net long exposure of $2,000, within our self-imposed 5 percent limit. But which two should be eliminated?

There are two different approaches to this question. One simple answer would be to eliminate the two smallest cap companies, because this

would have the salutary effect of raising, albeit slightly, the average capitalization of our undervalued list and take us a small step closer to better balance. The other possibility would be to try to determine which
four of the six banks/thrifts are the most undervalued and eliminate the
other two. Figure 6.18 lists all six.

Fortunately, looking at the fundamental data, at least one clear
choice about which to drop and which to keep can be made. FMSB looks
like it is the least undervalued based on having the worst revenue growth
and the highest PEG ratio (12 divided by 13, or 0.92.) Plus, it is the
smallest of the bunch. The next least undervalued is about a toss-up between HTHR and STSA. Because they have such similar fundamentals
perhaps the best way to break the tie is to drop the smallest cap stock,
which is HTHR.

After dropping FMSB and HTHR, our portfolio now is net long on the
Banking/Thrift industry by $2,000, an acceptable number. There are also
three insurance companies on the long list (see Figure 6.19). With none
on the overvalued list, it is probably prudent to drop one, even though
they are not all in the same segment of the insurance business. AGP offers health insurance while FNF and FAF sell real estate title insurance.

AGP looks like it is the most undervalued. Between FNF and FAF the
difference is not so clear. Based on earnings and expected earnings
growth it is a virtual dead heat. Revenue growth has been stronger at
FNF but some of that has been driven by acquisitions, as it has at FAF, so
we probably should not put too much emphasis on that. Based on the
PS ratio, FAF carries a much lower valuation, and that is enough to tip

FIGURE 6.18 LIST OF BANK/THRIFT STOCKS IN PORTFOLIO MODEL

Ticker	PE	Ind. PE	Forward PE	EPS Est. Growth	PS	Ind. PS	Rev. Growth	Ind. Rev. Growth
FMT	7	17	6	25	2.31	3.40	+18%	−3%
ITLA	11	17	10	15	2.57	3.40	+7	−3
FMSB	14	17	12	13	2.36	2.80	−1	−7
HTHR	13	17	12	15	2.23	2.80	+9	−7
STSA	15	17	13	18	2.45	2.80	+7	−7
WES	14	17	11	15	1.31	2.80	+12	−7

FIGURE 6.19 LIST OF INSURANCE COMPANY STOCKS IN PORTFOLIO MODEL

Ticker	PE	Ind. PE	Forward PE	EPS Est. Growth	PS	Ind. PS	Rev. Growth	Ind. Rev. Growth
AGP	15	17	14	19	0.60	0.70	+37%	+12%
FNF	6	13	10	12	0.73	0.90	+88%	+12%
FAF	6	13	10	12	0.39	0.90	+36%	+12%

the scales—we will drop FNF from the portfolio. Unfortunately that does not help the market cap imbalance, because FNF has the largest capitalization of all the undervalued companies. The average market cap now becomes $1.1 billion.

The only other change we might contemplate to improve the market-cap imbalance is to drop the largest of the large from the overvalued list. GE, with a market cap of $312 billion, contributes a great deal to the imbalance. By dropping that one stock, the average market cap on the overvalued list falls from $21.5 billion to $6.2 billion. Making those changes gives us a portfolio of 22 undervalued and 19 overvalued stocks. Not perfectly balanced and still skewed in terms of market cap but reasonably close to matched.

Hear is a summary of the six steps to be taken:

1. Run a model to develop a list of undervalued and overvalued stocks.
2. Calculate the average market cap for each stock.
3. Determine the total size of the portfolio (i.e., how much money will be invested in each stock).
4. Calculate the net industry exposure in dollar terms and set a limit of less than 5 percent of the total portfolio value.
5. If adjustments need to be made so that industry exposure is reduced, review the fundamental data for each stock in the overexposed industry group. Determine and remove the stock that is the least undervalued or the least overvalued.
6. In the absence of a compelling valuation argument, use market cap to help determine which stocks to drop or keep.

A Test

Of course, the obvious question is how our attempt to handpick the correct stocks from the initial set will actually work. In order to determine that, we will go through the same exercise using some of the original stocks our model produced in late 2002. Then we can review their subsequent performance in 2003.

As in the above example, there were a large number of banks/thrifts in the original list of 46 undervalued stocks generated at the end of 2002. Our challenge is to weed out six of the eight bank/thrift stocks (see Figure 6.20) using valuation criteria.

Based on the forward PE ratio and estimated earnings growth (PEG ratio), two stocks stand out: CIB and UPFC. Both firms were priced very low relative to the expected earnings growth. What's more, CIB has the lowest PS ratio and moderate revenue growth over the past 12 months, making it the hands down winner for "most undervalued." UPFC, in addition to its low PEG ratio had very strong revenue growth, with only IFC coming anywhere close to that sort of expansion. Taking all the elements together, UPFC should probably win second place.

If we were to rank all eight, in order of most undervalued to least undervalued, it would look something like this:

1. CIB—extremely low PEG, extremely low PS ratio, slight revenue growth

FIGURE 6.20 LIST OF BANK/THRIFT STOCKS 2002

Ticker	PE	Ind. PE	Forward PE	EPS Est. Growth	PS	Ind. PS	Rev. Growth	Ind. Rev. Growth
CIB	3	14	3	8	0.69	2.5	+2%	−7%
CCOW	13	14	11	14	2.07	2.5	+1	−7
GLDB	12	14	10	15	1.66	2.5	−4	−7
IFC	11	14	9	13	1.56	2.5	+14	−7
BPOP	13	14	11	14	2.20	2.5	−6	−7
FBC	6	14	7	12	1.42	1.9	−3	−6
STSA	10	14	8	10	1.15	1.9	−4	−6
UPFC	11	14	8	30	1.61	1.9	+18	−6

2. UPFC—extremely low PEG, moderate PS ratio, very strong revenue growth

3. IFC—low PEG, moderate PS ratio, very strong revenue growth

4. FBC—low PEG, moderate PS ratio, poor revenue growth

5. GLDB—low PEG, moderate PS ratio, poor revenue growth

6. STSA—high PEG, low PS ratio, poor revenue growth

7. CCOW—high PEG, high PS ratio, slight revenue growth

8. BPOP—high PEG, high PS ratio, poor revenue growth

Note the characterizations are relative terms. BPOP had a *relatively* high PEG ratio when compared to the other banks/thrifts. On an absolute basis it was still a low 0.79. But because we have to eliminate six stocks, we are forced to choose only the very lowest valuations.

How does this ranking compare with the actual price performance of these stocks in 2003? Quite well. If our thought process was on target, we would expect to see the most undervalued rise more than the least undervalued.

While not perfectly correlated, our effort to identify the two most undervalued stocks was successful. Both CIB and UPFC were the biggest gainers over the next 12 months (see Figure 6.21). All of the stocks outperformed the broad market, by a considerable amount, but there was a relationship between the fundamental factors we examined and subsequent performance.

In Chapter 7 we will use what we learned here to explore an entirely different way of building a market neutral portfolio—one that starts from the bottom rather than the top and that eliminates any worries about balancing industry exposure.

FIGURE 6.21 BANK/THRIFT STOCK PRICE CHANGE 2003

Ticker	Price Change in 2003
CIB	+159%
UPFC	+141
IFC	+94
FBC	+103
GLDB	+44
STSA	100
CCOW	+82
BPOP	+37

Summary

Creating a portfolio that has the ideal balance is a little bit art and a little bit science. The first decision for investors to make is whether to strive for a truly market neutral portfolio that has a some balance, or whether a long/short portfolio is more appropriate, along with its somewhat higher risk. A third alternative is a hybrid version, one that does not require complete balance but keeps the amount of money invested long equal to the amount of money invested short. Finally, as a variation on the market neutral approach, we can take the extra effort to hand-pick stocks based on their industry as well as valuation attributes and assemble a more carefully crafted portfolio.

The table in Figure 6.22 highlights risk characteristics for each approach. The level of risk is a relative assessment; for all four portfolio strategies the risk will be lower than is typical of a long-only portfolio.

Which approach an investor takes is inextricably linked to his or her tolerance for risk. Even a risk-tolerant investor, utilizing a long/short portfolio, should not have too much net industry exposure.

In a perfect world, and in a perfectly balanced portfolio, the betas of all the companies on the long side would match up with the betas of all the companies on the short side. So would the market capitalizations. In reality, making that happen is difficult. What's more, the payoff may not be worth the lost opportunity. Instead, investors should focus primarily on choosing the right portfolio strategy and controlling industry exposure.

FIGURE 6.22 RISK CHARACTERISTICS OF FOUR PORTFOLIO STRATEGIES

Portfolio Strategy	Market Risk	Industry Risk	Potential Returns
Market Neutral—Mechanical	Lower	Higher	Lower
Long/Short	Higher	Higher	Higher
Hybrid	Lower	Higher	Higher
Market Neutral—Handpicked	Lower	Lower	Lower

7

FROM THE BOTTOM UP

In Chapter 5 we outlined a method for identifying undervalued and overvalued stocks that takes a "top-down" approach. We started at the top by looking at the entire universe of publicly traded companies and then progressively narrowed down our list to a manageable number of stocks. We accomplished this by establishing some criteria and then searching the universe of stocks for individual companies that met those criteria.

As we saw in Chapter 6, we not only need to generate candidates to buy and sell short but also to create a balanced portfolio from the stocks that are turned up in this manner. A "raw" list of longs and shorts may create a portfolio that has too much exposure to a single industry and, thus, is unnecessarily risky. For example, if our search turned up 25 stocks that look undervalued and 10 of them are pharmaceutical firms, we probably need to prune our exposure to that one sector.

Building a top-down model is a terrific way of developing a portfolio. It consists of a two-step process: finding a group of undervalued and overvalued stocks and then carefully picking through them such that the resulting combination has balance in terms of industry exposure and, secondarily, market cap and beta. Top down is not the only way, however.

We can also approach the task of portfolio creation from the bottom up. Instead of starting with the whole universe of stocks, we can start with a single industry and survey the companies found within it. This allows us to get a sense of what the valuation norms are for the companies competing in the same market. Moreover, we may be able to pick out one stock in particular that is undervalued and another that is overvalued and put them together in a market neutral portfolio. Sometimes this is called a *paired trade* because it literally pairs up two stocks—one long and one short.

What we are really trying to do with this analysis is isolate two stocks that will perform, operationally speaking, in similar fashion in the coming year. At the same time we want two stocks that are incorrectly valued: one that is valued below the industry average and one that is valued above the industry average. If we can identify such a pair, we will have a successful market neutral strategy.

Of course, it is impossible to identify with any certainty two companies that will go on to perform in similar fashion. We do not have a crystal ball that we can gaze into and see that companies X and Y are going to sell the same number of widgets, reduce expenses by the same amount, suffer equally from increased raw material costs, etc. However, if we choose two companies that compete with each other, at least we know that they will both be dealing with many of the same economic factors—like whether overall demand for widgets is rising or falling in general.

Remember our earliest example of Ford versus GM? There was no way of knowing in advance, for example, that GM would increase sales more than Ford in 2002. But at least we could be sure that if steel prices shot up, or falling interest rates improved demand for cars, both companies would be similarly impacted. Certainly not to the same degree; different companies have different strengths, and perhaps GM has better supply chain management or longer-term contracts with steel suppliers. But by choosing two competitors, we improve the odds that they will experience similar performance characteristics.

Also, though it may not be a crystal ball, one way we gain insight into future performance is to look at past sales performance—the wind-in-the-sails factor we discussed in Chapter 3. If we see two competitors and one had much better sales gains in the past, we can speculate that this trend will continue.

To review then, our goal with a bottom-up analysis is to find: (A) two companies that appear likely to perform in similar fashion and (B) one of those companies is undervalued and the other is overvalued. Even better is finding a company that is undervalued *and* has a strong wind in its sails, or one that is overvalued and is becalmed.

Example #1

How this works can be illustrated with the following example. Using data from the end of 2001, we looked at all of the companies operating in the trucking industry. (The choice of trucking was mostly random, although we wanted an industry where there was virtually no question about proper classification, where the number of industry players was not too big and where valuations would not be dependent on the potential for technological breakthroughs. More about industry selection later.) The table in Figure 7.1 shows all of the trucking companies with

FIGURE 7.1 TRUCKING COMPANIES WITH $100 MILLION MARKET CAP

Company	Forward PE	EPS Growth Estimate	Sales Growth	Industry Sales Growth
Arkansas Best	13.8	5.7%	-12.6%	-2.6%
CNF	22.6	11.3	-6.3	-2.6
Consolidated Freight	NA	5.0	-2.6	-2.6
Covenant Transport	26.9	20.5	1.2	-2.6
Forward Air Corp.	31.0	21.3	10.6	-2.6
Heartland Express	23.6	12.3	7.5	-2.6
J.B. Hunt	25.3	8.9	-4.2	-2.6
Knight Transportation	26.9	20.4	22.0	-2.6
Landstar System	12.6	17.7	0.5	-2.6
Old Dominion Freight	8.0	15.0	6.6	-2.6
P.A.M. Transportation	10.5	6.0	7.5	-2.6
Roadway Corp.	13.4	10.7	-4.6	-2.6
Swift Transportation	27.3	17.7	9.6	-2.6
U.S. Xpress	32.3	10.8	1.4	-2.6
United Parcel	24.3	13.9	3.9	-2.6
USA Truck	22.9	11.0	12.3	-2.6
U.S. Freightways	15.9	14.0	1.0	-2.6
Werner Enterprises	20.7	14.4	6.6	-2.6
Yellow Corp.	14.4	9.0	-5.9	-2.6

a market capitalization of at least $100 million, operating at the end of 2001, along with a couple of key fundamentals.

Without jumping through a lot of analytical hoops, we can see from eyeballing the data that only two companies had a forward PE that was less than the future earnings per share growth estimate: Landstar and Old Dominion. In other words, they had a PEG ratio of less than one. All of the other firms had a forward PE greater than expected earnings growth and, thus, a PEG of greater than one. (Recall that PEG is forward PE divided by expected growth.) Of those two firms, Old Dominion has a slightly better sales record, so if we were to pick one company that looks the most undervalued, it would be Old Dominion.

As for the most overvalued company, if we calculate which company had the highest PEG ratio, three in particular stand out. The worst was U.S. Xpress with a forward PE about three times expected growth, but it was closely followed by J.B. Hunt at 2.84 and Arkansas Best at 2.42. In Figure 7.2 are the trucking companies with their PEG ratios calculated.

FIGURE 7.2 TRUCKING COMPANY WITH PEG RATIOS CALCULATED

Company	Forward PE	EPS Growth Estimate	PEG Ratio
Arkansas Best	13.8	5.7%	2.42
CNF	22.6	11.3	2.00
Consolidated Freight	NA	5.0	NA
Covenant Transport	26.9	20.5	1.31
Forward Air Corp.	31.0	21.3	1.45
Heartland Express	23.6	12.3	1.92
J.B. Hunt	25.3	8.9	2.84
Knight Transportation	26.9	20.4	1.32
Landstar System	12.6	17.7	0.71
Old Dominion Freight	8.0	15.0	0.53
P.A.M. Transportation	10.5	6.0	1.75
Roadway Corp.	13.4	10.7	1.25
Swift Transportation	27.3	17.7	1.54
U.S. Xpress	32.3	10.8	2.99
United Parcel	24.3	13.9	1.75
USA Truck	22.9	11.0	2.08
U.S. Freightways	15.9	14.0	1.14
Werner Enterprises	20.7	14.4	1.44
Yellow Corp.	14.4	9.0	1.60

It was almost a toss-up as to which one of the three companies looks most overvalued, because while U.S. Express has the highest PEG ratio, its sales record is not as bad as either J.B. Hunt or Arkansas Best. Of the three, probably either J.B. Hunt or Arkansas Best had the best (i.e., the worst) combination of declining sales and a high PEG ratio.

The net results of a long position in Old Dominion and a short position in either J.B. Hunt or Arkansas Best would have been excellent. Old Dominion went on to gain 118 percent over the next 12 months, and J.B. Hunt stock was up 9 percent. Arkansas Best shares were off 16.7 percent. An equal investment in Old Dominion/J.B. Hunt would have returned 54 percent and Old Dominion/Arkansas Best would have boasted a 67 percent return.

As an aside, none of the three short candidates identified was the best choice, but two of the three did fall in price. As the table in Figure 7.3 illustrates, there were even better shorts in 2002, but then hindsight is always 20/20.

FIGURE 7.3 PRICE CHANGE OF TRUCK COMPANIES 2002

Company	Price Change in 2002
Arkansas Best	−16.7%
CNF	−3.1
Consolidated Freight	−100.0
Covenant Transport	12.4
Forward Air Corp.	−44.8
Heartland Express	20.5
J.B. Hunt	9.0
Knight Transportation	3.5
Landstar System	56.1
Old Dominion Freight	118.3
P.A.M. Transportation	76.0
Roadway Corp.	−6.8
Swift Transportation	−12.2
U.S. Xpress	−7.8
United Parcel	12.7
USA Truck	−38.7
U.S. Freightways	−17.5
Werner Enterprises	11.4
Yellow Corp.	8.7

This initial success in the trucking industry is enough to encourage us toward further investigation. To better understand if it will work in other cases, we turn to another example using another old economy industry: Steel.

There were 13 different firms in the steel industry, listed in Figure 7.4, at the end of 2001 that had market caps of greater than $100 million. There were several others that had to be eliminated because there was no earnings growth estimate available for them.

As with the trucking companies, there were some dramatic differences in valuation. Despite having an only average sales record, AK Steel traded at a forward PE of 66, high by any standard, but particularly for a steel company. AK Steel's PEG ratio was the highest on the list at 8.64, and it certainly looked like it took the prize for being most overvalued.

Among candidates for most undervalued, Grupo IMSA looked promising with a PEG ratio of only 0.14. On the strength of its better than average sales and a PEG ratio of 0.73, Quanex also looked attractive. Without knowing what lay ahead, Quanex would probably be a slight favorite, only because Grupo IMSA had such a dismal sales record.

That particular pairing of a short position in AK Steel and a long position in Quanex would have been nicely profitable in 2002. AK Steel

FIGURE 7.4 STEEL FIRMS WITH $100 MILLION MARKET CAP

Company	Forward PE	EPS Growth Estimate	Sales Growth	Industry Sales Growth
AK Steel	66.5	7.7%	−12.1%	−13.4%
Allegheny Tech.	29.7	8.9	−9.4	−13.4
Carpenter Tech.	15.2	14.0	10.5	−13.4
Companhia Sideurgica	9.6	14.3	−34.8	−13.4
Grupo IMSA, S.A.	3.5	24.8	−27.3	−13.4
Nucor	27.5	11.4	−10.7	−13.4
Oregon Steel Mills	19.7	10.0	4.0	−13.4
Pohang Iron and Steel	8.2	9.0	−27.3	−13.4
Quanex	9.8	13.5	−1.1	−13.4
Schnitzer Steel	11.3	7.0	−12.5	−13.4
Steel Dynamics	31.7	21.7	−13.3	−13.4
U.S. Steel	NA	8.3	3.1	−13.4
Worthington Ind.	14.1	11.2	−13.4	−13.4

stock fell 32 percent and Quanex stock rose almost 20 percent. Taken together, it would have meant a positive return of 26 percent.

In Figure 7.5 is a summary of how all the steel stocks performed in 2002. Neither AK Steel nor Quanex were the *best* choices—those honors belonged to Allegheny Tech. as the best short and Schnitzer Steel as the best long—but the AK Steel/Quanex combination was quite good.

As with all of the examples developed in this book, we must sound a note of caution about extrapolating these results. Certainly examples from other time periods and other industries could be found where the results would be unimpressive. Both the trucking and the steel industry cases are included here as an illustration of how a stock pairing can be made using very simple fundamental data.

Introducing More Complexity

The best models often rely on a variety of criteria, so we took the basic idea a step further by adding an additional fundamental factor, price-to-sales ratio, and by examining a different industry from a more recent time frame. In Figure 7.6 are some fundamental data for 12 casino companies from the beginning of 2003 for which we could see earnings forecasts for 2004.

FIGURE 7.5 PRICE CHANGE OF STEEL FIRMS 2002

Company	Price Change in 2002
AK Steel	−32.2%
Allegheny Tech.	−60.6
Carpenter Tech.	−50.3
Companhia Sideurgica	−11.6
Grupo IMSA, S.A.	30.5
Nucor	−21.1
Oregon Steel Mills	−18.1
Pohang Iron and Steel	3.7
Quanex	19.6
Schnitzer Steel	34.9
Steel Dynamics	2.2
U.S. Steel	−28.0
Worthington Ind.	9.7

FIGURE 7.6 CASINO COMPANIES WITH FORWARD PE RATIOS

Company	Symbol	Forward PE	Expected Earnings Growth	PEG Ratio	Sales Growth	PS Ratio
Ameristar Casinos	ASCA	8	17%	0.48	29%	0.54
Argosy Gaming	AGY	7	12	0.53	34	0.55
Aztar Corp.	AZR	9	11	0.68	2	0.65
Boyd Gaming	BYD	9	17	0.52	9	0.79
Century Casinos	CNTY	7	32	0.20	-8	1.12
Harrah's Entertain.	HET	11	15	0.73	18	1.04
Int. Game Tech.	IGT	17	18	0.94	54	3.64
Isle of Capri	ISLE	6	12	0.51	6	0.36
Magna Entertain.	MECA	43	12	3.45	8	1.20
Mandalay Resort	MBG	11	15	0.74	-4	0.87
Park Place Entertain.	CZR	13	9	1.37	5	0.54
Station Casinos	STN	13	14	0.90	-8	1.34
Average		**14**	**15%**	**0.92**	**12%**	**1.05**

There are some points that immediately stand out with just a quick glance at the table in Figure 7.6. The forward PE ratios, which were based on 2004 earnings estimates, ranged from a low of 6 for Isle of Capri (ISLE) to a high of 43 for Magna Entertainment (MECA). MECA's high PE was not accompanied by a particularly high earnings growth rate, so the PEG ratio was 3.45, obviously far higher than any other firm.

Also, one company was coming off a remarkable sales gain over the previous 12 months, International Game Technology (IGT). Take note, however, that it was not all organic revenue growth but rather reflected an earlier acquisition. Revenue growth through acquisition is not bad, but it's not as impressive as generating more sales from the same facilities. IGT also carried the highest PS ratio by a significant margin.

Century Casinos (CNTY) stands out as having a low forward PE ratio and a very high projected earnings growth rate, resulting in the lowest PEG ratio. ISLE had the lowest PS ratio.

Because we are using old data, we have the luxury of seeing exactly what happened to the stocks prices in 2003 (see Figure 7.7).

Obviously it was a good year for casino stocks, with an average gain of 45 percent. But perhaps the most interesting question we can answer is "which of the fundamental factors worked best in predicting the sub-

FIGURE 7.7 PRICE PERFORMANCE OF CASINOS 2003

Company	Symbol	2003 Price Performance
Ameristar Casinos	ASCA	68%
Argosy Gaming	AGY	36
Aztar Corp.	AZR	60
Boyd Gaming	BYD	17
Century Casinos	CNTY	56
Harrah's Entertain.	HET	24
Int. Game Tech.	IGT	85
Isle of Capri	ISLE	59
Magna Entertain.	MECA	−16
Mandalay Resort	MBG	46
Park Place Entertain.	CZR	30
Station Casinos	STN	70
Average		**45%**

sequent rise or fall of share prices?" Was it the forward PE, the PEG ratio, past sales growth, the PS ratio, or a combination of the above?

The six lowest forward PE stocks gained an average of 49 percent in 2003, and the six highest gained 40 percent. That suggests forward PEs are a reasonably good determinant of future price appreciation. In this case the same stocks were also the lowest and highest PEG stocks. Past sales growth, at least by itself, was of no use. Indeed, it served as in inverse indicator in this case. The six stocks with the best past sales growth only had an average share price gain of 18 percent, and the six worst gained an average of 53 percent. PS ratio was not very helpful either. The six lowest PS ratio stocks were up 45 percent, and the six highest were up 44 percent.

If we wanted to pick the single most undervalued and overvalued stocks by *combining* all of these factors, we could create a point system based on being below or above the averages. Awarding a point for having a below-average forward PE, a below-average PEG ratio, an above-average sales record, and a below-average PS ratio would give us three candidates for "most undervalued": ASCA, AGY, and HET. Of those three, it would be a virtual toss-up between ASCA and AGY over which had the lowest PEG ratios.

Using the same methodology to pinpoint the most overvalued gives us a clear winner: MECA. The company had the highest forward PE, the highest PEG ratio, below-average sales growth, and an above-average PS ratio.

A market neutral investment consisting of buying shares in either ASCA or AGY and selling short MECA would have been very profitable. The ASCA/MECA combination would have generated a 42 percent return. The AGY/MECA pair would have gained 26 percent.

An "Illuminating" Example

The electric utility industry was considered, at one time, to be the last bastion of widows and orphans. Previously a highly regulated industry that was considered a conservative and safe place to invest, everything changed with the advent of deregulation in the late 1990s. With deregulation came hopes for big profits from energy trading. After the Enron scandal, those hopes were dashed and share prices crashed. In 2003 the industry began to shake off its malaise, and many utilities went back to what they had always done pretty well—generate electricity.

Again using data from the beginning of 2003, we identified the largest 20 electric utilities for which there were earnings estimates for the next year. They are listed in Figure 7.8, ranked in order of PEG ratio.

For such a supposedly staid industry, there was quite a lot of variance in valuations. PEG ratios ranged from 0.19 to almost 10. How strong a predictor of future stock price performance was the PEG ratio? The lowest 10 PEG ratio stocks went on to gain an average of 42 percent in 2003. The highest 10 PEG ratio stocks had an average increase of 9 percent. PEG ratio served as an excellent tool for separating the undervalued from the overvalued, and those starting valuations clearly made a difference in how the stocks went on to perform. Indeed, the lowest PEG ratio stock—AES Corp. (AES)—had an extraordinary rise of 208 percent.

Low forward PE stocks also significantly outperformed high forward PE stocks. Although the lists were quite similar to the low PEG/high PEG set, forward PE was a slightly better predictor of share price performance. The lowest 10 forward PE stocks gained an average of 44 percent and the highest forward PE stocks were up 8 percent.

There was also a correlation between past sales and 2003 price performance. The ten companies with the best past sales growth saw their stock prices rise 37 percent in 2003. The ten worst had share prices rise

FIGURE 7.8 TWENTY ELECTRIC UTILITIES RANKED BY PEG RATIO

Company	Symbol	Forward PE	Expected Earnings Growth	PEG Ratio	Sales Growth	PS Ratio
AES Corp.	AES	3	15%	0.19	15%	0.21
Empresa Nacional	EOC	10	12	0.87	15	1.53
Edison Int.	EIX	9	8	1.13	12	0.33
TXU Corp.	TXU	9	7	1.26	29	0.27
First Energy	FE	9	7	1.44	53	0.86
Entergy	ETR	12	8	1.45	−20	1.28
Duke Energy	DUK	12	8	1.46	45	0.75
Dominion Resources	D	12	8	1.51	−7	1.59
Public Service Enter.	PEG	10	6	1.70	2	0.91
Energy East	EAS	11	7	1.71	−9	0.91
Exelon Corp.	EXC	10	6	1.72	−1	1.18
DTE Energy	DTE	12	7	1.72	60	0.91
Teco Energy	TE	10	6	1.75	6	0.98
FPL Group	FPL	12	6	1.97	−2	1.30
NSTAR	NST	13	6	2.00	−14	0.88
American Electric	AEP	10	5	2.06	10	0.43
Cinergy	CIN	12	5	2.51	−20	0.55
Consolidated Edison	ED	15	4	4.03	−12	1.11
Ameren Corp.	AEE	15	4	4.06	1	1.42
Enel SpA	EN	19	2	9.50	−15	1.02
Average		**11**	**7%**	**2.20**	**12%**	**0.92**

14 percent. Similarly, low PS ratio stocks tended to outperform high-PS ratio stocks.

Recalling our point system from the previous example, there would have been three candidates for most undervalued and three for most overvalued. Undervalued possibilities would have been AES, TXU, and First Energy. Of the three, the most undervalued stock would have to have been AES because its forward PE and PEG ratio were so much lower than the others.

Most overvalued prospects would have been Ameren, Consolidated Edison, and Enel SpA (EN). EN looked like the most overvalued because of its super-high forward PE and PEG ratio, along with a prior revenue decline, and a higher-than-average PS ratio.

Had we combined those two stocks in a market neutral portfolio it would have been a very profitable investment. Buying shares in AES returned an astounding 208 percent in 2003. Selling short shares in EN would have resulted in a loss of 31 percent. Together, the two positions would have yielded a gain of 89 percent.

Of course, in hindsight it looks easy. Today it seems obvious that AES was undervalued and a good investment. At the time, however, an investment in AES was a dubious proposition. The company was struggling with a great deal of debt, there were reports of an impending energy trading investigation, and its Brazilian operations were close to default. Without some thoughtful fundamental analysis, no one in their right mind would have wanted to buy shares in AES.

What's more, it's not as if AES went rocketing higher in a straight line at the beginning of 2003. In fact, by mid-February the stock price had *fallen,* and any investor would probably have questioned the wisdom of having bought AES shares a month earlier. We bring this up to underscore how important it is to have a disciplined methodology that can stand the psychological tests that investing brings with it. Most investment decisions are difficult and usually subject to our own second-guessing. Unless there is some substantial reasoning that supports the initial decision, it is all too easy to convince ourselves later that we made a mistake.

For this reason, an investor must "own" the decision process to buy or sell short a stock. In other words, he must understand the reason, have tested it, and believe in it. Otherwise, at the first sign of trouble, he will be inclined to abandon the strategy and then it certainly won't work. It would have taken courage to hold shares of AES in February 2003, but obviously that courage was rewarded with an incredible gain by year-end (see Figure 7.9).

The Paper Trail

Paper products are largely a commodity product and profits are heavily impacted by energy costs, overall industry capacity, and demand. At the beginning of 2003, there were hopes that the industry slump that began in 2000 was at an end. Prices were firming up along with demand, so there was a sense of optimism surrounding the industry.

FIGURE 7.9 PRICE PERFORMANCE OF ELECTRIC UTILITIES 2003

Company	Symbol	2003 Price Performance
AES Corp.	AES	208%
Empresa Nacional	EOC	54
Edison Int.	EIX	76
TXU Corp.	TXU	25
First Energy	FE	11
Entergy	ETR	0
Duke Energy	DUK	4
Dominion Resources	D	16
Public Service Enter.	PEG	38
Energy East	EAS	0
Exelon Corp.	EXC	27
DTE Energy	DTE	−15
Teco Energy	TE	−6
FPL Group	FPL	9
NSTAR	NST	8
American Electric	AEP	11
Cinergy	CIN	13
Consolidated Edison	ED	0
Ameren Corp.	AEE	10
Enel SpA	EN	31
Average		**26%**

There were 14 large-cap paper products companies at the beginning of 2003 and for which 2004 earnings estimates were available (see Figure 7.10).

Once again, low forward PE and low PEG ratio stocks far outperformed their opposite number. Low forward PE paper stocks rose an average of 50 percent, and low PEG ratio stocks rose 51 percent. Conversely, high forward PE stocks were up 27 percent and high PEG ratio stocks climbed an average of 25 percent.

Past sales growth and PS ratios were not as much help in predicting the next year's stock price movement. Stocks with poor past revenue growth did well, and those with previously strong growth were up less. Low PS ratio stocks performed about as well as high PS ratio stocks.

Using the same point system as in the previous examples leaves us with quite a few choices on the overvalued side. Boise Cascade, Bowater, International Paper, and Kimberly Clark all look like they are particu-

FIGURE 7.10 LARGE-CAP PAPER PRODUCTS FIRMS 2003

Company	Symbol	Forward PE	Expected Earnings Growth	PEG Ratio	Sales Growth	PS Ratio
Aracruz Celulose SA	ARA	6	15%	0.41	−20%	3.49
Wausau-Mosinee	WMO	10	22	0.44	2	0.62
UPM Kymmene	UPM	8	14	0.57	4	0.80
Albany International	AIN	8	10	0.79	−3	0.81
Georgia Pacific	GP	6	6	1.02	−3	0.17
Caraustar Industries	CSAR	8	7	1.12	−2	0.29
Stora Enso	SEO	10	9	1.15	−8	0.73
Smurfit Stone	SSCC	9	7	1.24	−6	0.49
Sonoco Products	SON	13	9	1.35	6	0.81
MeadWestvaco	MWV	15	11	1.39	49	0.85
Kimberly-Clark	KMB	13	9	1.48	9	1.64
International Paper	IP	12	7	1.70	−9	0.70
Boise Cascade	BCC	12	7	1.76	−2	0.21
Bowater	BOW	18	8	2.23	9	0.95
Average		**11**	**10%**	**1.19**	**1.9%**	**0.89**

larly overvalued. Of the four, Bowater's high forward PE and high PEG ratio make it the most likely choice. The most undervalued stocks appear to be either UPM Kynmere or Wausau-Mosinee, and it would be difficult to choose between them. How the stocks performed in 2003 is summarized in Figure 7.11.

A market neutral investment in WMO/BOW would have returned 4 percent; UPM/BOW would have gained 7 percent. Neither of these results was particularly impressive, but they were profitable investments.

Patterns

Reviewing these three examples, we begin to see a couple of patterns emerging. Low PEG ratio and low forward PE ratio stocks always outperformed high PEG ratio and high forward PE ratio stocks and by a wide margin. Past sales growth, at least by itself, was of no value in helping us decide which stocks are better to own and which to sell short. Low PS ratios were positively correlated with better stock price appreciation

FIGURE 7.11 PRICE PEFORMANCE OF PAPER PRODUCTS FIRMS
2003

Company	Symbol	2003 Price Performance
Aracruz Celulose SA	ARA	91%
Wausau-Mosinee	WMO	19
UPM Kymmene	UPM	26
Albany International	AIN	64
Georgia Pacific	GP	87
Caraustar Industries	CSAR	44
Stora Enso	SEO	30
Smurfit Stone	SSCC	20
Sonoco Products	SON	10
MeadWestvaco	MWV	25
Kimberly-Clark	KMB	28
International Paper	IP	55
Boise Cascade	BCC	28
Bowater	BOW	11
Average		**38%**

in the case of electric utility stocks, but there was not much correlation in the case of casino or paper stocks.

When it came to trying to pick *the* single most undervalued and overvalued stocks from an industry, using a multifactored approach was successful. When making selections based on all four factors, the returns were positive in each case (see Figure 7.12).

FIGURE 7.12 RESULTS OF MULTIFACTORED STOCK SELECTION
METHOD

Paired Investment	Industry	Net Gain
ASCA/MECA	Casinos	42%
	OR	
AGY/MECA	Casinos	26%
AES/EN	Electric Utilities	38%
WMO/BOW	Paper	4%
	OR	
UPM/BOW	Paper	7%

However, a strategy that used only the lowest and highest PEG ratio and ignored PS ratios and past sales growth was successful too and would have dramatically improved the results in one instance—the Paper industry. Because the absolutely lowest PEG stock among paper companies, ARA, had a phenomenal gain in 2003, including it in a market neutral pair would have been very successful, as illustrated in Figure 7.13.

Unfortunately, the best investment decisions don't always conform to such simple rules. If we turn back the clock to the beginning of 2002 and apply this "buy the lowest PEG and sell short the highest PEG" rule to the same three industries, the results are not as impressive. Indeed, that strategy would have lost money in all three instances as the lowest PEG stocks in Casinos, Electric Utilities, and Paper declined further, or rose less, than the highest PEG stocks.

Using a *multifactor approach* would have been more successful in 2002 in these three industries. For example, in the Casino industry evaluating multiple criteria would have led us to buy Isle of Capri and sell short Churchill Downs for a net loss of about 5 percent. (Recall that the S&P 500 declined 23 percent in 2002.) The lowest PEG/highest PEG rule would have bought MTR Gaming and sold short Churchill Downs for a net loss of 29 percent. The same was true for the Electric Utilities and Paper industries—using multiple criteria led to better decisions.

These different results obtained in two different years illustrate the importance of testing any strategy over a period of time. Investors can easily develop a strategy that seems to work and then be disappointed at its performance over a longer time frame. Intuitively we can imagine that any methodology relying on more than one criterion, or rule, is probably more stable and less volatile than reliance on a single factor. To put it another way, it seems unlikely that any one fundamental data point is capable of consistently leading us to optimum investment decisions. So

---

FIGURE 7.13 MARKET PERFORMANCE MARKET NEUTRAL PAIR WITH PEG

Paired Investment	Industry	Net Gain
CNTY/MECA	Casinos	36%
AES/EN	Electric Utilities	38%
ARA/BOW	Paper	40%

even though using PEG ratios alone gave us the best result in 2003, *over the two-year period* we would have been better served by considering all the variables.

Finally, the type of industries chosen for this type of bottom-up analysis is important. For one thing, the industry classification should be definitive. For example, there is little debate about whether a company included in, say, the steel industry is indeed a steel producer. The same cannot be said for some electronics firms that may be classified in the same industry group but operate in different specialty areas and thus face very different competitive forces. Do Pericom Semiconductor and Cisco, both considered "networking device" companies, really face the same external dynamics?

Also, earlier in the book we discussed the difficulty of assessing biotechnology company valuations based on fundamentals. Biotech companies have the capability of breakthroughs or breakdowns based on what happens in the *lab* rather than what happens with their balance sheets each quarter. Being "undervalued" or "overvalued" doesn't have much meaning when a new cancer treatment drug has just been disapproved or approved by the FDA.

To a lesser, but still significant, extent the same is true for many technology-centric industries. Semiconductor, data storage, networking, even computer software firms can experience dramatic shifts in stock price based on a new innovation. A new semiconductor chip or a new software application can abruptly increase the value of one company while decreasing the value of others. Our method of selecting stocks based on valuation works best when companies live up to their expected operational performance and there are no surprises. To the extent that there *are* positive or negative surprises, they can either help or hurt the stock performance, but one of our goals is to minimize the unknowns. Thus, we are better served by avoiding investments where operational surprises are more likely to occur.

When we think about industries that are less likely to experience breakthroughs, or become victims of competitor breakthroughs, what do we imagine? Industries like the ones used above: Trucking, Steel, Casinos, Electric Utilities, and Paper. It seems unlikely that a casino will suddenly develop a unique competitive advantage that leaves other casinos in the dust. The same would be true for a whole of host of sectors, such as Basic Materials, Transportation, Energy, etc.

It is more likely that the companies operating in those fields will perform along the lines that analysts are predicting. To be sure, it is quite common in even the most mundane business for a management team to excel and surprise everyone with its great results, or, conversely, for a company to completely drop the ball and miss its targets by a mile. But if we are playing the odds (and what good investor is not?) we can avoid some pitfalls by staying away from industries where sudden technological innovation can drastically change the landscape and largely invalidate our initial valuation.

With that in mind, any bottom-up analysis starts with selecting the right industries. There are plenty to choose from. Common sense tells us to *avoid* industries relating to computer hardware, software, networks, and storage, biotechnology, electronic instruments, and communications equipment. Warren Buffett has famously stayed away from "technology" investments, professing to not understand them. It's more likely that he understands that their business can change almost overnight.

The selection of industry for the five examples above was predicated on the following three criteria:

1. The number of companies was reasonable.
2. Inclusion in the industry was not a subject for debate or nuanced in any way.
3. The industry was not one prone to technological breakthrough or failure.

Summary

Rather than working from the top down and selecting undervalued and overvalued candidates from the broad universe of publicly traded companies, it is also possible work from the other direction—the bottom up. By doing so, investors will automatically create a balanced portfolio in terms of industry risk.

In conducting basic back-testing, a multifactored model produced the best results over two different years. Collectively, forward PE ratio, projected earnings growth, past sales growth, and price-to-sales ratio did a good job of pointing the way toward stocks that were undervalued and overvalued. Moreover, in each of five examples the selected undervalued stocks rose in value more than the overvalued stocks, creating a profitable paired investment.

This bottom-up approach probably works best in industries that are not subject to rapidly shifting technology or trends. Investors should be careful in developing their own methodology to test ideas across different time frames and market environments.

8

A FEW SHORT WORDS

If there is one impediment to implementing a market neutral strategy for most investors, it is the idea of selling a stock short. It can seem scary, counterintuitive, and just flat-out like a bad idea, all at the same time. For all of these reasons, and because short-selling is an unfamiliar practice to many investors, this chapter will address the subject in a few short words.

How Selling Short Works

Two hypothetical investors, Larry and Mary, each have separate brokerage accounts at the same firm. Larry has in his account 200 shares of XYZ Corp. because he thinks it's a company with a bright future. Mary, on the other hand, believes XYZ Corp. is a fading star, whose best days are behind it. She is so convinced that XYZ is a loser that she decides to sell 200 shares short and calls her broker with that instruction.

The broker looks around at all the firm's accounts and spies Larry's 200 shares of XYZ. He borrows the shares from Larry and sells them in the market on Mary's behalf. At the time XYZ shares are selling for $15. Several months go by and Mary's view of XYZ proves correct. The stock falls to only $12 per share, and Mary decides that XYZ may have faded about as much as it is going to. Calling her broker again, she tells him to "cover the short," meaning that the shares will be purchased and returned to Larry.

Because the shares Mary now buys are worth only $12, she keeps the difference from the initial price. Her profit on the short sale, not including commissions, is 200 × $3, or $600. Larry is almost certainly unaware that his shares were ever loaned out, and his account is unaffected by the transaction, except, of course, his investment in XYZ is worth less than it used to be. (Note that we do not include commissions in our calculations, but we do so not because we want to minimize the impact of trading costs. There is always some cost for the transaction, but it can range from as much as $75 per trade to almost nothing in the case of managed accounts with flat fee/unlimited trading privileges.)

Let's suppose that during the time Mary had borrowed the shares, XYZ paid a dividend to shareholders. Larry is expecting to receive the dividend, and it is Mary's obligation to pay it to him. She is responsible for any dividend payments all during the time she has the shares out on loan. If XYZ's dividend was $0.07 per share, the broker will arrange for Mary to pay Larry $14 (200 shares × $0.07). Again, Larry will be none the wiser about where it came from, just that he was properly paid his dividend.

Let's further suppose that XYZ is really quite a small company, and its shares are not widely held. What would happen if, during the time Mary has borrowed the shares, Larry decided to sell his shares? This would seem to present a problem because the shares in Larry's account are on loan to Mary. So, the broker would look elsewhere internally to see if the shares could be borrowed from someone else's account. If that is not possible, the broker might have relationships with other brokerage firms that would allow shares to be borrowed from accounts held there. In either case, the problem would be averted, and neither Larry nor Mary need ever hear about it. However, if XYZ shares are so narrowly held that the broker just can't find any to loan Mary, her short position will be closed out at XYZ's then-current price. Mary probably won't be too happy about this, but there is not much she can do, short of shopping around for a different brokerage firm that has greater access to shares and then moving her account.

Using the same scenario, it's easy to imagine what happens when, instead of falling, the price of XYZ shares goes up. Suppose Mary sold shares short at $15 and then XYZ comes out with better-than-expected earnings, causing the stock to rise to $18. If Mary covers at that price, her loss would be $600 (200 shares × $3 per share).

This is a simplified description of what happens when a stock is sold short. Although short-selling is a much-maligned practice, it is not terribly complicated. Shares are borrowed from a brokerage and then returned at a later date at the then-current price. If the price is lower, the investor makes a profit, and if the price is higher, the investor pays the difference and takes a loss.

A Bad Rap

Short-selling has a bad reputation for several reasons. For one thing, even professional mutual fund managers fret about selling short, and the record among them is spotty. Note this excerpt from a mutual fund manager's newsletter, AIM Opportunities Fund, May 2003: "Short sales involve greater risk than long funds in that they rely on the manager's ability to accurately anticipate the future value of a security." Depending on one's perspective, the comment is either humorous or a bit chilling. It seems to imply that when this manager *buys* stocks, he doesn't try to accurately anticipate the stock's future value. Or, it could be that he just finds selling a stock short more difficult to do. In either case, this comment highlights the perceived difficulty, even among the experts, of short sales.

Then there is the undeniable fact that stocks tend to go up over time, and selling short, by definition, is a form of swimming against the tide. Some stocks will decline in price every day, but overall, any bet that a stock will fall has the odds stacked at least a little bit against it.

Another frequently cited complaint is that selling short creates a situation where the potential loss is unlimited. Almost every article written about short-selling in the popular media makes some reference to this possibility of infinite losses. As far as it goes, it is a technically correct statement. There is no upward bounded limit on the price of a stock. Theoretically, XYZ shares could trade ever higher, and Mary's losses would grow ever bigger. Imagine someone in 1994 who underestimated the importance of the Internet and sold short router giant Cisco. Holding that short position for the next ten years would have resulted in a loss of

1,200 percent; i.e., a $10,000 short sale would have cost $131,000 to cover by the end of 2003!

In reality, if Mary has some modicum of sense, she would act to limit the potential damage. If XYZ's price climbed significantly, perhaps even doubling, Mary would almost certainly begin to question her original assessment of the company and cover her short position. She would lose money in that event, not something to be taken lightly: if XYZ shares doubled, Mary would lose $3,000 or 100 percent of her initial investment. But it is unrealistic to worry that Mary's account would suffer a decline of *infinite* proportions.

Another step that can be taken to limit the size of a loss is to place a stop-loss order when the original transaction is made. Mary has the option to tell her broker to close her short position if XYZ shares reach some predetermined price. If her tolerance for loss was $500, she would instruct her broker to cover if XYZ reached $17.50 per share.

Finally, another fault found with short-selling has a more philosophical basis. American capitalism is founded on the notion of owners (shareholders) giving company managers money with which to grow the business. The owners reap the rewards of growth through dividends and/or share appreciation. Because short-selling is based on the expectation that a company's value is going to decline, it seems to many people like an unseemly or distasteful way to profit.

Fair enough. But short-sellers provide a valuable service to the market, making it more efficient than it would be without them. They provide liquidity by deploying capital on the other side of purchase transactions. And because of the work they do in identifying overvalued businesses, short-sellers act as a check on what is sometimes unbridled and unjustified enthusiasm for a company. There are many examples of short-sellers who uncovered problems inside company financials long before anyone else did and sounded the alarm. By doing so, they have sometimes been known to uncover fraud and save at least some investors from disaster.

Two Types of Short-Sellers

Short-sellers tend to come in two major varieties. The "forensic-accounting" type is the one that makes the headlines, spotting problems on company balance sheets that others have missed. By digging deep into the numbers and identifying unhealthy trends, or transactions that made no sense, these sharp-eyed accounting mavens have been able to profit from deteriorating fundamentals, or even fraudulent behavior. In some cases, they have been just ahead of the authorities and the bankruptcy judge.

This same group has been accused of spreading disinformation in order to create fear among investors and drive the price of a stock down. By releasing a damning research report to the media, some professional short-sellers hope to create a panic and then cover their own short positions at a substantial profit. No one should forget that these professionals have an economic interest in seeing share prices tumble and can be guilty of spinning or manipulating the facts in order to buttress their position. As with all investors, sometimes they do get it wrong.

It is also true that professional short-sellers often do not want anyone to know they have taken a short position. If short-sellers are attempting to influence investor behavior by disseminating negative information about a company, they would not help their cause if their motive was obvious. What's more, if their identity is known, professional short-sellers sometimes find themselves unable to gather information because company management refuses to meet and discuss the business.

The other type of short-seller is just an ordinary, garden-variety sort who identifies companies trading at an elevated valuation and attempts to make money on an inflated stock price. This group is not looking for scandalous activity or wrongdoing so much as overly optimistic forecasts made against a backdrop of mediocre past company performance. It is a style much more akin to what has been discussed in this book and can be practiced by many investors.

The companies targeted by these more low-key short-sellers are often operating successful businesses. They haven't done anything illegal. They aren't cooking the books. Rather, for whatever reason, the market has mistakenly awarded the stock of these companies a high premium that is not deserved based on past operating results or future prospects. The valuation-oriented short-seller is less likely to make headlines but is equally capable of making a profit.

The Height of Shorts

Like most everything else on Wall Street, measures have been developed to gauge how pronounced short-selling is, by individual company and collectively for the market as a whole. Each month, the U.S. stock exchanges compile a summary of "short interest," or how many shares are sold short, for every stock.

By itself, the number is not very useful. For example, what does it really tell us to know that the short interest in Microsoft as of January 2004 was almost 194 million shares? It seems like a really big number of shares sold short. But because Microsoft is such a large company and its stock trades so heavily, that level of short interest may not be so big relatively speaking.

In order to put some perspective on the size of the short interest, a more helpful statistic is the number of shares sold short divided by the average daily trading volume. Called the "short interest ratio," it offers more insight. The *short interest ratio* tells investors how many days, with average volume, it would take for all of the short positions in a stock to be covered. Because Microsoft was averaging over 50 million shares of trading volume a day in January 2004, the short interest ratio was 3.81.

In contrast to Microsoft's short interest ratio, one of the most heavily shorted Nasdaq stocks in January 2004 was Autonomy Corp., where the short interest ratio was over 32! In other words, if the investors who had shorted Autonomy covered their positions, it would take 32 days, at normal trading volume, to buy back just the shares that were sold short. That represents a high level of pessimism about the stock. As an aside, the view of Autonomy had been much worse. In November 2003 the short interest was a remarkable 82.

The level of short interest in a stock and its significance is a subject of great debate. On the one hand, many Wall Street professionals take a contrarian view of high levels of short interest. The thinking is that because all of those shares sold short must ultimately be bought back, a high level of short interest is actually a bullish indicator. Sometimes called a *short squeeze*, if a stock with high short interest starts to rise, those investors with short positions get nervous and begin to buy shares back, thereby causing the stock to rise further and motivating more short-sellers to buy shares back. This upward cycle can cause a stock price to rocket higher in a fairly short period of time.

On the other hand, there is some academic research (mentioned in Chapter 5) that comes to the opposite conclusion. In October 2002, Desai, et. al., published a paper in the *Journal of Finance* that presents evidence contradicting the conventional wisdom. In "An Investigation of the Informational Role of Short Interest in the Nasdaq Market," the authors suggest that heavily shorted firms subsequently have abnormally negative returns. Other empirical studies, most notably Asquith and Muelbroek in 1995, have also reached this conclusion.

Desai and his colleagues determined that when a large number of shares of a stock are sold short, it is a harbinger of bad things to come. The study they conducted on Nasdaq stocks found that companies with at least 2.5 percent of their shares sold short underperformed stocks with less short interest. What's more, the greater the short interest, the more likely there was a subsequent period of underperformance. This finding and it's contradiction of conventional wisdom is fascinating. Perhaps one way of reconciling these two opposite views is in terms of time frame. It may be that stocks with a high short interest may be subject to brief and intense price increases over the short term, but over the longer term they tend to underperform.

A Twist on Short Interest

Aside from knowing what the short-interest ratio is, it is also possible to examine the change in short interest from one month to the next. Because the data is reported by the exchanges on a monthly basis, investors can determine whether short interest is increasing or decreasing from one month to the next. Rather than looking at short interest by itself, it may be more useful to analyze large changes in short interest.

Curious about whether large increases in short interest might have some bearing on future stock price performance, we conducted a very small test using data from late 2001 through 2003. We selected companies that experienced the greatest increases in short interest from one month to the next and then tracked the price performance of those stocks over the next 13 weeks (see Figure 8.1). The companies all had a market capitalization of over $100 million and saw short interest increase by five times the previous month's level.

FIGURE 8.1 PERFORMANCE OF STOCKS WITH HIGH SHORT INTEREST

Number of Stocks with Extremely Large Increases in Short Interest	Percent Outperforming the S&P 500 over the Subsequent 13-Week Period	Average Gain/Loss (Percent)
17	71%	8.3%
17	88	13.0
16	87	9.1
17	82	4.1
16	56	−12.8
10	60	−10.8
13	69	−10.2
23	39	4.9
9	0	−4.7
9	22	10.1
13	69	0.3
11	55	−1.4
15	60	11.8
15	53	8.7
16	50	6.1
Average	**57.4%**	**2.4%**

Surprisingly, the share price of stocks fitting these criteria actually tended to go up, meaning that a very large increase in short interest was a slightly bullish indicator.

In all but 4 of the 15 months, the percentage of stocks outperforming the S&P 500 was greater than 50 percent. In 10 of the 15 months, a long portfolio made up of these stocks would have been profitable.

This is a very small sample and does not begin to address the question of whether high short interest is bullish or bearish. It does offer fertile ground for further study by other researchers. It also suggests that climbing on the bandwagon of a newly popular short target may be a bad idea. Investors should take a look at changes in short interest before taking a position in a stock.

A Couple of Short Rules

Not everyone is permitted to sell stocks short, or more correctly, not every type of brokerage account can be used to short stocks. For example, any kind of retirement account, like a 401(k), does not qualify. In order to sell short, the brokerage account must be set up as a margin account. A margin account allows an investor to borrow from the brokerage, either in the form of money or securities.

The margin requirement for short sales is 150 percent of the dollar amount sold short. Take the case of our hypothetical investor, Mary. Because she sold short $3,000 worth of stock, her broker would require that she maintain a $4,500 credit balance. If the price of XYZ shares were to rise, and Mary doesn't have enough cash in her account, she will be contacted by her broker and asked to deposit more funds. Margin calls occur on short sales just as they do with long holdings purchased on margin. Because different brokerage firms have varying rules and requirements that may exceed the exchange's minimums, investors should find out the specifics from a broker representative.

Another regulation that probably is not much of a factor for most investors is called the *uptick rule*. This rule states that a stock cannot be sold short unless the previous trade was at least slightly higher than the one before it, or, if the previous trade was the same as the one before it, but the one before that was higher. The uptick rule is likely to be a consideration for short-term traders who are attempting to act on some immediate negative momentum and not so meaningful for those who are taking a longer-term short position.

"Put" Another Way

Although it is not available with all stocks, there is sometimes an alternative to selling shares short. Through the use of "put options," investors are able to achieve the same effect as a short sale, and using this method has some definite pluses and minuses.

Simply put, an *option* gives someone the right to buy or sell shares at some predetermined price, called the "strike price," and to do so at a specific date in the future. The value of a *call option* increases when the price of the underlying stock goes *up*. The value of a *put option* increases when the price of the underlying stock goes *down,* and it is put options that we are interested in here. To help explain how this works, we will revisit Mary and her favorite short candidate, XYZ Corp.

Instead of selling short 200 shares of XYZ when it was trading at $15, Mary could have purchased two put options on XYZ. Because one option is the equivalent of 100 shares, two put options represent 200 shares. For purposes of this exercise we will assume that Mary purchased two puts with a strike price of $15 and she paid $3 each, or a total of $600. Remember that because one put represents 100 shares, Mary's out-of-pocket expense is 200 × $3, or $600. We will also assume that her put option expires six months from when she purchased it, but it could be a shorter or longer time frame. Longer-dated options are called *long-term equity anticipation securities* (LEAPS) and will expire anywhere from ten months to three years but always in January.

For her $600, Mary now has the right to put 200 shares of XYZ stock to someone else for $15 per share sometime in the next six months. It's as if she could force someone to pay her $15 per share no matter what the actual price of the stock is. This makes her put more valuable if the share price declines. If XYZ shares are only trading at, say, $11 per share, and if Mary can force someone to pay her $15 per share, then Mary has something pretty valuable.

If XYZ shares fall from $15 to $11 in the span of several months, Mary's put option will rise considerably in value. It would be reasonable to expect that her puts could be sold for something on the order of $5, or $1,000, which would mean she had more than a 67 percent gain on her $600 investment. How do we arrive at that estimated value?

The way option prices are determined by the market is complicated business and beyond the scope of this book. But some of the arithmetic is quite transparent. There are two components that make up the value of an option:

1. *The cash value.* If XYZ stock is selling for $11 per share, then we know Mary's option is worth $4 in cash value. That's because she can force someone to pay $15 when the stock is only worth $11.
2. *The premium value.* At the outset, Mary paid $3 when the cash value of the option was $0. This amount is called the premium, or the *time value* of the option. It is what an investor must pay for the right to sell in the future. Mary receives some premium over the $4 in

cash value because of the possibility that the stock will decline further before the deadline expires. As time goes by, and the expiration date that was originally six months away gets closer, the premium, or time value declines. We can guess that if a few months have passed, the premium has declined from $3 to perhaps $1. The cash value of $4 plus the premium value of approximately $1 makes a total of $5. Because Mary owns two puts, the value of her investment would be 200 × $5, or $1,000.

The *premium value of an option declines* from the moment it is purchased until it is sold or expires. The rate at which premium value declines is nonlinear. It tends to decline at an accelerating rate the closer the option gets to expiration. It also declines as the cash value increases. For example, if XYZ stock falls to $8 (in options parlance it is "deep in the money") the premium value declines to a negligible amount.

The *cash value of the option rises or falls* based on the price of the underlying stock. If XYZ stock falls to $8, the cash value of Mary's put options is $7, or the difference between the strike price and the price of the stock. If XYZ stock stays at $15, or rises above that price, then the cash value is $0. The speed with which the time value erodes accelerates the closer the option gets to expiration.

The Trouble with Options

The decline in premium value is the biggest drawback to using put options instead of selling a stock short. An option is a wasting asset, and its value will depreciate unless the stock price falls. If nothing happens with XYZ and it is still trading at $15 or more in the next six months, the put option becomes worthless and the loss would equal 100 percent of Mary's initial $600 investment.

Because of the time element found in put options, not only must an investor correctly predict the downward direction of the underlying stock, but she must also predict that it will occur within a specific time frame. This makes it doubly hard to make a profit. It's one thing to look at a company and surmise that it is not doing well. It's another matter to forecast how soon that poor performance will be reflected in the price of the stock.

The fact that put options represent a wasting asset, and that they add a level of complexity to the whole effort of being market neutral, is enough to dissuade many investors from using them. Indeed, those who invest in options are a very small percentage of the investing public.

In addition, getting to the fair value of an option is difficult. The calculation requires the use of a mathematically rigorous formula called Black-Scholes and involves an estimate of how volatile the underlying stock is, or will be. One Web site that can help in valuing options is Schaeffers Research (http://www.shaeffersresearch.com).

Finally, the value of stock options themselves is quite volatile. On a percentage basis, they will experience wide swings in price depending on the price of the underlying stock. Not everyone has the disposition to accept those gyrations.

The Advantage of Options

On the positive side, there are some advantages to using put options instead of selling a stock short. First, it eliminates the "unlimited loss of investment" problem. By buying puts, Mary could lose only her $600 investment, whereas shorting XYZ stock could have resulted in a bigger loss.

Second, if Mary gets it right, the return on her investment is excellent. While it is a difficult challenge to get both the direction *and* the timing correct, the reward for doing so is bigger than it is for just getting the direction right. Her hypothetical 67 percent return in the example above is testimony to that.

Third, recall that when the stock of a dividend-paying company is sold short, the short-seller is required to make good on that dividend. No such requirement exists for holders of put options. So, put options can cost a little bit less than selling short if the underlying stock pays a dividend.

Looking out three months, the table in Figure 8.2 compares what would have happened if Mary had sold short shares of XYZ or if, instead, she had purchased two put options. It shows the amount of money made or lost under three different scenarios: if XYZ dropped to $11 per share, stayed the same at $15 per share, or rose to $19 per share. None of the results accounts for commissions.

Note that if XYZ shares fall, the gains would have been greater buying puts than selling the shares short. The loss with put options would

FIGURE 8.2 SHORT SALE VERSUS PUT OPTION RESULTS

Beginning Price of XYZ	$15	$15	$15
Price of XYZ 3 Months Later	$11	$15	$19
Profit/Loss on 200 Share Short Sale	$800	$0	-$800
Estimated Profit/Loss on Purchase of 2 Puts	$1,000	-$100	-$550

also have been greater if XYZ stock didn't move. Because this table only addresses where things might stand three months from the start, there is still some residual time value in Mary's puts. Remember that the puts won't expire for another three months. Even if XYZ stock climbed to $19 per share, and the chance of the puts ever being profitable had greatly diminished, there would still be some remaining value in the option itself. The estimate here is that the puts would still be worth about $0.25 apiece or $50 total.

To reiterate, it is clear that using put options instead of selling shares short has several important differences. It can accelerate returns and it can accelerate losses, but only to a point. The owner of put options has a cap on losses and can lose no more than what was originally invested.

As a Practical Matter

Every investor faces a difficult decision when considering whether to utilize stock options in his or her portfolio. Options are not for everyone. The complexity and the volatility may make options unsuitable for the casual market participant. What's more, options are not the sort of investment vehicle an investor can purchase and then ignore. Because of the time element, options require more ongoing attention.

Using put options for a market neutral portfolio also raises the question of exactly how "neutrality" is achieved. In our examples so far, we have viewed being market neutral as having the same amount of dollars long as the dollars short. That scheme must be modified if put options are substituted for selling shares short. It wouldn't make any sense to have $600 worth of put options on an overvalued stock and $600 worth of shares in an undervalued stock. Not, at least, if the goal is to be market neutral. Put options are like a short sale on steroids because each option represents 100 shares.

Let's suppose that Mary had not only noticed that XYZ Corp. was overvalued, but also that XYZ competitor, UVW Inc., was undervalued. For simplicity, suppose further that UVW was also trading at $15 per share, just like XYZ. If Mary had purchased two put options on XYZ for $600 and at the same time bought $600 worth (40 shares) of UVW stock, her miniportfolio would be far from neutral. She would instead have a very imbalanced pair of positions, because she has the equivalent of 200 shares short and 40 shares long.

If the XYZ shares do nothing (that is, if the puts Mary purchased become worthless over the next six months) her 40 shares of UVW stock will have to rise 100 percent just for her to break even. Conversely, if Mary wanted to take a more balanced approach, she would have purchased 200 shares of UVW, or $3,000 worth of stock. Under that scenario, if she loses her $600 investment in XYZ puts, UVW stock would need to rise a more moderate (although still significant) 20 percent for her to break even. The table in Figure 8.3 summarizes how UVW shares would have to perform in each case.

Perhaps the easiest way to achieve a neutral balance is to think in terms of the value of shares controlled by the put options, rather than the purchase price of the put options. Because the XYZ puts represent 200 shares of a $15 stock, a balanced approach would require purchasing 200 shares of UVW, also at $15.

Using options offers some advantages but also creates a new set of challenges. Generally, investors who are not able to devote some time to actively managing their portfolio are probably ill-served by options. More active investors may find that the opportunity for higher returns outweighs the additional effort and volatility.

FIGURE 8.3 MARKET NEUTRAL SHORT SALE VERSUS PUT OPTION RESULTS

Dollar Value of Initial Purchase of UVW	$600	$3,000
Dollar Gain Required to Break Even on XYZ loss	$600	$600
% Gain on UVW Needed to Break Even on XYZ loss	100%	20%

A Shorting Shortcut

There is one other way to approach the development of a hedged portfolio. While it does not truly result in a market neutral portfolio, it can accomplish one of the primary goals, namely reducing market risk. This shortcut technique also has the advantage of being easier to implement.

Instead of selling short individual stocks, it is possible to sell short the broad market, using some index as a "proxy" for all stocks collectively. This would call for an investor to buy undervalued individual stocks and then sell short an index with the same amount of money. The hope is that under this approach, if the broad market rises, the undervalued stocks will rise even more, resulting in a profit. Or, if the overall market declines, the idea is that it will fall further than the undervalued stocks, again creating a profit. This strategy does not address sector risk—a portfolio constructed in this way will still have exposure to a potential decline in any one industry group. However, it does take a step toward reducing a portfolio's market risk.

The method used to sell an index short can be quite complicated or quite simple. The complicated route would involve buying put options on some stock index: the Dow Jones Industrial Average or the S&P 500, for example. (The broadest possible index is the Wilshire 5000, representing over 5,000 publicly traded firms which are headquartered in the U.S., but options are not available on this index.) As previously discussed, put options are complex and volatile, and this is especially true of index put options. But for sophisticated investors they can be an effective tool.

For those preferring the simplest route, it is quite easy to purchase a mutual fund that moves in an inverse manner relative to a market index. A number of these mutual funds in operation are designed to move in the opposite direction of some benchmark index. Perhaps the best known are in the Rydex family of funds. For example, Rydex operates the Ursa Fund (RYURX) that changes in value in exactly the opposite way as the S&P 500. If the S&P 500 index goes up, the Ursa Fund drops in value by the same percentage amount. If the S&P 500 falls, the Ursa Fund rises by the same amount.

There are similar funds available through Potomac Funds, who has a Dow Jones Industrial Average inverse fund, an S&P 500 inverse index fund, and a Russell 2000 (small cap) inverse index fund. ProFunds has similar offerings. The minimum investments in these funds are usually fairly substantial, $25,000 in the case of Rydex.

These funds are sometimes called "bear funds" because they make money when the market falls. There are also bear funds that are actively managed, meaning that a portfolio manager is making judgments about which stocks are going to fall. The Rydex, Potomac, and ProFunds mentioned above are all mechanistic, with no active decision making and a performance that is always the inverse of an index.

If investors want to create a hedged portfolio without selling short individual stocks, it makes more sense to use one of these inverse index funds rather than an actively managed bear fund. First, any actively managed fund introduces a new variable into the equation; namely, the skill of the portfolio manager. How good is the manager at picking stocks that are going to fall? Second, an investor does not want to worry about whether the undervalued stocks that he or she selected for the *long* side of the portfolio will match up with the stocks being shorted in an actively managed fund. Generally, it's better to use an inverse index fund as a way to reduce market risk and not have to be concerned about sector exposure.

Using one of the inverse index funds essentially cuts an investor's work in half. Instead of looking for overvalued stocks, he or she can use the fund as a proxy for the short side of the portfolio. Of course, for this to work, the long side of the portfolio has to perform well. The undervalued stocks must go up at a faster rate or decline at a slower rate than the broad market. If that condition is met, then an effective hedged portfolio will be the result.

What's more, using these funds overcomes, indirectly, the current restrictions on selling stocks short. A margin account is not required in order to purchase these funds. An inverse index fund, then, can be used as a hedge in any type of brokerage account, making some form of a hedged portfolio possible for more people.

Will this strategy work? Again, that really depends on the long side of the portfolio and the method used to pick undervalued stocks. The disadvantage of this approach is that a combination portfolio made up of individual long stocks and an inverse index fund does not address industry risk. Care must be taken on the long side not to have any sort of industry concentration, but to instead have a very broadly diversified group of stocks.

Summary

There is a perception that selling stocks short is both complicated and dangerous. It is neither. There are a few important rules to master, with assistance from the broker handling the transaction. When applied as part of a broader portfolio strategy, selling short can make a great deal of sense.

Using put options as a proxy for short sales has some advantages. However, options require considerably more oversight because, all other things unchanged, their value declines over time. What's more, options can create anxiety among some investors due to high levels of volatility. They are not for everyone.

Finally, for those investors who do not have the ability or willingness to short individual stocks, there are inverse index mutual funds. Even though the resulting portfolio is not really market neutral in the strict sense of the term, using these funds allows investors to hedge their long holdings and reduce market risk.

9

A DIFFERENT SORT
OF MODEL

At the risk of overwhelming the reader with too many ways of developing a market neutral or long/short stock selection method, this chapter will walk through the development process, from idea to implementation to result. This book's emphasis on stock selection methods is based on the fact that it is the single most important factor contributing to success when establishing a market neutral portfolio. A market neutral or long/short portfolio will fail if it is unable to capture abnormal returns.

The top-down strategies developed in Chapter 4 and then analyzed further in Chapter 5 were moderately complex. The following case study was created with simplicity in mind and is drawn from easily accessible data. Everything used here was freely available through a single Internet source, Microsoft's MoneyCentral.

Case Study

The premise for this model is that there is evidence that stocks with low price-to-sales (PS) ratios outperform stocks with high PS ratios. In order to keep things simple, the universe of stocks used to develop the model was limited to the 30 Dow Jones Industrial Index stocks.

When looking at the Dow 30, it is easy to see that it represents a wide cross section of industries. Because it is, after all, designed to reflect a range of businesses in the United States, its diversity is not surprising. However, if one is to build a stock selection method using PS ratios, it must take into account that those ratios will vary considerably based on the company's industry classification.

The table in Figure 9.1 shows the Dow 30 stocks and their PS ratios at the beginning of 2004.

What is not obvious from looking at this single snapshot is that many of these PS ratios are persistently high and others persistently low. Auto manufacturers and commodity producers are in industries with generally low PS ratios, and software and semiconductor companies are in industries with typically high PS ratios. If a model just called for buying Dow stocks with low PS ratios and selling short Dow stocks with high PS ratios, then General Motors and International Paper would *always* be on the long list and Microsoft and Intel would *always* be on the short list. The selection method has to be more subtle than that and go on to make some determination about whether a PS ratio is *relatively* high or low.

FIGURE 9.1 PS RATIOS DOW 30 2004

Company	PS Ratio	Company	PS Ratio
Alcoa Inc.	1.53	Honeywell International	1.26
Altria Group	1.39	Int. Business Machines	1.81
American Express	2.44	Int. Paper Co.*	0.67
AT&T Corp.*	0.46	Intel Corp.	7.34
Boeing Co.	0.66	J.P. Morgan Chase	3.07
Caterpillar Inc.	1.32	Johnson & Johnson	3.83
Citigroup	4.38	McDonald's Corp.	1.91
Coca-Cola Co.	5.99	Merck & Co.	3.48
E.I. DuPont de Nemours	1.69	Microsoft Corp.	9.09
Eastman Kodak Co.*	0.56	3M Corp.	3.71
Exxon Mobil Corp.	1.13	Procter & Gamble Co.	2.87
General Electric Co.	2.36	SBC Communications	2.07
General Motors Corp.	0.16	United Technologies	1.50
Hewlett-Packard Co.	0.97	Wal-Mart Stores	0.89
Home Depot	1.27	Walt Disney Co.	1.79

*Eliminated from the index in April 2004.

One way of making a judgment about whether one of these PS ratios is high or low is to look at it in the context of its industry average. That is, how does Microsoft's PS ratio compare with the average PS ratio for all software companies? We could conclude that if it was lower than the industry average, shares would be undervalued. However, that approach is problematic when used with the Dow stocks. Inclusion in the Dow Jones Industrial Average is reserved for companies that are considered leaders in their field. It's possible that, relative to other members of its industry, a Dow-member stock might carry a premium valuation by virtue of its status.

For example, at the beginning of each of the last three years, Microsoft's PS ratio towered over the average software competitor by anywhere from four to ten times. It was much the same story with Home Depot for the last few years, where its PS ratio exceeded the average competing home improvement retailer by anywhere from one and a quarter to ten times. Consequently, comparing PS ratios across industry averages might not be very useful; Dow stocks can consistently carry relatively higher PS ratios compared to other industry players.

However, another way of deciding if a PS ratio is relatively high or low is to examine it in the historic context of the company itself. What has the PS ratio been in the past, and where is it today relative to its "normal level?" Is Alcoa's PS ratio of 1.53 at the beginning of 2004 about what it usually is, or abnormally high or low? This seems like a more effective measure than an industry comparison and a better way of determining whether a Dow stock is being valued more or less highly than usual.

With that in mind, it made sense to review the PS ratio for each stock and compare it to what the average PS ratio had been for the three prior years. The three-year average was arbitrary; a longer duration average could have been used, but it would be less sensitive to changes. A shorter duration of two years did not seem like much of an "average" and would be extremely sensitive. The general hypothesis was that Dow stocks trading above their three-year-average PS ratio were likely to be overvalued and those trading below their three-year average were likely to be undervalued. It seemed reasonable to expect that the PS ratio for each stock would, over time, revert back to what had been its three-year "norm."

Specifically, taking the current PS ratio, adding to it the PS ratios from the prior two years, and dividing by three creates a three-year-average PS ratio. Importantly, the average is a rolling average, so that each year it self-adjusts and creates a new "normal" PS ratio. Thus, as markets change, the average PS ratio changes with it.

Taking the notion a step further, the practical question becomes this: what would happen if shares were purchased in stocks where the PS ratio was below the three-year average and shares were sold short when the PS ratio was above the three-year average? Thus, the rule:

- If the current PS ratio is < the three-year-average PS ratio, then buy.
- If the current PS ratio is > the three-year-average PS ratio, then sell short.

By following this rule, the theory is that an investor can buy shares of Dow stocks when they are abnormally low-priced and undervalued. At the same time, shares that are priced abnormally high can be sold short.

One potential difficulty with this system is that it might overlook long-term shifts in a company's business dynamics. SBC Communications, for example, has been undergoing such a shift for a number of years, as it has moved from being one of a few regional Bell operating companies to one of many telephone service providers. First the introduction of wireless calling and, more recently, Internet-based telephony, has made it more difficult for SBC to achieve profitable growth, and its PS multiple has been steadily shrinking. Only time will tell if this is a permanent shift or if SBC will develop new businesses to compensate. However, the steady decline in PS over several years' time has tended to make SBC appear undervalued since the beginning of 2001, according to this model. Unfortunately, SBC's shares have fallen about 50 percent in that time.

Acknowledging this possible shortcoming does not mean the model is ineffective. Indeed, as we will see below, it has been very effective over the five-year time period examined: 1999 to 2003.

Figure 9.2 details the data from the beginning of 1999 and what the PS ratio rule would have signaled for the coming year.

The first thing to observe is how few of the Dow stocks would be purchased and how many would be sold short. Following the rule would definitely create a portfolio heavily skewed to the short side and *not* a market neutral portfolio. Why were there few stocks at the beginning of 1999 indicated to buy and so many to sell short? Investors may recall that at the time, most stocks were in the midst of a big rally and valuations were

FIGURE 9.2 THE PS RATIO RULE

Company	December 1998 PS Ratio	3 Prior Year Average PS Ratio	Rule
Alcoa Inc.	0.89	0.87	Sell short
Altria Group	1.75	1.58	Sell short
American Express	2.42	2.14	Sell short
AT&T Corp.	1.02	0.79	Sell short
Boeing Co.	0.57	1.71	Buy
Caterpillar Inc.	0.78	0.86	Buy
Citigroup	1.37	1.38	Buy
Coca-Cola Co.	8.78	7.82	Sell short
E.I. DuPont de Nemours	2.41	1.84	Sell short
Eastman Kodak Co.	1.73	1.58	Sell short
Exxon Mobil Corp.	1.76	1.35	Sell short
General Electric Co.	3.34	2.69	Sell short
General Motors Corp.	0.25	0.28	Buy
Hewlett-Packard Co.	1.30	1.32	Buy
Home Depot	2.95	2.00	Sell short
Honeywell International	1.64	1.50	Sell short
Int. Business Machines	2.07	1.45	Sell short
Int. Paper Co.	0.70	0.65	Sell short
Intel Corp.	7.49	5.74	Sell short
J.P. Morgan Chase	1.85	1.59	Sell short
Johnson & Johnson	4.77	3.92	Sell short
McDonald's Corp.	4.19	3.34	Sell short
Merck & Co.	6.47	5.55	Sell short
Microsoft Corp.	18.56	13.4	Sell short
3M Corp.	1.90	2.18	Buy
Procter & Gamble Co.	3.28	2.57	Sell short
SBC Communications	3.65	2.87	Sell short
United Technologies	0.95	0.77	Sell short
Wal-Mart Stores	1.39	0.89	Sell short
Walt Disney Co.	2.29	2.33	Buy

climbing. PS ratios had been steadily rising for the past several years and so the then-current ratios were often above their three-year averages.

Looking at the subsequent price performance, the low PS ratio stocks did slightly outperform the high PS ratio stocks in 1999, but only barely. The 7 undervalued stocks were up, on average, 20.9 percent, and the 23 overvalued stocks were up 20.6 percent on average. Suppose an investor put $1,000 in each stock—$7,000 long and $23,000 short. Such an off-centered portfolio, tilted heavily to the short side, would have performed poorly in the bull market environment of 1999. The long side of the portfolio would have generated a gain of $1,463, but the short side of the portfolio would have lost $4,738. Taken together, the loss would have been 10.9 percent (see Figure 9.3).

But remember in Chapter 6 we looked at two other ways to construct a hedged portfolio: (1) alter the criteria a bit so that an equal number of stocks are long and short and thus create a market neutral portfolio, or (2) use a hybrid approach and invest the same amount of dollars in the 7 longs stocks as in the 23 short stocks (i.e., $15,000 in each group).

To test these alternatives, the model was adjusted slightly to generate an equal number of long and short stocks by adding 8 more stocks to the undervalued side of the portfolio. The 8 were chosen by selecting those whose PS ratios were *closest* to their three-year average, even though they did slightly exceed it. By modifying the rule for buying stocks, a balanced portfolio was created with 15 longs and 15 shorts. However, these two new groups of stocks did not, on average, perform so well as the original groups. The 15 undervalued stocks gained 19.1 percent, and the 15 overvalued stocks gained 22.2 percent. Altering the criteria produced a not-so-impressive net loss of 1.5 percent.

Then there was the hybrid solution. In that scenario, with the original 7 stocks long and 23 stocks short, but with equal dollars invested in each group, the portfolio was ever-so-slightly positive. The table in Figure 9.4 summarizes all three sets of results along with the change in the Dow index itself.

None of these results occurring against a backdrop of the Dow rising 25 percent appears very impressive. Even with the hybrid approach,

---

FIGURE 9.3 PS RATIO RULE PORTFOLIO PERFORMANCE

1999 Results	Gain/Loss
Undervalued Stocks	+20.9%
Overvalued Stocks	+20.6%
Combined Long/Short Portfolio	−10.9%

FIGURE 9.4 PERFORMANCE OF THREE PORTFOLIO STRATEGIES

Portfolio Structure	1999 Gain/Loss
Long/Short	−10.9%
Market Neutral (Altering Criteria)	−1.5%
Market Neutral (Hybrid)	+0.1%
Long Only—DJIA	+24.7%

it is hard to get excited about a return that is so close to breakeven. But with the latter offering somewhat more encouraging results than the long/short or altered market neutral, what would happen if the same methodology was applied in subsequent years?

In Figure 9.5 is a summary of what the model would have recommended at the end of 1999 and the results for each component stock of the Dow Jones Industrial Index in 2000.

Once again, this model was giving short-sale signals far more frequently than it was generating buy signals. This time, as the year 2000 got underway, there were 24 stocks to sell short and only 6 to buy. Compared to what happened in 1999, however, the results achieved by following the model were much more positive. On average, the long stocks rose 17.1 percent and the short stocks fell 13.3 percent. That is exactly the result an investor would hope for. A hybrid portfolio with equal dollars long and short in the two groups would have returned 15.2 percent and done so with considerably less risk than a long-only portfolio. The Dow index as a whole was down 5 percent in 2000.

As before, the hybrid structure trumped both the long/short and the altered market neutral structures. A long/short portfolio of 24 stocks short and 6 stocks long would have returned about 14 percent. Alternatively, creating a portfolio with 15 stocks short and 15 stocks long by modifying the criteria slightly would also have given positive results. The modification reduced the number of stocks sold short by only selecting the 15 that were the *furthest over the three-year-average PS ratio*. With this modified set of criteria the resulting market neutral portfolio would have returned 9.1 percent (see Figure 9.6).

FIGURE 9.5 HYBRID STRATEGY PERFORMANCE IN 2000

Company	December 1999 PS Ratio	3 Prior Year Average PS Ratio	Rule	Gain/ Loss in 2000
Alcoa Inc.	1.87	1.22	Sell short	−19.6%
Altria Group	0.68	1.32	Buy	+99.8
American Express	3.49	2.75	Sell short	+8.6
AT&T Corp.	1.07	0.96	Sell short	−64.3
Boeing Co.	0.65	0.76	Buy	+50.7
Caterpillar Inc.	0.85	0.86	Buy	−8.1
Citigroup	2.13	1.68	Sell short	+27.4
Coca-Cola Co.	7.27	8.26	Buy	+1.6
E.I. DuPont de Nemours	2.58	2.24	Sell short	−30.5
Eastman Kodak Co.	1.46	1.51	Buy	−34.8
Exxon Mobil Corp.	1.74	1.58	Sell short	+2.4
General Electric Co.	4.58	3.54	Sell short	−3.9
General Motors Corp.	0.45	0.30	Sell short	−29.9
Hewlett-Packard Co.	1.76	1.52	Sell short	−39.0
Home Depot	3.41	2.73	Sell short	−27.8
Honeywell International	1.93	1.69	Sell short	−18.5
Int. Business Machines	2.20	1.85	Sell short	−25.1
Int. Paper Co.	0.95	0.77	Sell short	−28.5
Intel Corp.	9.33	7.13	Sell short	−26.6
J.P. Morgan Chase	1.91	1.76	Sell short	−4.5
Johnson & Johnson	4.72	4.47	Sell short	+10.4
McDonald's Corp.	4.11	3.72	Sell short	−14.2
Merck & Co.	4.78	3.94	Sell short	+27.1
Microsoft Corp.	23.4	18.5	Sell short	−61.1
3M Corp.	2.49	2.20	Sell short	+19.5
Procter & Gamble Co.	3.09	3.01	Sell short	−32.7
SBC Communications	3.34	3.23	Sell short	+10.0
United Technologies	1.29	0.97	Sell short	+24.5
Wal-Mart Stores	1.48	1.21	Sell short	−22.1
Walt Disney Co.	2.30	2.34	Buy	−6.4

FIGURE 9.6 MODIFIED HYBRID STRATEGY PERFORMANCE IN 2000

Portfolio Structure	Gain/Loss in 2000
Long/Short	+14.1%
Market Neutral (Altering Criteria)	+9.1%
Market Neutral (Hybrid)	+15.2%
Long Only—DJIA	−5.0%

By the beginning of 2001, as we can see in Figure 9.7, there was a shift. The number of stocks with PS ratios *below* their three-year average (i.e., undervalued) increased dramatically. We might expect this after stock prices generally fell in 2000. When stock prices fall more than revenues, PS ratios will decline. Collectively the 30 Dow Industrials saw revenues increase an average of 10 percent in 2000. Consequently, because stock prices fell and revenues rose among the Dow stocks, PS ratios gen-

FIGURE 9.7 PORTFOLIO PERFORMANCE RESULTS 2001

Company	December 2000 PS Ratio	3 Prior Year Average PS Ratio	Rule	Gain/ Loss in 2000
Alcoa Inc.	1.26	1.34	Buy	+9.1%
Altria Group	1.21*	1.21*	Buy	+18.2
American Express	3.08	3.00	Sell short	−30.3
AT&T Corp.	0.40	0.70	Buy	+31.9
Boeing Co.	1.13	0.78	Sell short	−33.1
Caterpillar Inc.	0.81*	0.81*	Buy	+17.2
Citigroup	2.14	1.88	Sell short	−4.8
Coca-Cola Co.	7.40	7.82	Buy	−17.3
E.I. DuPont de Nemours	1.78	2.26	Buy	−8.4
Eastman Kodak Co.	0.82	1.34	Buy	−26.8
Exxon Mobil Corp.	1.67	1.72	Buy	−5.6
General Electric Co.	3.68	3.87	Buy	−13.9
General Motors Corp.	0.39	0.36	Sell short	−6.5
Hewlett-Packard Co.	1.86	1.64	Sell short	−32.0
Home Depot	2.45	2.94	Buy	+2.9
Honeywell International	1.53	1.70	Buy	−26.4
Int. Business Machines	1.82	2.03	Buy	+28.7
Int. Paper Co.	0.70	0.78	Buy	−0.2
Intel Corp.	5.99	7.60	Buy	−1.7
J.P. Morgan Chase	1.46	1.74	Buy	−23.8
Johnson & Johnson	5.02	4.84	Sell short	+22.4
McDonald's Corp.	3.11	3.80	Buy	−18.9
Merck & Co.	5.35	5.53	Buy	−28.0
Microsoft Corp.	18.4	20.0	Buy	+34.8
3M Corp.	2.85	2.41	Sell short	+5.4
Procter & Gamble Co.	1.87	2.75	Buy	+7.9
SBC Communications	3.14	3.38	Buy	−19.9
United Technologies	1.41	1.22	Sell short	−8.0
Wal-Mart Stores	1.33	1.40	Buy	+7.3
Walt Disney Co.	3.18	2.59	Sell short	−33.5

*Arbitrarily, in the case of equal ratios, the model is instructed to buy.

erally declined. At the beginning of 2001, a situation existed where PS ratios had fallen but the three-year averages were still fairly elevated.

The net results of the strategy were again positive in 2001. The 21 stocks that the model indicated should be purchased were down 1.6 percent on average, while the 9 stocks to be sold short were down 13.4 percent, providing a sizeable gain. The hybrid construction, with, for example $15,000 spread out over the 21 long stocks and $15,000 spread out over the 9 short stocks, would have yielded a return of 5.9 percent.

A long/short portfolio, with 70 percent of the dollars long (21 stocks) and 30 percent of the dollars short (9 stocks), would have returned 2.9 percent (see Figure 9.8). Adjusting the criteria slightly to sell short the 15 stocks that have a PS ratio above, *or closest to the three-year-average PS ratio,* would have returned 3.2 percent. Once again, the hybrid structure was the most successful and all three forms surpassed a long-only investment in the index.

At the end of 2001, the model suggested an even more skewed set of longs versus shorts. At that point, there were 23 longs and 7 shorts (see Figure 9.9).

In this year, the market neutral returns would have again been just barely positive, much like in 1999. The return of a hybrid portfolio would have been 0.7 percent, as the long selections fell on average 18.5 percent and the short selections fell by 19.9 percent. By comparison, the overall Dow Jones Industrial Average fell 16.8 percent, slightly less than either group because of the way the index is calculated.

The long/short structure would have returned –9.5 percent. With a modified set of 15 stocks long and 15 stocks short, the long stocks would have declined 18.2 percent, and the short stocks would have fallen 19.4 percent, giving that portfolio configuration a small total return of 0.6 percent (see Figure 9.10).

FIGURE 9.8 PERFORMANCE OF FOUR STRATEGIES IN 2001

Portfolio Structure	Gain/Loss in 2001
Long/Short	2.9%
Market Neutral (Altering Criteria)	3.2%
Market Neutral (Hybrid)	5.9%
Long Only—DJIA	–5.9%

FIGURE 9.9 PORTFOLIO PERFORMANCE RESULTS 2002

Company	December 2001 PS Ratio	3 Prior Year Average PS Ratio	Rule	Gain/ Loss in 2002
Alcoa Inc.	1.32	1.48	Buy	−37.6%
Altria Group	1.10	1.00	Sell short	−7.3
American Express	2.10	2.89	Buy	−5.5
AT&T Corp.	0.50	0.66	Buy	−29.3
Boeing Co.	0.56	0.78	Buy	−16.8
Caterpillar Inc.	1.02	0.89	Sell short	−12.4
Citigroup	2.16	2.14	Sell short	−26.1
Coca-Cola Co.	5.84	6.84	Buy	−4.0
E.I. DuPont de Nemours	1.72	2.02	Buy	−2.9
Eastman Kodak Co.	0.65	0.98	Buy	+27.9
Exxon Mobil Corp.	1.63	1.68	Buy	−12.1
General Electric Co.	3.17	3.81	Buy	−39.0
General Motors Corp.	0.39	0.41	Buy	−23.1
Hewlett-Packard Co.	0.72	1.45	Buy	−23.6
Home Depot	2.19	2.68	Buy	−52.6
Honeywell International	1.17	1.54	Buy	−28.9
Int. Business Machines	2.43	2.15	Sell short	−38.0
Int. Paper Co.	0.74	0.80	Buy	−14.5
Intel Corp.	7.92	7.75	Sell short	−56.4
J.P. Morgan Chase	1.42	1.60	Buy	−36.1
Johnson & Johnson	5.46	5.07	Sell short	−6.3
McDonald's Corp.	2.28	3.16	Buy	−39.6
Merck & Co.	2.80	4.31	Buy	−1.4
Microsoft Corp.	15.5	19.1	Buy	−25.0
3M Corp.	2.88	2.74	Sell short	+7.4
Procter & Gamble Co.	2.11	2.36	Buy	+12.5
SBC Communications	2.86	3.11	Buy	−29.8
United Technologies	1.11	1.27	Buy	−4.5
Wal-Mart Stores	1.23	1.35	Buy	−11.8
Walt Disney Co.	1.55	2.34	Buy	−27.3

FIGURE 9.10 PERFORMANCE OF FOUR STRATEGIES IN 2002

Portfolio Structure	Gain/Loss in 2002
Long/Short	−9.5%
Market Neutral (Altering Criteria)	0.6%
Market Neutral (Hybrid)	0.7%
Long Only—DJIA	−16.8%

We can examine one more year's worth of data, that for 2003 (see Figure 9.11). We would expect, with the broad market falling so much in 2003, that the model might once again offer more longs than shorts—unless revenues for the Dow stocks also fell dramatically.

The "buys" far outpaced the "shorts." In fact, of the five years examined, 2003 had the least number of short candidates. More important is how those shorts performed, rising an average of only 2 percent during

FIGURE 9.11 PORTFOLIO PERFORMANCE RESULTS 2003

Company	December 2002 PS Ratio	3 Prior Year Average PS Ratio	Rule	Gain/ Loss in 2003
Alcoa Inc.	0.95	1.18	Buy	+61.7%
Altria Group	1.03	1.11	Buy	+46.0
American Express	1.94	2.37	Buy	+30.7
AT&T Corp.	0.54	0.48	Sell short	−21.2
Boeing Co.	0.51	0.73	Buy	+25.5
Caterpillar Inc.	0.78	0.87	Buy	+78.6
Citigroup	1.96	2.09	Buy	+39.3
Coca-Cola Co.	5.54	6.26	Buy	+14.8
E.I. DuPont de Nemours	1.76	1.75	Sell short	+7.9
Eastman Kodak Co.	0.78	0.75	Sell short	−29.7
Exxon Mobil Corp.	1.31	1.54	Buy	+17.7
General Electric Co.	1.86	2.90	Buy	+25.1
General Motors Corp.	0.30	0.36	Buy	+46.8
Hewlett-Packard Co.	0.85	1.14	Buy	+26.8
Home Depot	0.85	1.83	Buy	+65.2
Honeywell International	0.92	1.21	Buy	+38.6
Int. Business Machines	1.64	1.96	Buy	+13.0
Int. Paper Co.	0.67	0.70	Buy	+24.6
Intel Corp.	3.83	5.91	Buy	+95.1
J.P. Morgan Chase	1.11	1.33	Buy	+47.4
Johnson & Johnson	4.39	4.96	Buy	−7.4
McDonald's Corp.	1.32	2.24	Buy	+56.2
Merck & Co.	2.45	3.53	Buy	−13.2
Microsoft Corp.	10.3	14.8	Buy	+3.0
3M Corp.	2.95	2.89	Sell short	+36.7
Procter & Gamble Co.	2.89	2.29	Sell short	+16.2
SBC Communications	2.09	2.70	Buy	−4.3
United Technologies	1.04	1.19	Buy	+48.8
Wal-Mart Stores	0.86	1.14	Buy	+5.3
Walt Disney Co.	1.21	1.98	Buy	+37.6

the year. The longs were up an average of 33 percent. How the different portfolio configurations would have worked is seen in Figure 9.12.

Is this a model worth considering? Absolutely. The caveat is that further testing should occur over a longer time period. This data set only covers five years, too short a time from which to draw unassailable conclusions. And even with more successful testing, there are no guarantees that this high-low PS model will work in the future.

The market neutral "hybrid" structure was the most successful of the three variations in each year except 2003, and it posted a gain in all five years (see Figure 9.13). Demonstrating positive returns regardless of the overall market environment is one of the hallmarks of a good market neutral strategy. The most disappointing result came in 1999 when we would have hoped for a slightly higher return. In years when the market is exceedingly bullish, we know that a market neutral portfolio will lag, but its performance in 1999 was particularly weak. Using the model over all five years and compounding the results each year would have resulted in a 41.6 percent gain. An investment in the Dow index itself would have produced a 16.6 percent gain over the same time frame.

FIGURE 9.12 PERFORMANCE OF FOUR STRATEGIES IN 2003

Portfolio Structure	Gain/Loss in 2003
Long/Short	27.2%
Market Neutral (Altering Criteria)	5.5
Market Neutral (Hybrid)	15.5
Long Only—DJIA	25.3

FIGURE 9.13 MARKET NEUTRAL PORTFOLIO RESULTS 1999–2003

Year	Market Neutral Gain/Loss	DJIA Gain/Loss
1999	0.1%	24.7%
2000	15.2	−5.0
2001	5.6	−5.1
2002	0.7	−17.2
2003	15.5	25.3
Cumulative Total	**41.6%**	**16.6%**

What Lies Ahead

Perhaps of even greater interest is what this particular model foretells for 2004. During the year there were three new stocks added to the Dow Jones Industrial Index (American Int. Group, Pfizer, and Verizon) and three were deleted (AT&T, Eastman Kodak, and International Paper). In Figure 9.14 is a summary of the portfolio as it would have been constructed after those changes were made in April 2004.

Once again, the portfolio created is more short than long. In the past, the hybrid portfolio composition, calling for an equal investment in the 12 longs and the 18 shorts, was the most successful. Time will tell whether it will once again generate a positive return in 2004.

Data Mining and Model Development

A phenomenon known to researchers as *data mining* describes the practice of looking for, and finding, patterns in data. However, sometimes those patterns are not really there at all. Or rather, the patterns are there but were arrived at in such a convoluted manner that they have no real validity—they are coincidental. Overly zealous data mining can sometimes be proof that if we look at enough numbers for a long enough time, we will ultimately find a relationship among them. It is one of the most dangerous threats to the development of a sound investment model.

It is easier to mistakenly find patterns when the approach to stock selection is backward-looking. For example, trying to "reverse engineer" the stocks that recently went up or down and determine what they had in common is an easy way to see patterns where none exists. Suppose an investor had a list of the 50 stocks that had fallen the furthest in the most recent calendar year. One way to develop a model would be to look for what characteristics those 50 stocks shared at the beginning of the year. Doing so, however, is likely to generate all sorts of what appear to be shared characteristics that are nothing more than random occurrence.

A better idea is to look forward. First consider what factors might influence whether a stock rises or falls. Then, after proposing some set of factors, test the idea to see what happened to the stocks fitting those parameters. By generating the factors first, and then determining their effectiveness, investors can avoid the temptation to see patterns that aren't there.

FIGURE 9.14 PROJECTED MARKET NEUTRAL PORTFOLIO 2004

Company	December 2003 PS Ratio	3 Prior Year Average PS Ratio	Rule
Alcoa Inc.	1.53	1.27	Sell short
Altria Group	1.35	1.16	Sell short
American Express	2.40	2.15	Sell short
American Int. Group	2.38*	2.57	Buy
Boeing Co.	0.67	0.58	Sell short
Caterpillar Inc.	1.27	1.02	Sell short
Citigroup	3.23	2.45	Sell short
Coca-Cola Co.	5.91	5.76	Sell short
E.I. DuPont de Nemours	1.65	1.71	Buy
Exxon Mobil Corp.	1.10	1.28	Buy
General Electric Co.	2.32	2.45	Buy
General Motors Corp.	0.44	0.38	Sell short
Hewlett-Packard Co.	0.93	0.83	Sell short
Home Depot	1.24	1.43	Buy
Honeywell International	1.25	1.11	Sell short
Int. Business Machines	1.79	1.95	Buy
Intel Corp.	6.89	6.21	Sell short
J.P. Morgan Chase	1.69	1.41	Sell short
Johnson & Johnson	3.66	4.50	Buy
McDonald's Corp.	1.84	1.81	Sell short
Merck & Co.	4.57	3.27	Sell short
Microsoft Corp.	8.58	11.48	Buy
3M Corp.	3.66	3.16	Sell short
Procter & Gamble Co.	2.67	2.56	Sell short
Pfizer	6.04*	6.74	Buy
SBC Communications	2.11	2.35	Buy
United Technologies	1.59	1.25	Sell short
Verizon	1.52*	1.72	Buy
Wal-Mart Stores	0.91	1.00	Buy
Walt Disney Co.	1.50	1.42	Sell short

*April 2004 PS ratio

Unfortunately, countless patterns have been observed in historic stock market data that resulted in trading systems that did not work in practice. In order to guard against just such a trap, investors should consider the observations of two Brigham Young University finance professors, McQueen and Thorley. In a 1999 paper entitled "Mining Fool's

Gold," they point out that erroneous data mining is likely to be at work when: (1) the trading rule is overly complex; (2) there is no coherent theory underlying the rule; and (3) the pattern does not exist during the time periods outside the sample. In addition, they suggest that when transaction costs and taxes are considered, quite often what were positive results become unimpressive.

Investors in pursuit of their own methodology for selecting undervalued and overvalued stocks should ask themselves if they have simply engaged in erroneous or overzealous data mining. It is a bad sign if one starts with a simple concept but, in order to make it work, gradually adjusts it into a convoluted mess. As for the model just outlined, which we will call DOWPS (Dow price-to-sales), here is what we know: the trading rule is not overly complex. It does not, for example, say that the stocks to be sold short should have a PS ratio higher than their own three-year average and higher than the average of all the Dow 30 stocks, but lower than the forecasted PS ratio, etc. It is a simple and straightforward rule.

Nor does the DOWPS model lack an underlying coherent theory. Research suggests stocks with lower PS ratios will perform better than stocks with higher PS ratios. The DOWPS model simply lets us know whether a PS ratio is relatively high or low, based on a stock's three-year history.

Finally, we don't know whether the DOWPS pattern exists outside of the small sample we examined. Five years of data is encouraging, but 40 years would be convincing. Clearly this is a shortcoming of the DOWPS model—it has not been tested long enough to generate much confidence. But even with 40 years worth of data, there is some risk that what has worked before will cease to work. Markets change, behavior changes, and there just is no such thing as a sure thing.

As an aside, another potential model worth considering is similar to the DOWPS but substitutes price-to-book (PB) ratios for PS ratios. It generated results over the same period that were very similar to the DOWPS model, slightly better in some years and slightly worse in others.

Anomalies

Even Malkiel, the well-known apologist for the theory that stock prices are always perfectly calibrated, acknowledges there are anomalies, or exceptions, to the efficient market hypothesis. An example of this is the *January effect* that describes the tendency of stocks (particularly small-cap stocks) to fall at the end of the calendar year and then rise in the first month of the next year. The explanation for this effect has been that investors sell off losing stocks at the end of the year in order to capture the tax loss and then put their money back to work in the market in January. The January effect seems to have faded in the last few years, and January is not currently the month with the historically highest returns—that honor goes to November (for the S&P 500).

Another anomaly is sometimes called *window dressing,* and it describes the tendency of winning stocks to continue to rise on the last day of the calendar quarter. The theory is that mutual fund portfolio managers want their quarter-end portfolios to look their best and will be sure to buy more shares in the stocks they hold that are already up for the quarter. One corollary result of this practice is that mutual fund NAVs tend to be artificially high on the last day of the quarter.

The DOWPS model outlined above may be an exception to the efficient market hypothesis. Or, the fact that the Dow stocks tended to revert back to their historic PS ratios for those five years could be coincidence. The efficient market hypothesis tells us that the pattern will not be sustained and that PS ratios really have no bearing on what a stock's price might do in the future.

The question for investors is whether what appears to be an anomaly might really be just a random occurrence. Was the January effect for real? Most likely it was. But what about the old AFL and NFL rule? That rule states that when the winner of the Super Bowl is a team that has its roots in the original American Football League, it foretells a bearish year for stocks. Since 1967, when the first Super Bowl was played, through 2003, the "rule" worked in all but seven years. That's about an 80 percent success rate. It gets a little confusing these days with football teams that have shifted from one city to another (are the Baltimore Ravens, who moved there from Cleveland and won the Super Bowl in 2001, an NFL-rooted team or an AFC expansion team?) but no one can argue that this predictor has been correct far more often than not.

The dean of tracking odd correlations found between the stock market and just about anything else is Yale Hirsch, publisher of the *Stock Trader's Almanac* (http://www.stocktradersalmanac.com). Here is an example of one of his observations, as published in the May 2003 issue of his newsletter:

> On May's first trading day the Dow has been up 8 of the last 10. The days before and after Mother's Day have bullish implications but May expiration has been dangerous. Memorial Day week was up 12 years in a row from 1984 through 1995 but it's been down five of the last seven years with sizeable losses the last four years.

If there is some pattern that has shown itself, Hirsch has identified it. What has happened to the stock market in election years, different months of the year, different days of the week, etc., is all chronicled by Hirsch, with the expectation that history repeats itself.

There is no certain way for investors to decide if a pattern represents a coincidence or something more, but the burden of proof should be high. Any theories should be met with skepticism and required to pass the three-part test of McQueen and Thorley: the trading rule should be simple; there must be a rational, coherent theory behind it; and it should work in time periods outside the sample.

Suppose we observe that when the market is down on Friday, the following Monday is also down 75 percent of the time. A simple trading rule can be constructed from that information. But is there a rational, coherent theory behind it? Is there some explanation for why the market would consistently decline on Mondays after a bad Friday? Are traders depressed going into the weekend and then carrying their malaise over into Monday? That seems unlikely, and such a trading rule would fail to pass the test.

Even when an anomalous pattern does pass the test, there is also a chance that it won't last. One criticism of efforts to find and exploit exceptions is that too much success can bring an end to the very inefficiency being exploited. If a large number of people with a large number of dollars begin to act on some anomaly, then they will effectively eliminate it. If enough investors read this book and begin buying shares of Dow 30 stocks whose PS ratios are less than their three-year average, the price of those shares will rise, become fairly valued, and then cease to demonstrate the better-than-average returns they have for the last few years.

Despite those caveats, a long line of investors have made fortunes, both small and large, by finding stocks that were incorrectly priced by the market. As Warren Buffet famously said, "I'd be a bum on the street with a tin cup if the markets were efficient."

Summary

A model developed using PS ratios for the Dow 30 Industrials worked well over the five years tested. The basic rationale is that stocks with low PS ratios tend to be undervalued and those with high PS ratios tend to be overvalued. In order to decide if a PS ratio is low or high, the model compares the current ratio with the rolling three-year average.

Constructing a portfolio using this rule resulted in a positive return in five out of five years. Cumulatively, the return was 40.5 percent for the five years ending in 2003 while a long-only investment in the index itself would have returned −16.6 percent. As with most any long/short or market neutral portfolio, the risk exposure was reduced.

The problem with developing any sort of model that seeks undervalued and overvalued stocks is that it may not be what it seems. Human beings are very skilled at seeing patterns that don't exist. Many trading rules or systems work sporadically or for a short period of time. Even when some types of stocks are consistently mispriced, there is some risk that enough others will discover the inefficiency and cause it to disappear.

10

MUTUAL FUNDS

Face it, as fun and potentially profitable as it may be to develop a market neutral portfolio of one's own, many investors don't have the time to do it themselves. Make no mistake about it, doing the research, creating a portfolio, and monitoring it can (and should) take considerable effort. For investors who enjoy this sort of thing, it will be a labor of love. For others, there are alternatives.

Of course, as outlined later in Chapter 12, hedge funds can serve as an effective investment vehicle for qualified investors. But they are only available to investors who are "qualified" through high net worth and/or income. They also come with a hefty fee structure.

A more practical alternative to hedge funds for most investors are the available mutual funds. They tend to have much lower barriers to entry, with minimum investments ranging from $1,000 to $25,000. In the following pages are profiles of a number of mutual funds that hedge their portfolios in some fashion. However, note that a market neutral mutual fund may not necessarily be truly neutral, at least as we have defined it. Rather, it is a term broadly used among mutual funds to mean some hedging is taking place.

The obvious advantage to using a mutual fund is that it requires a lot less "care and feeding" than putting together one's own long/short portfolio. There is some cost associated with owning a fund, whether it is an outright sales charge or the costs of running the fund, which are charged against investor's returns. However, for many people, those costs are a small price to pay so long as the fund performs well.

Moreover, some investors are just more comfortable having a professional money manager looking out for them. For every person who has the confidence to pick individual stocks, there are several other people who do not feel they have the expertise required. Mutual funds can be a terrific answer for such investors.

Not all of the funds discussed here are market neutral, by any stretch. Some truly do have a pure neutral style: they are dollar neutral and beta neutral. A couple of others have a long or short bias. What they all have in common is a charter that allows them to be long and short and a willingness to hedge against market risk. The list of funds here is not exhaustive; there are more than the 20 mutual funds profiled below that practice some type of hedging. However, certainly some of the largest and well-known long/short funds are included, and investors should find more than enough alternatives.

Performance

The critical importance of good stock picking with any market neutral portfolio has been stressed throughout this book. The message is the same for hedged mutual funds. Among other types of equity mutual funds, which are usually long-only, the historical tendency of the stock market to rise over time will tend to hide poor stock selection. Long-only funds, given enough time, will tend to go up along with the broad market. That will not necessarily happen with market neutral funds, where there is little correlation with the overall stock market. The manager's skills are completely on display, and if the stock picking is not good, then the fund will perform poorly.

Finding funds with long track records in this category is not easy because, as we will see below, many of these funds are relatively new. Looking back much beyond five years produces a very small number of funds. In fact, only six of the funds examined here existed prior to 1998. And if we review performance records from the last several years, we see results that are quite variable.

Part of this can be explained by the fact that a tax law change in 1997 made market neutral mutual funds more feasible. Prior to the elimination of what was called the "short/short rule," funds were not allowed to generate more than 30 percent of their returns from short positions, making it difficult to implement a long/short strategy. In any case, the median age of these funds is about five years.

In 2002, for example, of our 20 profiled mutual funds, 18 were in operation for the full year. One of the funds reviewed below, the Schwab Hedged Equity fund, was only just launched in 2002, and the Rydex SpHinx fund was launched in 2003.

A wide-ranging set of returns was achieved in 2002 within the group (see Figure 10.1). At the high end of the performance spectrum, Comstock Capital Value Fund (DRCVX) was up 35.9 percent and at the low end Choice Long/Short (CHLAX) was down 29.4 percent. Those divergent results make it clear that choosing the right fund is awfully important and will mean the difference between success or failure. Note from the graph in Figure 10.1 that there is an almost perfectly equal distribution, or S-shaped curve, among winners and losers.

Generally, the category as a whole acquitted itself well in 2002. As one way to judge, an equal investment in all 18 funds would have returned

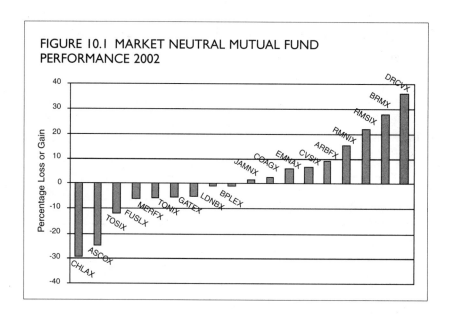

FIGURE 10.1 MARKET NEUTRAL MUTUAL FUND PERFORMANCE 2002

2 percent for the year. Given that the S&P 500 lost 24 percent over the same time frame, most investors would have been grateful for such a result. So while there was considerable variability among the funds, overall they served investors well in a difficult year for the stock market.

Take note that two funds that are included in the above summary and profiled below. AIM Opportunities (ASCOX) and Comstock Capital Value (DRCVX) are on either ends of the spectrum, in terms of both performance and style. Both funds hedge their portfolios, but ASCOX has a strong long bias and DRCVX an equally strong short bias. Neither can be called market neutral, and in a bear market year like 2002 ASCOX had poor results while DRCVX led the pack.

Foul Weather Friends?

While results in 2002 were generally good, it is equally important to see how these funds perform in a generally rising market. As investors are all too aware, bull markets have been pretty infrequent the last few years, but 2003 gives us a good environment in which to see how hedged mutual funds might do when optimism prevails (see Figure 10.2). Out of the 19

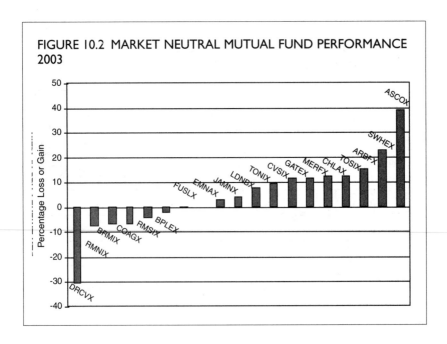

FIGURE 10.2 MARKET NEUTRAL MUTUAL FUND PERFORMANCE 2003

funds with full-year results, 11 made a profit, 8 had a loss and an equal investment in all 19 would have produced a gain of just under 5 percent.

Our hedged but biased funds were again at the extremes, but with places switched. In 2003, the AIM Opportunities Fund (ASCOX) was at the top of the charts with a gain of 39 percent, and Comstock Capital Value (DRCVX) came in dead last with a loss of 30 percent. In 2003 that which was last became first.

That dramatic shift in performance illustrates a concern voiced by Morningstar analyst Dan McNeela who covers this category of mutual fund. He worries that investors will be too captivated by the most recent performance of these funds and not consider how they might perform over the long haul. After three years, from 2000 to 2002, when market neutral funds performed well relative to the broader market, he believes that investors might be "ready to look past some of the previous struggles" that these funds have had.

There *is* a tendency among investors to somewhat blindly rush into funds that have the best track record in the previous year or two. That is why in evaluating fund performance investors are smart to review at least three years worth of data. We are fortunate to have two back-to-back years representing market extremes. If a fund is able to perform well in both bullish and bearish periods, it is fulfilling an important goal: providing positive absolute returns regardless of the market backdrop.

Some might argue that three years worth of performance is not enough. However, if we go back further than three years our analysis runs the risk of suffering from something called "survivorship bias." This occurs because we know that some market neutral funds that were in business before 2000 have subsequently withdrawn from the market, primarily because of poor performance. To only incorporate the survivors in a performance assessment almost certainly skews the results more positively than they actually would have been if we included all the funds operating pre-2000.

Is it reasonable to expect a positive return among market neutral mutual funds all of the time, year in and year out? Absolutely. Among hedge funds, it is not uncommon to see steady gains, year after year, in all market environments. For example, in 2002 an index of market neutral hedge funds compiled by CSFB/Tremont was up 7.4 percent. In 2003 it was up 7.1 percent. By those standards hedged mutual funds disappoint.

Katheryn McDonald, Portfolio Manager for AXA Rosenberg, observes that one factor that has weighed negatively on the long-term performance of market neutral mutual funds is simply a timing issue. The tax law change and the subsequent launch of many funds in 1997 and 1998 coincided with what most observers now consider an equity bubble. As might be expected for this investment class, performance lagged behind the phenomenal, and most would say, irrational, rise in equities.

McDonald brings up a good point. Perhaps some of these mutual funds simply suffer from bad timing and were launched at an inopportune moment. However, since 1998 there has been only one year in which hedged mutual funds performed better than market neutral hedge funds (see Figure 10.3).

Nonetheless, if McDonald's view is accurate, then it is probably too soon in the history of these mutual funds to decide whether they will live up to their potential of good performance in all kinds of market environments. What is needed is a longer period of time during which the markets behave in a normal fashion, more in keeping with the long-term historical record.

The good news is that there are a couple of funds that have achieved positive returns in both bullish and bearish environments, which is what market neutral funds are really supposed to do. We will turn to a brief performance review towards the end of this chapter.

The Jury Is Still Out

Morningstar's McNeela is generally lukewarm about the market neutral mutual fund category, partly because there are so few offerings.

FIGURE 10.3 HEDGE FUND PERFORMANCE 1998–2003

Year	Average Hedged Mutual Fund	CSFB/Tremont Market Neutral Index
1998	3.9%	13.3%
1999	6.2	15.3
2000	17.3	15.0
2001	5.0	9.3
2002	2.1	7.4
2003	4.9	7.1

What's more, fewer still have a long operating history. "My general sense is that most market neutral mutual funds are a tough fit for investors, and I have not been overly optimistic about encouraging people to get in to them." Part of his concern stems from investors not necessarily understanding the funds. Clearly there is some education required in order for many investors to grasp exactly what the strategy is.

Another doubter is Phillip Toews, President and CEO of the Toews Funds. He suggests that market neutral mutual funds "still have to prove themselves" and that any active portfolio management that "relies on anything other than the long-term growth of the stock market presents a risk." His own funds utilize a more passive, mechanistic management style that he believes is easier for investors and financial planners to accept.

One thing is certain: relative to the thousands of mutual funds currently in existence, the market neutral category is remarkably small. That may be because the category has seen few unqualified successes and a number of funds have closed their doors. Both Heartland and Dreyfus have shut down previous offerings, and several smaller funds have also folded in the last couple of years.

As with any market neutral approach, the goal of these funds is to reduce volatility and produce positive returns in any environment. Unfortunately, few have been able to achieve this admirable goal. It's not entirely clear why, but certainly the high fee structure usually associated with these funds doesn't help.

While the average mutual fund expense ratios are between 1 percent and 1.5 percent, the average expense ratio for 19 of the 20 funds below, is 2.1 percent. (One fund, SPhinX, is so new no expense data is available.) In addition, some funds also carry a sales charge, or load, of between 1 percent and 5 percent. With expenses running that high, the fund must really perform well just to keep up with the broader market or other funds. Even a good performance, when combined with those higher fees, can produce a lackluster return.

There are three reasons behind these higher expense ratios. First, because the funds tend to be small, the expenses tend to be high relative to assets and thus the ratios are high. Second, the dividends paid on short positions are included as an operating expense. Third, shorting stocks often requires more frequent trading. The turnover statistics for market neutral funds are usually two or three times the average of all mutual funds. More trades translate into a higher cost of doing business.

Though expenses tend to be higher, everything comes down to performance. If a fund can still turn in a strong performance, even with a relatively high expense ratio, no one is likely to complain.

These funds also tend to be tax inefficient and may be best suited for tax-deferred accounts. With all of that trading going on, a disproportionate amount of the gains are short term in nature and subject to higher tax rates.

Part of a Well-Balanced Diet?

To say that a market neutral mutual fund belongs in every portfolio is a little like a doctor prescribing medication without seeing the patient. Such decisions should be made in consultation with a doctor, or in this case a financial planner. The "patient's" financial situation, age, and goals all need to be considered before a responsible recommendation can be made.

With that said, many financial planners are ignorant about market neutral investing. Any investor who is interested in the subject may actually need to educate their advisor. Continuing with the doctor/patient analogy, it is not uncommon these days for patients to bring a new treatment to the attention of their physician. That doesn't mean the treatment is right for the circumstances, but some degree of self-determination and involvement in the decision is appropriate.

The biggest reason for having a market neutral component in an investor's overall portfolio is the fact that it will not correlate with other equity investments. In other words, it will behave differently than most other equity holdings, often moving in a different direction. This lack of correlation is really just another form of diversification. While it almost certainly isn't a good idea to put all of one's assets in a market neutral portfolio, if an individual has equity investments, then it probably makes sense for that individual to have some type of market neutral investment as well. It's the same logic that causes many investors to have some money in different asset classes: some in bonds, some in real estate, some in stocks, etc.

The Funds

What follows is a brief performance review of a number of market neutral mutual funds.

AIM Opportunities

There are actually three different AIM Opportunities Funds: I, II, and III. The difference is the size of company each fund invests in, small-cap, mid-cap, or large-cap. For longs, the managers look for five-year earnings and revenue growth of over 15 percent, among other things. For short candidates, they look for things like rising inventory-to-sales ratios and accounts receivable-to-sales ratios.

The use of short-selling is somewhat limited at the AIM Opportunities Funds, amounting to a maximum of 25 percent of net assets. Even though these funds are not market neutral, they are included here because they do hedge. The manager's stated goal is to reduce volatility, but not necessarily always to show a positive return. Reviewing the track record of this fund, it does look a whole lot more long than short. Its bull market performance was strong in 2003, and in 2002 it acted much like the S&P 500, losing almost 25 percent (see Figure 10.4).

FIGURE 10.4 AIM OPPORTUNITIES I PERFORMANCE

AIM Opportunities I (ASCOX)

Bear Market Performance—2002	−24.8%
3-Year Performance (2001–2003)	−5.0%
Bull Market Performance—2003	+39.2%
Expense Ratio	1.29%
Sales Charge	Yes
Assets Under Management	$472M

Arbitrage Fund

When acquisitions are announced, the company being acquired typically trades just below the announced acquisition price until the deal is closed. This fund, like the Merger Fund listed later, capitalizes on that small difference in price. If the fund believes there is a strong likelihood of the deal getting done, it buys shares of the target company. If the transaction is in an all-stock form, Arbitrage Fund will sell short shares of the acquiring company to protect against any decline in value. More about this technique is discussed in Chapter 11.

The Arbitrage Fund has a less established history than the Merger Fund, but in the short time it has been around it has distinguished itself with solid, low-risk performance (see Figure 10.5).

FIGURE 10.5 ARBITRAGE FUND PERFORMANCE

Arbitrage Fund (ARBFX)

Bear Market Performance—2002	+9.3%
3-Year Performance (2001–2003)	+36.9%
Bull Market Performance—2003	+15.2%
Expense Ratio	1.95%
Sales Charge	No
Assets Under Management	$248M

Laudus Rosenberg

Unlike many of the funds profiled here, Laudus Rosenberg actually has a "family" of long/short funds. For individual investors, there are three different funds available.

All three funds use a similar model for selecting long and short positions, whereby the managers essentially conduct a breakup analysis in order to make a fair value assessment of a company relative to its peers. According to Katheryn McDonald, one of those managers, the goal of this process is to quantify which companies will generate the maximum amount of earnings per dollar of share price for the long side of the portfolio. Conversely, a similar calculation is made to identify short opportunities by calculating the maximum amount of earnings loss per dollar of share price.

Because the methodology used is similar in each of the funds, albeit with a slightly different weighting given to different criteria, the real difference comes down to what universe of stocks is used as a pool for selection. The Global Long/Short draws from all equities (see Figure 10.6), the Large/Mid-Cap Long/Short draws from the top 500 U.S. companies by market capitalization (see Figure 10.7), and the Value Long/Short (see Figure 10.8) focuses on small-cap and mid-cap firms that are found in the Russell 2500 Index.

FIGURE 10.6 GLOBAL LONG/SHORT PERFORMANCE

Laudus Rosenberg Global Long/Short (RMSIX)

Bear Market Performance—2002	+22.0%
3-Year Performance (2001–2003)	NA
Bull Market Performance—2003	–4.2%
Expense Ratio	2.92%
Sales Charge	No
Assets Under Management	$21M

FIGURE 10.7 LARGE/MID-CAP LONG/SHORT PERFORMANCE

Laudus Rosenberg Large/Mid-Cap Long/Short (RMNIX)

Bear Market Performance—2002	+15.4%
3-Year Performance (2001–2003)	+18.4%
Bull Market Performance—2003	–7.5%
Expense Ratio	3.07%
Sales Charge	No
Assets Under Management	$28M

FIGURE 10.8 VALUE LONG/SHORT PERFORMANCE

Laudus Rosenberg Value Long/Short (BRMIX)

Bear Market Performance—2002	+27.9%
3-Year Performance (2001–2003)	+32.9%
Bull Market Performance—2003	–6.6%
Expense Ratio	2.69%
Sales Charge	No
Assets Under Management	$122M

Boston Partners

While having one of the more successful track records since it was first created back in 1998, this fund is closed to new investors. Boston Partners continues to accept funds from existing customers but does not feel it has the capacity to handle additional money from new clients. The fund has a value orientation when it comes to selecting stocks. The fund screens a universe of 5,000 stocks to come up with 200 to 300 stocks per week that are then subjected to an in-depth analysis.

According to Paul Heathwood, principal at Boston Partners, the fund looks for companies that have high valuations, poor cash flow, and weak balance sheets for the short side of the portfolio. Indeed, he believes that "if we had to point to our edge, it would be on balance sheet analysis that we think can serve as a predictor to future problems on the income statement." For the long side of the portfolio, the same concepts are applied in reverse.

One characteristic that is unique to Boston Partners is that they accept a certain level of sector risk by not necessarily matching up longs and shorts by sector. Heathwood says that "we are willing to have sector exposure, long or short, of a maximum of 20 percent of the portfolio and they come out of our bottom-up stock selection." (See Figure 10.9.)

FIGURE 10.9 BOSTON PARTNERS LONG/SHORT EQUITY PERFORMANCE

Boston Partners Long/Short Equity (BPLEX)

Bear Market Performance—2002	−0.8%
3-Year Performance (2001–2003)	+21.3%
Bull Market Performance—2003	−2.2%
Expense Ratio	3.32%
Sales Charge	No
Assets Under Management	$73M

Calamos

The Calamos Market Neutral Fund, like Boston Partners, has been around longer than many market neutral mutual funds, and like Boston Partners it is closed to new investors. The fund is unique in how it achieves market neutrality: rather than buying undervalued stocks and shorting different, overvalued stocks, Calamos focuses on the convertible bonds of individual companies.

The strategy is to buy corporate bonds that can be converted into stock and at the same time short the shares of that stock. By doing this,

Calamos essentially locks in the interest payment that comes with the bond and protects against loss of principal through the short position.

This is probably the market neutral fund that Morningstar's Mc-Neela is most upbeat about, and he expresses surprise that there are not other funds using the same methodology, particularly in light of the fact that Calamos is closed (see Figure 10.10).

FIGURE 10.10 CALAMOS MARKET NEUTRAL PERFORMANCE

Calamos Market Neutral (CVSIX)

Bear Market Performance—2002	+6.6%
3-Year Performance (2001–2003)	+26.3%
Bull Market Performance—2003	+9.4%
Expense Ratio	1.50%
Sales Charge	Yes
Assets Under Management	$694M

Caldwell & Orkin

This fund is not market neutral but instead might take a net long or net short position at any given time. Unlike some funds listed here, Caldwell & Orkin views its benchmark as the S&P 500 rather than a T-bill's rate of return. Accordingly, the fund is willing to take on some additional risk in order to exceed the S&P 500's rate of return. The three-year track record is only so-so, and the fund remains closed to new investors, as it has been since 1998 (see Figure 10.11).

FIGURE 10.11 CALDWELL & ORKIN MARKET OPPORTUNITY PERFORMANCE

Caldwell & Orkin Market Opportunity (COAGX)

Bear Market Performance—2002	+2.9%
3-Year Performance (2001–2003)	−7.5%
Bull Market Performance—2003	−6.6%
Expense Ratio	1.41%
Sales Charge	No
Assets Under Management	$248M

Charles Schwab

One of the biggest and best known discount brokerage firms offers a handful of their own mutual funds. The newest offering is the Hedged Equity Fund, which relies on Schwab's proprietary stock ranking system, buying top-rated stocks and selling short the lowest-rated stocks. Information about this fund is scant because it was launched in late 2002 (see Figure 10.12). It should be noted that this fund has one of the higher initial minimum investments: $25,000.

FIGURE 10.12 SCHWAB HEDGED EQUITY PERFORMANCE

Schwab Hedged Equity (SWHEX)

Bear Market Performance—2002	NA
3-Year Performance (2001–2003)	NA
Bull Market Performance—2003	+22.9%
Expense Ratio	2.0%
Sales Charge	No
Assets Under Management	$47M

Choice Funds

Choice created its long/short fund relatively recently, having launched it in February 2001. Given its performance, perhaps it was a fund better left unlaunched. In a bear market year when the S&P 500 dropped well over 20 percent, one would expect a market neutral fund to outperform the benchmark, and at least lose *less* money. Choice was not able to attain even that modest goal. Then, in 2003 the fund again underperformed the broad market. Unless, and until, Choice can develop a better track record, it would seem like a fund to avoid (see Figure 10.13).

FIGURE 10.13 CHOICE LONG SHORT FUND PERFORMANCE

Choice Long Short Fund (CHLAX)

Bear Market Performance—2002	−29.4%
3-Year Performance (2001–2003)	NA
Bull Market Performance—2003	+12.5%
Expense Ratio	3.16%
Sales Charge	Yes
Assets Under Management	$9M

Comstock

The Comstock Capital Value Fund, which joined the Gabelli fund family several years ago, is actually more of a bear market fund than a market neutral fund. However, the fund managers, who have been at this for quite some time, claim that they are able and willing to turn bullish when the market fundamentals warrant it. They just haven't seen any reason to be positive on stocks for quite some time. In the meantime the fund has been largely in cash and short positions.

The managers' negative outlook has provided plenty of positive returns over the last few years. But this is clearly not a fund that has performed well in all market environments; in 2003 the fund was down over 30 percent (see Figure 10.14). In fact, the fund had negative returns every year from 1994 through 1999.

FIGURE 10.14 COMSTOCK CAPITAL VALUE PERFORMANCE

Comstock Capital Value (DRCVX)

Bear Market Performance—2002	+35.9
3-Year Performance (2001–2003)	+14.8%
Bull Market Performance—2003	−30.4%
Expense Ratio	1.70%
Sales Charge	Yes
Assets Under Management	$97M

Franklin Templeton

The well-regarded Franklin Templeton family offers a long/short alternative that was closed to new investors until March 2003. Newer investors may wish it had remained closed because the most recent performance has been lackluster. In its first full year the fund was up an astonishing 55 percent, but since then it's been all downhill.

The fund allows itself the latitude to be net long or net short, depending on what the managers perceive as the best opportunity. For example, in late 2003 the fund was net long in minerals companies and net short in manufacturing. Overall, the fund was 69 percent long and 48 percent short (more than 100 percent because of leverage) at the beginning of 2004 (see Figure 10.15).

FIGURE 10.15 FRANKLIN TEMPLETON US LONG SHORT PERFORMANCE

Franklin Templeton US Long Short (FUSLX)

Bear Market Performance—2002	−6.2%
3-Year Performance (2001–2003)	−7.9%
Bull Market Performance—2003	−0.3%
Expense Ratio	2.45%
Sales Charge	Yes
Assets Under Management	$124M

Gateway Fund

There is seemingly no end to the different hedging strategies funds have developed. Gateway hedges by selling call options on the S&P 500 while simultaneously holding the underlying S&P 500 stocks. This generates positive returns but also limits the possible upside if the index rises dramatically. With some of the cash flow produced by selling calls, the fund turns around and buys put options on the S&P 500 to protect against declines in the index.

The net effect has been a low-volatility portfolio with losses coming in much lower than the S&P 500 in down years. In years when the market was way up, Gateway's returns have lagged too. While Gateway fails the test of always producing positive returns, it has provided a great deal of downside protection during the last few bearish years and may be one of the most stable funds listed. The fund is the oldest and largest of all those profiled here, having started in 1977 and now with about $1.4 billion under management (see Figure 10.16).

FIGURE 10.16 GATEWAY FUND PERFORMANCE

Gateway Fund (GATEX)

Bear Market Performance—2002	–4.9%
3-Year Performance (2001–2003)	+2.4%
Bull Market Performance—2003	+11.6%
Expense Ratio	0.97
Sales Charge	No
Assets Under Management	$1,458M

James Funds

This is a very small fund family, operating four funds from their offices in Ohio. Dr. Frank James uses a quantitative approach to selecting stocks for both the long and short portfolios in the market neutral portfolio.

James's emphasis is on fundamental factors, like price-to-book and price-to-earnings ratios. Dr. James believes that his firm's unique ability lies in determining how much weight to place on each of approximately 20 primary factors they use. The fund is usually perfectly neutral, but is occasionally allowed to skew net long or net short. (See Figure 10.17.)

FIGURE 10.17 JAMES MARKET NEUTRAL PERFORMANCE

James Market Neutral (JAMNX)

Bear Market Performance—2002	+1.6%
3-Year Performance (2001–2003)	+6.7%
Bull Market Performance—2003	+3.2%
Expense Ratio	2.23%
Sales Charge	No
Assets Under Management	$11M

Lindner Funds

Lindner is another very small fund company with six different offerings, one of which is a market neutral fund. The fund itself is actually managed by Standish Mellon and makes its stock selections from a universe of approximately 1,200 companies drawn from the Russell 1000 and the S&P 500. According to Sean Fitzgibbon, Vice President at Standish Mellon Asset Management, companies are evaluated on the basis of valuation, technical indicators, and business momentum, as defined by earnings and revenue performance.

Different criteria are emphasized more or less heavily depending on the industry classification. "In technology, we tend to be a lot more focused on business momentum, and in financials, we weigh more on valuation factors" says Fitzgerald. In addition, Standish Mellon relies on a team of analysts to conduct a reality check on the quantitative assessment.

The Lindner Market Neutral is almost perfectly balanced between long and short positions, and the fund holds approximately 100 stocks long and 100 stocks short. By having the same amount of dollars long as short, by sector, the fund keeps its sector risk exposure to a minimum. (See Figure 10.18.)

FIGURE 10.18 LINDNER MARKET NEUTRAL PERFORMANCE

Lindner Market Neutral (LDNBX)

Bear Market Performance—2002	−1.0%
3-Year Performance (2001–2003)	−4.8%
Bull Market Performance—2003	+4.1%
Expense Ratio	3.28%
Sales Charge	No
Assets Under Management	$12M

Merger Fund

Merger Fund has a unique style, even among this unique genre. Only the Arbitrage Fund uses the same strategy, and like that fund, these managers identify arbitrage opportunity between companies that have announced a merger/acquisition. There is not a great amount of risk in these scenarios, unless a deal gets called off for some reason. The success of the fund ultimately depends on how accurately the managers are able predict the closure of the transaction. Obviously the fund also depends on there being a certain level of merger and acquisition activity.

One key difference between this fund and the Arbitrage Fund is longevity; the Merger Fund has been around since 1989, as have its managers. Until 2002 the fund had a perfect track record of producing positive returns every year (see Figure 10.19).

FIGURE 10.19 MERGER FUND PERFORMANCE

Merger Fund (MERFX)

Bear Market Performance—2002	−5.7%
3-Year Performance (2001–2003)	+7.3%
Bull Market Performance—2003	+11.6%
Expense Ratio	1.38%
Sales Charge	No
Assets Under Management	$1,457M

Phoenix Investment Partners

This is a large fund family with 11 different branded investment subsidiaries. The Capital West arm offers three different versions (Classes A, B, and C) of its market neutral fund, the difference being the various permutations on sales charges. Only the Class A fund is profiled here (see Figure 10.20). This fund has the dubious distinction of being one of the most expensive to own in terms of fees and charges.

Phoenix uses a quantitative approach to identify the best long and short candidates. While the fund strives to be sector neutral, it does sometimes allow individual groups to skew net long or short. According to the managers, the fund will always have the same amount of dollars long as short.

The emphasis on fundamentals at Phoenix becomes apparent when we look at some portfolio statistics. For example, in late 2003, the average forward PE for stocks in the long portfolio was 19, and the average for the short portfolio was 29. Clearly the managers are trying to purchase

---

FIGURE 10.20 PHOENIX MARKET NEUTRAL PERFORMANCE

Phoenix Market Neutral (EMNAX)

Bear Market Performance—2002	+5.7%
3-Year Performance (2001–2003)	+12.6%
Bull Market Performance—2003	–0.1%
Expense Ratio	3.85%
Sales Charge	Yes
Assets Under Management	$102M

---

undervalued stocks and sell short overvalued stocks. The performance record of the fund is mixed; it has done pretty well over the past three years, but it was not particularly successful in the 2003 bull market.

One bothersome fact about this fund is the number of portfolio managers it has seen. The third management team came on board in July 2002, according to Morningstar, and then in May 2003 two previous managers rejoined the fund. That's a lot of change for a fund that is seven years old, making it tough for investors who value a consistent approach.

Rydex

This fund family may be best known for its inverse index funds as well as its sector funds, but Rydex has been a mutual fund innovator in a variety of ways. One of the latest is through the launch of the SPhinX Fund in mid-2003. The fund is so new there is very little data available on it, but it is worth including here because it is unique and fits into this category of mutual funds so perfectly.

Standard and Poor's created a hedge fund index in 2002 that tracks 40 different hedge funds, across three different broadly defined subinvestment styles and a total of nine different strategies. It is not the only such hedge fund index, but the Standard and Poor's name gives it a certain amount of credibility. It is "an investable benchmark that is designed to be representative of the broad-based investment experience of the hedge fund marketplace," according to promotional material published by Standard and Poor's.

Rydex, in turn, has obtained a license through its partner PlusFunds and has created a fund that tracks the index. Much like an investment in a fund of hedge funds, there are suitability requirements for investors in the form of a minimum net worth or income. The minimum investment is $25,000. What is fascinating about this fund is that it creates a single vehicle for investing in a diversified group of hedge funds that is simple to access. This will be a fund worth watching.

Toews Funds

Toews offers two hedged funds, one for the S&P 500 and another for the Nasdaq 100. These funds fall into the market neutral category only loosely, but they do provide hedging and are included here because they take an interesting approach. Toews also has the lowest expense ratio of all the funds reviewed here.

These funds attempt to track their respective indexes while at the same time provide some downside protection. Toews looks for intermediate-term market trends, essentially moving into cash when the respective broad market is trending down and then reflecting the respective index when the market is trending up.

As a result of this methodology, the Toews funds may have greater upside in a bull market than other, more truly market neutral funds. Toews' approach really amounts to a simple market timing system, and the funds have not been around long enough to really judge how well the timing mechanism works. The timing mechanism itself is based on price action alone, not on fundamental data or a complicated technical analysis.

According to Phillip Toews, President and CEO, most financial planners who have invested in the funds use both rather than choose one or the other. "A 70 percent TOSIX and 30 percent TONIX combination correlates strongly with a large-cap growth portfolio. We're seeing advisors move a portion of their clients' portfolios out of large-cap growth funds and into this sort of combination." (See Figure 10.21 and Figure 10.22.)

FIGURE 10.21 TOEWS S&P 500 HEDGED PERFORMANCE

Toews S&P 500 Hedged (TOSIX)

Bear Market Performance—2002	−11.8%
3-Year Performance (2001–2003)	NA
Bull Market Performance—2003	+12.5%
Expense Ratio	1.50%
Sales Charge	No
Assets Under Management	$35M

FIGURE 10.22 TOEWS NASDAQ 100 HEDGED PERFORMANCE

Toews Nasdaq 100 Hedged (TONIX)

Bear Market Performance—2002	−5.3%
3-Year Performance (2001–2003)	NA
Bull Market Performance—2003	+7.9%
Expense Ratio	1.50%
Sales Charge	No
Assets Under Management	$17M

How They Stack Up

In evaluating all of these funds, we really need to consider how well they have lived up to the goal of producing positive returns in all market environments. On that basis, we have to discard two funds that have had quite remarkable returns in some years: AIM Opportunities and Comstock Capital Value. These funds would probably be the first to acknowledge that they are not really market neutral, and their performance underscores that view, but they are included here because they make some effort to hedge against market risk. AIM Opportunities can be up to 25 percent short, for example, and makes an effort to reduce volatility, but it is more of a growth fund than anything else. Comstock is, or has been for quite some time, a fund with a strong short bias. An investor will only be successful in either of these funds because the broad market is rising, in the case of AIM Opportunities, or falling, in the case of Comstock.

A couple of funds with decent records are closed to new investors. Among those, the Calamos Fund scores points for having such a consistent performance, year after year. Clearly, these managers know how to produce a steady return. Investors can only hope that it will reopen sometime in the future or that another fund will emulate their convertible bond strategy.

Both the Gateway and the Toews funds are intriguing because they offer hedging that does not rely on a portfolio manager's stock picking skills. Both funds limit the downside risk through the use of mechanical means but are designed to participate in a market upturn. Toews's trend-following system is too new to have been thoroughly tested, but the funds bear watching. Neither Gateway nor Toews are likely to be winners in a bear market, but they do offer equity exposure and some good insurance against big declines.

Except for a stumble last year, the Merger Fund has a truly exemplary track record. The dearth of mergers and acquisitions in 2001 and 2002 has made this fund's job more difficult. If there is resurgence in merger activity, it seems likely that the Merger Fund will regain its footing and continue its pattern of generating positive returns with lowered risk. Even though it has not been around as long, the Arbitrage Fund has had even more impressive results. In fact, Arbitrage has the single best three-year record of all the funds surveyed.

Another fund that has the distinction of having produced gains in each of the three periods examined—for the last three years and during both bull and bear market years—is the tiny James Fund. Even though gains have been modest, James scores points for its consistency during a tumultuous time in the stock market.

Finally, the Laudus Rosenberg Value Fund had the second-best overall record for the past three years. It is worrisome that the fund performed so poorly in 2003 but perhaps not surprising because the fund also declined in 1999, the last year for a bull market. There is no denying that even with that slip in 2003, profits for the last three years were almost 33 percent.

The Future

What lies ahead for market neutral mutual funds? Of course no one knows for sure, but it seems likely that there will be more of them in the future. In some ways, this class of funds is in its infancy. To date, the existing funds have attracted a small amount of investment capital and very little attention from investors, analysts, or the media.

As the operating history of market neutral mutual funds extends and as both investors and financial planners have more data to observe, they will gain a more prominent place in portfolios. Laudus Rosenberg's McDonald says that she would not be surprised to see a tenfold increase in the number of market neutral funds offered over the next ten years.

One reason to expect more market neutral mutual funds is that investors are seeking protection from the stock market declines of the past few years. A market neutral mutual fund is likely to appeal to that sentiment. New offerings, though, must be judged with caution. One fact that should be clear from this book is that a manager's stock selection skill, or lack thereof, is highly accentuated in a market neutral strategy. A new fund with a new manager will have something to prove before most financial planners and investors are comfortable with it, and rightly so.

With more funds and a longer history, perhaps some standardization will also begin to take shape. Unlike the hedge fund industry, there is no generally accepted classification system among mutual funds.

As briefly mentioned earlier, mutual funds don't seem to adhere to a strict definition of long/short versus market neutral. Recall that a long/short portfolio can be net long or net short at any given time, while a market neutral portfolio is perfectly balanced, having the same amount of assets long as short. Among mutual funds, that distinction does not seem to hold sway, and it would be a mistake to read anything into a name. Investors will have to look deeper into the fund prospectus and marketing material. Even then, it is not always clear how much long or short bias a fund has.

This is no small distinction. Strictly speaking, a true market neutral fund that is perfectly balanced between long and short positions probably carries slightly less risk and has less upside. This is because the fund has less exposure to the direction of the market and less opportunity to get it wrong or right. A fund that is more long than short, or vice versa, has a bit more risk as well as more upside and downside (see Figure 10.23).

Another difficulty with these funds is that there is no effective benchmarking in place. Morningstar classifies the few market neutral funds it covers as "domestic hybrid." This designation is not really very specific to the unique characteristics of a market neutral fund, nor is it terribly

---

FIGURE 10.23 LONG/SHORT BIAS MARKET NEUTRAL FUNDS

Fund	Bias	Fund	Bias
AIM Opportunities	Long	Franklin Templeton	None
Arbitrage Fund	None	Gateway Fund	Long
Laudus Rosenberg	None	James Funds	None
Boston Partners	None	Lindner Funds	None
Calamos	None	Merger Fund	None
Caldwell & Orkin	None	Phoenix Investment	
Charles Schwab	None	Partners	None
Choice Funds	Long	Rydex	None
Comstock	Short	Toews Funds	Long

---

useful to know how a market neutral fund performed compared to domestic hybrid funds. Morningstar's quandary, however, is that there simply aren't enough market neutral funds to warrant a separate classification. That too may change as more funds are available.

We can hope that a better benchmarking system develops as the market begins to pay more attention to this unique genre of funds. Until there are more funds, a category of "hedged" mutual funds probably makes the most sense. Eventually, more narrowly defined performance data can evolve.

The other development that may change the landscape is the creation of the S & P hedge fund index and the subsequent launch of the SPhinX mutual fund. This fund is a real innovation, and, as it develops a track record, more investors and financial planners are likely to take advantage of it. It seems likely that there will be more of these sorts of funds launched, tied to other hedge fund indexes.

Finally, with some noted exceptions, such as the Arbitrage, James, Lauder Rosenberg, and Merger funds, the performance of many of these funds leaves something to be desired. The disparity between the general record of these mutual funds and the record of hedge funds is too great to ignore. Is it possible that, to date, hedge funds have attracted more talented or more experienced portfolio managers? To be sure, market neutral funds are quite different from the typical mutual fund. The portfolio managers who are successful must be just as adept at picking stocks to sell short as stocks to buy and perhaps that skill set is in short supply.

Another explanation may lie in the respective pay scales. Successful hedge fund managers can earn significantly more than mutual fund managers, and the disparity may have drawn, in broad terms, more talent to the hedge fund industry. Let's not forget that it is the investor, however, who pays for that talent in the form of high hedge fund fees.

In any case, hedged mutual funds deserve more attention. Fund companies should turn their attention to developing more offerings and improving performance; mutual fund analysts and the media should bring the funds currently available to light; and investors should pay attention.

Summary

A number of mutual funds offer some form of hedging to individual investors or their financial planners. Relative to the scale of the hedge fund industry, it is a remarkably small universe. With some notable exceptions, the performance of mutual funds compared to hedge funds also suffers by comparison. A few funds with several years of success behind them are open to new investors, but not as many as one might expect. A credible case can be made that this should and will change.

11

ALTERNATIVE TACTICS

Hedging in the financial markets can take many forms, and sometimes the term *alternative investments* is used to generally describe such nontraditional asset classes. The very first forms of equity hedging were done much as this book has described them: finding some stocks that were undervalued to buy while selling short other, overvalued stocks. And even before the first equity hedge fund was formed, farmers hedged their crops in the futures markets against sudden price changes or weather catastrophes. In the modern era, dozens of new forms of hedging have evolved, ranging from the simple to the sophisticated.

Many of these methods are beyond the reach of, or not practical for, individual investors or financial planners. For example, *arbitrage* plays are designed to take advantage of small discrepancies in the prices of related instruments. Often, arbitrage tends to be fairly complex and requires a level of resources not available to individual investors, either in the form of capital, expertise, or computer horsepower. By definition, arbitrage is supposed to be a "riskless" transaction. In truth, a transaction with no risk is quite rare; reduced risk is more likely.

To explain the notion of arbitrage we will start with a simple example. Suppose you own a car, say a 2002 Honda Accord. You know through research that your car is worth approximately $10,000, based on its "Blue

Book" value along with its condition and mileage. One day as you are perusing the eBay auction site, you see another 2002 Honda Accord that is in identical condition, has the same features, etc., but is priced for sale at $8,000.

You could react to this discovery in several ways. You might immediately and reasonably conclude that there is something wrong with the car on eBay. Or you might contact the owner to learn more about the vehicle, in order to reassure yourself that it is indeed in good condition. If you were satisfied on the latter point, you could purchase the eBay car for $8,000 and at the same time put your own Accord up for sale on eBay for $10,000. If you were successful you would make a profit of $2,000 (less transaction costs) with very little risk. That is the essence of arbitrage—simultaneously exploiting differences in price between like assets.

The biggest reason why arbitrage is difficult to implement is probably quite obvious. Others who see the $8,000 Accord for sale on eBay are likely to also recognize that it is incorrectly priced and bid the price up to its fair market value. In a world of transparent price discovery, true arbitrage is rare. Of course, if the car is in fact of inferior quality, then there is no mispricing taking place and no arbitrage.

Generally, the more closely alike the assets are the better it is for an arbitrageur, but finding them is not easy. If we want to search for arbitrage opportunities in the stock market, we should start by looking for assets (i.e., stocks) that are identical or near-identical.

Statistical Arbitrage

One place to look might be situations where there are two classes of stock traded for the same company. There may be a combination of common stock and preferred stock, or different share classes with different types of voting rights. An example of the latter can be found with Neiman Marcus, the well-known retailer. Neiman Marcus shares come in two forms—Class A and Class B common stock. Shares trade under two different symbols, NMG.A and NMG.B (or NMGa and NMGb, or NMG/A and NMG/B depending on the symbology used by the market data provider).

According to the company, there is no difference in the shares except for voting rights. Note the following statement from the Neiman Marcus investor relations department:

Class A Common Stock, formerly known as the NMG Common Stock, trades under the symbol NMG/A, and has the right to elect 18 percent of the Company's Board of Directors. The shares designated as Class B Common Stock trade under the symbol NMG/B and represent those shares that Harcourt General spun off to its shareholders. Class B stock has the right to elect 82 percent of the Company's Board of Directors. Otherwise the two classes are identical.

For most investors, the voting distinction is not important, so this looks like a pair of assets that are effectively identical.

Arbitrageurs would be interested in situations where the price of NMGa shares diverged from the price of NMGb shares. If one rose or fell more than the other, an opportunity to earn a profit with little or no risk could be created by buying shares in one and selling short the other. As the chart in Figure 11.1 illustrates, the stock prices do move in lockstep.

In fact, it is difficult to discern virtually any difference between the two. NMGa shares have consistently traded at a slight premium to NMGb shares. A statistical analysis tells us that the stocks' movements have a correlation of 99 percent and that NMGa has been valued, on average, 6.9 percent higher. However, a closer look reveals occasions when the relationship between the two has diverged. For example, in July of

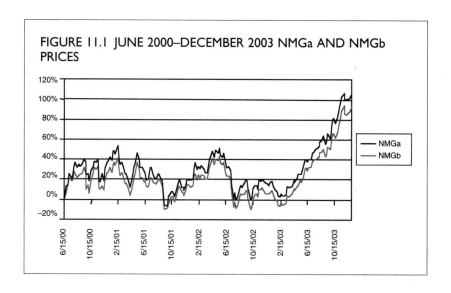

FIGURE 11.1 JUNE 2000–DECEMBER 2003 NMGa AND NMGb PRICES

2000 the stocks briefly traded at the same price. Then, in September of 2000, NMGa's premium went as high as 11.8 percent. The chart in Figure 11.2 shows these changes in relative value quite well.

An arbitrageur might have purchased shares of NGMa in November 2001 when the differential veered away from the normal 6.9 percent and, at the same time, sold short shares of NGMb. At the time, NMGa shares were selling for $30.83 and NGMb shares for $29.43. A $10,000 investment in each would have meant buying 324 shares of NMGa and shorting 340 shares of NMGb. By the end of January 2002 the differential had reverted back to its norm and had even exceeded it. Selling the NMGa shares at $35.41 would have resulted in a gain of $1,473, and covering the short on NMGb shares would have generated a loss of $1,081. Together, there was a net gain of $392 or almost 2 percent.

The same strategy in reverse could have been applied in September 2002 when the differential skewed the other way. Then, buying shares in NMGb for $27.61 and selling short shares in NMGa at $30.29 would have been the plan. Two months later, in November, there would have been a gain of 3.7 percent on NMGb and a loss of 1 percent on NMGa. The net gain would have been 1.3 percent.

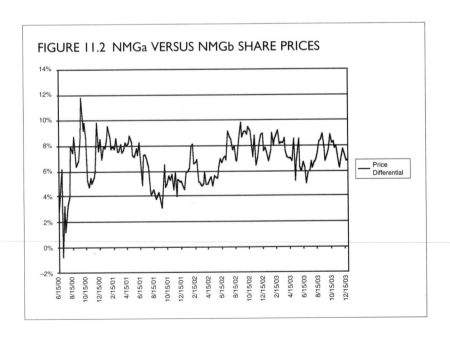

FIGURE 11.2 NMGa VERSUS NMGb SHARE PRICES

As is typical with arbitrage plays, none of the gains would have been all that large. Instead, this sort of strategy is characterized by relatively low risk and relatively low return. Clearly for the profits to be very meaningful, large amounts of capital need to be deployed, which puts this sort of strategy out of the reach of many investors.

Sometimes this sort of arbitrage is referred to as "paired trading" or as "statistical arbitrage," and it is another common type of market neutral investing. In one sense the name is a misnomer because it does carry some risk. In a nutshell, *statistical arbitrage* plays the odds that two stocks that have historically moved together will return to their historical pattern, if and when they diverge from each other.

The idea can be applied in situations other than those where there are different classes of stock in the same company. Sometimes two different companies operate in such a similar manner that their stocks tend to shadow each other. If two stocks have moved closely together in the past, but one stock begins to move differently, either higher or lower than its partner, then there is some likelihood that over time the two stocks will revert back to moving in tandem. Statistical arbitrage, as its name suggests, relies on the fact that such a reversion is statistically likely to occur. It is a very technically oriented strategy and has nothing to do with fundamental valuations. Rather, it uses past price movements and relationships to predict future price movements.

As an example, two stocks that have moved very closely together in the past are Freddie Mac (FRE) and Fannie Mae (FNM). Each company is a so-called government-sponsored enterprise (GSE) and operates under a Congressional mandate to purchase, package, and resell mortgages, providing liquidity to the U.S. housing market. Because they both operate in the same regulatory and economic climate, largely performing the same tasks, one would expect their stock prices to behave similarly.

We can see from the chart in Figure 11.3 that for the ten years ending in 2002, the stocks have moved in virtual lockstep fashion. Statistically, the weekly changes in price for one stock are highly correlated to changes in price for the other. While it is not quite as high as the Neiman Marcus example, it comes close at 98 percent.

Again, a statistical arbitrageur would watch these two stocks closely and look for occasions when one stock would move relatively higher or lower than the other. FRE stock has almost always been priced higher

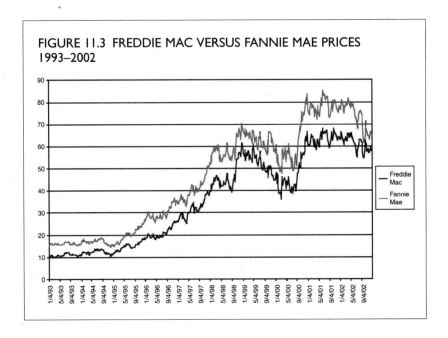

FIGURE 11.3 FREDDIE MAC VERSUS FANNIE MAE PRICES 1993–2002

than FNM stock, and the differential between the two has been quite stable. If the price of FRE stock suddenly moved higher than it normally had been when compared to FNM, the arbitrageur would sell FRE short and buy FNM. The hope would be that FRE stock would subsequently fall and/or FNM stock would rise so that the difference in their prices would come back to what it had been historically.

For the first two years of this data set, 1993 and 1994, the difference in weekly prices between the two stocks was typically about 40 percent. In other words, the price of a share of FNM had, on average, cost 40 percent more than a share of FRE. However, in January of 1995 that differential began to drop, and over the next eight months FNM only cost, on average, 30 percent more than FRE. A statistical arbitrage play would have called for buying shares of FNM in January at about $15.75 and selling shares of FRE short at around $11.75. The FNM premium was about 34 percent. By the end of August 1995, the differential did indeed revert back to 40 percent. Prices in both stocks rose over those eight months, but FNM shares rose more. As the chart in Figure 11.4 highlights, FNM stock was up 31 percent and FRE stock was up 23 percent. A statistical arbitrageur would have lost 23 percent of the money sold short in FRE and made 31 percent on the money used to purchase FNM. Assuming

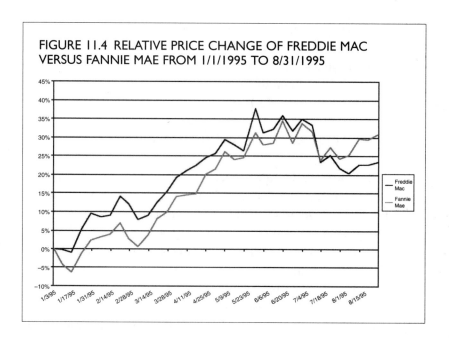

FIGURE 11.4 RELATIVE PRICE CHANGE OF FREDDIE MAC VERSUS FANNIE MAE FROM 1/1/1995 TO 8/31/1995

an equal dollar amount invested in each, the total return would have been about 4 percent.

There were other times when the differential between FNM and **FRE** strayed outside the normal range and created opportunities for profit among arbitrageurs. One caution on this strategy, however, is that investors must constantly be on guard for some structural shift that more or less permanently changes the dynamics between the two stocks. The baseline differential should be constantly reevaluated as a sort of warning system. In the case of these two stocks, the FNM premium gradually began to erode after 1997. For example, in the two years ending in December 1998, the FNM premium averaged only 29 percent. When looking for deviations from the historical norm, investors must regularly recalculate what the historic norm is and make adjustments accordingly.

Indeed, long-term structural changes to the historic relationship are the biggest risk to a statistical arbitrage strategy. If Congress were to change the GSE status of only one of the two, for example, the stock of that company would almost certainly move in a different direction from the other and do so permanently.

A couple of Web sites have information that might be useful in pursuing this strategy. One is called, appropriately enough, Pairs Trading (http://www.pairstrading.com) and the other is ValuEngine (http://www .valuengine.com). For a subscription fee, both sites provide lists of stocks that tend to move together. More information about both of these sites can be found in the Appendix.

Merger and Acquisition Arbitrage

Another form of arbitrage occurs when there is a merger or acquisition (M&A). A company announces that it is going to acquire another firm, the target, at some set price per share. Usually, the target company's shares will immediately rise to just below the announced acquisition price. (Until the deal is pretty far along, sometimes the shares will actually go higher because the market believes that another, higher offer will materialize.) But, up until the deal is consummated, it is common for the target company's shares to trade at a slight discount to the stated acquisition price. The reason for the discount is that there is some chance that the acquisition could be called off. It might run into regulatory trouble, or it might be structured with some conditional financing, or perhaps it faces a tough shareholder vote. To the extent that there is even a small chance of the deal's failure, the target company's shares will trade below the acquisition price.

In addition, there is the time value of money. Investors would not be willing to own shares of the target company prior to the acquisition closing unless they are going to earn some return on their funds. Thus, the longer it is until closing, the bigger the difference between the actual share price and the stated acquisition price.

Whatever the reason, until money changes hands and the shares are tendered, some amount of uncertainty surrounds the deal. M&A arbitrage is designed to capitalize on this uncertainty. M&A arbitrageurs capture a profit by buying the shares of the target company and earning "the spread" between the current price and the announced deal price. If the acquisition is designed as an exchange of stock, then often the arbitrageur will sell short the shares of the company buying the target. The short position will offset any decline in value of the acquiring company's shares.

Professionals who operate in this field become expert at judging whether a particular acquisition has a good chance of being closed or not. Because of the regulatory and legal framework surrounding mergers and acquisitions, it is a specialized practice that requires some unique expertise and is therefore difficult for most individual investors to replicate on their own. For those who have mastered the game, however, the rewards are excellent. Recall that two of the best performing mutual funds reviewed in Chapter 10—the Arbitrage Fund (ARBFX) and the Merger Fund (MERFX)—are engaged in this very strategy.

Note that this form of arbitrage is dependent upon an agreed-upon acquisition. There are occasions when a hostile takeover bid is placed, and investors will immediately bid up the target company's shares. However, if there is resistance on the part of the target company, then the obstacles to the deal are much higher and an investment is not so much arbitrage as it is speculation.

In early 2004 news began to circulate that AT&T Wireless (AWE) had been approached about being acquired. The company eventually confirmed that discussions were under way, and the stock price began to rise dramatically. By mid-February a deal was announced that called for Cingular Wireless to purchase AT&T Wireless for $15 per share, in cash, and with expectations that the transaction would close toward the end of the year. AWE shares did not rise to $15 but instead hovered in the range of $13.50 to $13.75, meaning that an investor could earn a low-risk return of between 9 percent and 11 percent by buying shares and waiting for the closing. The risks to that strategy included possible government interference (antitrust concerns) or some failure to secure financing, both somewhat unlikely occurrences. Mostly investors were being compensated for having their money tied up for nine or ten months.

The same principle applies when the acquisition is predicated on the exchange of stock rather than cash. Another combination that was announced in early 2004 was Juniper Networks' purchase of NetScreen Technologies for $4 billion in stock. After the deal was announced, Juniper shares closed the day at $26.18 and NetScreen shares were at $35.94. The terms of the agreement called for NetScreen shareholders to receive 1.404 shares of Juniper for each share of NetScreen. A quick calculation reveals that an investor could have bought shares in Net-Screen for $35.94 in anticipation of receiving $36.75 when the transaction closed a few months later. That represents a 2.2 percent gain.

However, in this case, there is the risk that Juniper's share value could decline, resulting in less value for NetScreen shareholders. The way an arbitrageur protects against this is to buy shares in NetScreen and to sell short Juniper, thus locking in the 2.2 percent price differential. Because the deal was expected to close no later than June 2004, investors would earn 2.2 percent over about four month's time. Annualized, that works out to a 6.6 percent return, with very little risk.

Convertible Arbitrage

There is also *convertible arbitrage,* a strategy that tries to take advantage of price differentials between convertible bonds or convertible preferred stock and the underlying common stock of the same company. Convertibles can be exchanged for shares of common stock, usually when the common stock price reaches some predetermined target, and in the meantime the bonds or preferred shares pay an interest rate. The arbitrage play typically involves buying the convertible and selling short the common stock at the same time. If the company struggles, any loss in the convertible is offset by the gain in the short position. In times of market volatility, there can be occasions where the stock price falls further than the corresponding convertible price or where the stock price rises less than the price of the bond.

Take, for example, the relative performance of Ford common stock and Ford convertible preferred stock that was issued in January 2002. At the time, an investor could purchase $50 of preferred stock that would also pay 6.5 percent interest per year. Along with the interest payment, each preferred share carried with it the right to be converted into 2.8249 shares of Ford common stock, which was then trading at $14.45. In other words, buying a share of $50 preferred gave the owner an annual income stream of $3.25 and an option to own 2.8249 shares of common stock. In January 2002, it would not have been worth converting the preferred because it would have meant exchanging a $50 asset for another one worth only $40.82 (2.8249 × $14.45).

However, the arbitrage strategy would have called for buying the preferred and shorting the common. Two years later that strategy would have proven quite profitable. By January 2004 the preferred shares were worth $56, and an investor would have earned an additional $6.50 in interest. At the same time, Ford common shares had risen to $15.96 and had earned a total of $0.80 in dividends. An equal $10,000 investment would have meant buying 200 shares of preferred and shorting 692 shares of common. The long gain would have amounted to $2,500 (200 × $6.00 in capital gains and $6.50 in interest) and the short position would have generated a loss of $1,599 (692 × $1.51 in capital loss and $0.80 in dividends paid out). The net gain would have been $901, or 4.5 percent.

Like all of the above alternative investment strategies, convertible arbitrage requires a specialized knowledge base. One of the most successful practitioners is the Calamos organization, which manages the Calamos Market Neutral Fund profiled in Chapter 10 as well as other mutual funds and closed end funds.

Even More

Aside from these strategies, there are a multitude of other, even more complex hedging tactics for instruments other than equities. They are beyond the scope of this book and, frankly, beyond the scope of most individual investors or financial planners on a do-it-yourself basis. For example, there are *fixed income arbitrage* tactics that involve buying and selling bonds that are at different places on the yield curve, or strategies that look for differentials between interest rate swaps and Treasury bonds.

Then there is *currency arbitrage* that takes advantage of small differences in exchange rates. By buying one currency in one market and simultaneously selling it in another, traders can lock in small profits virtually risk-free. Another form is called *index arbitrage* that exploits the occasional difference between the value of a stock index, like the S&P 500, and the futures contract on that same index. Because of trading costs, this can only be a profitable strategy for large institutions using large sums of money and a computerized program trading system. Practically speaking, these techniques cannot be replicated by the individual investor or financial planner.

Where these tactics do come into play is when one is choosing a hedge fund or a fund of hedge funds. Investors will want to have some familiarity with these approaches and what they mean in terms of risk versus reward. In the case of funds composed of hedge funds, the management firm is responsible for selecting participating funds that have a good track record and, more important, ensuring that the funds represent a diversified set of strategies. *Style purity* is a term used to describe how faithful a hedge fund manager is to a particular strategy, and a fund of funds will take steps to see that included funds do not stray too far.

More information about different styles of hedge funds appears in Chapter 12. The specific tactics briefly described here feed into a slightly broader classification system. Unfortunately, there is enough variation among managers and how they operate that it is difficult to say that fund type X is always going to differ in terms of risk from fund type Y. Differences tend to be based more on the manager than anything else.

Summary

There are three less common forms of equity market neutral investing: statistical arbitrage, merger and acquisition arbitrage, and convertible arbitrage. Unlike the more traditional form that buys undervalued and shorts overvalued stocks, these three techniques go beyond conventional valuation models.

Because of the technical requirements for large amounts of capital and/or specialized knowledge, these arbitrage strategies are not well-suited for individual investors or financial planning professionals. However, an understanding of their basic precepts is important when examining the full spectrum of hedge funds—a subject we turn to in the next chapter.

12

OF HISTORY AND HEDGE FUNDS

In 1948 a freelance reporter, doing work for *Fortune* magazine, was offered a very routine assignment: head down to Wall Street and put together a story on the various technical methods of investing currently being used by the pros. "We'll call it 'Fashions in Forecasting,'" the reporter's editor said. Catchy, but it was pretty standard fare, a routine sort of story. Even the reporter's name was routine: Jones. No one could have guessed that this mundane assignment would ultimately lead to revolutionary changes in the investment world.

It wasn't what was written in the article, which appeared in *Fortune* in 1949, that changed the world, but rather the fellow who wrote it. Because after Alfred Winslow Jones interviewed all the experts he could find for his story, he reached a rather presumptuous conclusion. He decided most of the experts didn't know all that much, and he could produce investment returns that were better than what these experts were doing. Moreover, Jones decided he could make a living doing it. It turned out he was right, and to a degree that would have surprised even him.

His conclusion at the time was all the more outrageous because A.W. Jones was a sociologist by training, not a financier. He had earned a Ph.D. from Columbia University, but he wasn't studying under the famous finance professors Graham and Dodd (although he did talk with Graham from time to time). Rather, he was studying human behavior, and he undertook a thesis project that resulted in a book called *Life, Liberty, and Property,* which was about the working class in Akron, Ohio. Jones interviewed 1,700 individuals in 1938 and asked them about their attitudes toward large corporations. Surprisingly, he discovered that most of his subjects maintained a positive attitude toward big companies, despite labor strife and the existing aftereffects of the Great Depression.

The book was well-received, and it led to Jones's first encounter with *Fortune* magazine. He was asked to adapt the book into an article for the magazine and then went on to be hired by *Fortune* as a full-time staff reporter. His "beat" was far-ranging, and he also wrote for *Time* on a variety of topics. Although he left *Fortune* as a full-timer, he was occasionally asked to do a story here and there, and that's what led to his assignment on "Fashions in Forecasting."

Jones would be a worthwhile historical subject in his own right. Prior to earning his Ph.D., he had graduated from Harvard, worked on a steamship, and been vice-consul to Germany while Hitler was gaining popularity. In the late 1930s he took his new wife to Spain and reported on the Spanish Civil war.

After writing his story on market forecasting, Jones formed an investment partnership with several friends; they all pooled their money and came up with $100,000, 40 percent of which was Jones's. That may not seem like a great deal of seed money, but in today's dollars that would be like assembling start-up capital of about $750,000. Clearly, this was more than a lark.

In the early years, Jones experimented with several different investment strategies, but he increasingly began to focus on an idea he had. Because Jones believed that it was quite possible to misjudge the direction of the market, he came up with a plan to deal with that occurrence. In fact, in his earlier interviews with Wall Street brokers, he learned that no one was really able to predict the market's direction. Jones idea was that he would consistently take some portion of his capital and use it to sell stocks short. The amount of exposure he had would vary; often more long than short, but sometimes more short than long. No matter what, he would always have some money "hedged."

This was pioneering stuff in part because most investors of the day took defensive positions by holding cash or bonds. Shorting stocks was not typically done as a matter of managing risk but was instead often viewed with suspicion—perhaps not all that unlike selling short today. As

Jones put it, he was using "speculative techniques for conservative ends." Another element of Jones' strategy was to leverage his portfolio by borrowing against it in order to further magnify his returns.

And those returns were really something. Between 1949 and 1966, when *Fortune* checked in with Jones to see how he was doing, his investment partnership climbed from $100,000 to an astounding $4,900,000. That works out to about a 27 percent per year gain! Over the same time period, the Dow Jones Industrial Average gained an average of about 11 percent per year. That's why the follow-up article that appeared in *Fortune* in April 1966 was called "The Jones Nobody Keeps Up With." Nobody *was* keeping up with him.

Jones is often credited with some other financial innovations, but in fact he merely extended and further popularized some concepts that were already in use. For example, he was not the first to establish his investment fund as a partnership, even though such a structure was not terribly common in the 1950s. Nor was he the first investment manager to pay himself a percentage of the profits. Forty years ago even some mutual funds paid their managers out of the returns they made. But it does seem to be true that Jones was the first to use what is now a fairly standard fee structure: 1 percent of assets under management and 20 percent of the profits.

The 1966 *Fortune* article spurred quite a bit of activity in the nascent hedge fund industry. According to John Van, of Van Hedge Fund Advisors, 140 new funds were started in the years immediately following its publication. However, these new players were not as adept as Jones and did not generate the sort of profits investors were hoping for. They tended to be more aggressively bullish and got caught in a couple of market downturns in 1968 to 1970 and again in 1973 to 1974. The 30 largest funds experienced a drop in assets of 70 percent by the early 1970s. When Tremont Partners (which tracks hedge funds) was formed in 1984, the firm identified a total of only 68 funds.

There was not much discussion about, or media coverage of, hedge funds in the 1980s, even though new ones continued to develop. Despite the fact that many investors in hedge funds were institutions with large constituencies (university endowments or pension funds), the occasional media story that appeared typically focused on hedge funds being for wealthy individuals. The tenor of many such articles stemmed from the limitations on entry into hedge funds, which in turn were based on the use of the partnership structure Jones had put in place.

Limited partnerships are restricted to fewer than 100 investors, according to the Investment Company Act of 1940. If a money manager wants to assemble a hedge fund and can only have a maximum of 99 investors, the manager will surely want to include only those investors who can contribute a significant amount of money. But even if the money manager did not naturally want to limit investors to only the wealthiest, the same 1940 legislation required that investors be accredited. To be accredited, an investor must have an annual income of over $200,000 ($300,000 for a couple) or a net worth of at least $1,000,000. Hence the accurate perception that hedge funds were only for a select few.

Using the limited partnership structure results in a number of trade-offs too. For the hedge fund manager, it means not having to disclose very much about the fund's investments, unlike mutual funds that have to publish their top holdings every quarter. Hedge fund managers tend to be very secretive about their strategies, so this lack of required disclosure is appealing to them. It also means having the latitude to invest in just about any way, shape, or form the manager chooses, so long as the offering memorandum (the document that lays out the fund's operating parameters) is broadly constructed. If investors are informed ahead of time that the fund has broad discretion, then the fund can be completely opportunistic. Another trade-off for limited partnerships is a restriction on advertising. Because there can be none, hedge funds have always relied on word of mouth, referrals, and, increasingly, hedge fund consultants, to attract investment.

The bottom line is that hedge funds are not subject to a great deal of oversight because of their legal status as limited partnerships. In exchange for less supervision, the funds have given up the right to promote themselves and agree to accept money only from individuals who have substantial assets or income.

Evolution

By the early 1990s, there were about 2,000 hedge funds in existence, including a couple that had gained a high-profile reputation. Julian Robertson's Tiger Management and George Soros' Quantum Fund were remarkably successful funds that kept getting bigger and bigger. And a funny thing happened as the assets ballooned: they had to branch out into more than just buying and selling short equities. There were simply too many billions of dollars for the large funds to invest only in stocks. What had previously been a hallmark of hedge funds, being small and nimble, turned into a liability for a few of these behemoths.

Robertson's Tiger Management serves as a perfect example. Julian Robertson was a master stock picker. He was so good at buying and selling stocks that by 1996 his fund was managing $7.2 billion, having grown from $8 million in 1980. With so much money to deploy, his investment policy evolved to the point of taking a minimum long position of $125 million and a minimum short position of $70 million. Smaller positions just were not substantial enough to have an impact on the fund's performance. Obviously such a high threshold ruled out a lot of companies and a lot of good ideas.

But what really changed the landscape for the Tiger Fund and for many other hedge funds was the advent of what was called "macro investing." As the assets in hedge funds began to swell and managers began to look further afield for new investment opportunities, a new style of hedge fund began to evolve. It started with global equities, but it grew to encompass all manner of international markets and instruments.

What came to be called "global macro strategy" was a serendipitous development. The increased use of computers to analyze all sorts of financial data coincided with the need to find new places to invest more and more money. A cottage industry of "quantitative analysis" grew up around hedge funds, and fund managers began to spend as much time traveling overseas as they did at home. If there were not enough investment opportunities at home, then they would broaden their horizons.

As the name implies, *global macro investing* is a top-down strategy that tries to capitalize on big trends in currencies, interest rates, and equities. Practitioners examine government policies, trade deficits, exchange rates, real estate prices, etc., and how they interact with each other across different regions or nations. Sometimes fund managers are able to spot circumstances that seem likely to result in a particular outcome. An oft-cited example is the 1992 prediction by George Soros that the British government would devalue the pound. Soros invested $10 billion of mostly borrowed money in that idea, and when he was proved right, his investors made a 20 percent return. That's when Soros was dubbed "The Man Who Broke the Bank of England."

Another example of global macro investing that carried a high profile was practiced by a fund called Long Term Capital Management (LTCM). Because its 1998 failure continues to color perceptions of hedge funds even today, it is worth reviewing its history. The fund was started by a former Solomon Brother bond genius named John Meriwether in 1994. LTCM had no trouble attracting investors, and having a couple of Nobel laureates on the management team didn't hurt. The first few years of operation were unqualified successes as the fund used its sophisticated models to act, as Myron Scholes put it, "like a giant vacuum cleaner sucking up nickels from all over the world." After an only moderately good year in 1997, the fund returned some capital to investors, and in 1998 the fund was highly leveraged, with about $4.8 billion in capital and $120 billion in assets.

That spring and summer, the fund began to predict that the difference between most Western countries' interest rates and most developing countries' rates would become narrower. The reason for this belief was based on LTCM's mathematical model for identifying mispriced bonds. But what the models didn't seem to account for was what happened when Thailand switched to a free-floating currency. Suddenly there was little of the demand for Thai assets that their government expected. This spurred an Asian currency crisis and then shortly thereafter, the Russian government defaulted on its bonds. When those two unrelated events occurred, there was little interest in owning developing countries' debt, and the interest rate spread moved in exactly the opposite direction from what LTCM had originally anticipated. The interest rates on Western debt dropped, and the rates on less-developed countries' debt soared.

The amount of leverage employed by LTCM played a big role in what happened next. If a fund is trading $120 billion but has only $4.8 billion in hard capital, a fairly small loss can wipe out the fund. Simplifying, it would only take a loss of 4 percent on the $120 billion to bankrupt the fund. The losses incurred by LTCM were astronomical, as high as $550 million on one day, and by September the fund had reached the end of its rope. Although seeking an infusion of capital, nothing materialized. The Federal Reserve, concerned that a failure by LTCM would pose a threat to the U.S. economy, agreed to bail out the fund and take over supervision of the operation. A consortium of banks provided funds, and LTCM began the process of winding down its investments and ultimately closing its doors.

Several facts surrounding this event are quite striking. First, even a casual student of hedge funds would have to ask, "Where was the hedge?" These global macro strategies can be largely unidirectional, with no hedging at all. If one of the primary benefits of hedge funds is to reduce risk and volatility, global macro funds don't seem to live up to that promise. Instead, at least in some cases, the managers make big bets on a macro-economic theme and pursue high rewards with concurrent high risk.

Second, the amount of leverage used was astonishing. Applying leverage (i.e., borrowing money and adding those borrowed funds to the investment) will really juice up gains, but it will also accelerate losses. Again, this is not the sort of approach that one might expect from a hedge fund, if one assumes that hedge funds are designed to produce solid returns in all market environments, as Jones had originally conceived.

Jones did use leverage in his fund, but he kept it limited to about 50 percent. For every $1 of capital, he might borrow 50 cents. Compare that to LTCM, where for every $1 of capital the firm borrowed $250. Clearly, somewhere between Jones in the 1950s and LTCM in 1998, the definition of, and practices by, hedge funds expanded. They went beyond Jones's fairly simple and straightforward proposition that if one cannot predict the direction of the market, then better to position a portfolio so that it can prosper without making that prediction.

A final notable fact about what happened with LTCM was the vast amount of negative media attention that became focused on the fund. All of the news stories and analyses were justifiably critical of what happened. But the fallout from LTCM spilled over to all hedge funds. Investors who heard the term "hedge fund" suddenly had a negative perception, and the industry suffered some damage to its reputation. Whatever the investing public had thought about hedge funds before, if they thought anything at all, it changed for the worse in 1998.

Styles

In order to better understand the full panoply of hedge funds, it is easiest to consider them in broad terms of style, even though individual funds don't necessarily fit into nice neat definitions or may use multiple styles. Some styles carry less risk than the original Jones approach, and some carry more. Although on the scale of things, Jones would probably be considered fairly conservative today. Each style evolved as markets became more global, as data became more accessible, and as computing horsepower became more readily available.

There are several different hedge fund classification schemes. In the fall of 2002, Standard and Poor's (S&P) created a hedge fund index, consisting of 40 different funds from a broad spectrum of types. Even though it is still new, the index has the potential to gain enough momentum and heft to become a widely recognized gauge of hedge fund performance. Because of this, and because it is as good a categorization as any other, the S&P styles are described here.

At the top level, S&P divides hedge funds into three broad categories: Arbitrage, Event-Driven, and Directional/Tactical. Then within each category, S&P further subdivides the funds into narrower specialties with the result being nine distinct strategies (see Figure 12.1).

Arbitrage funds share the common approach of exploiting small differences among securities that are similar to each other. *Event-Driven funds,* as the name suggests, try to take advantage of price changes related to one-time corporate events, like a bankruptcy, merger, or an IPO. *Directional funds* are much more likely to make some prediction about the broad direction of a particular market or instrument and then make investments that will benefit from a movement in that direction. For a little more detail on how some of these approaches work, see Chapter 11.

The problem with this classification, and every other similar sort of breakdown, is that it does not allow us to draw many conclusions about the level of risk present in a particular hedge fund style. Remember that hedge funds are free of much regulatory oversight and typically will give themselves a broad charter to make investments as the manager sees fit. Because of this fairly loose set of parameters, it is difficult to generalize about a particular category of fund style.

FIGURE 12.1 STANDARD AND POOR'S HEDGE FUND CLASSIFICATION

Arbitrage	**Event-Driven**	**Directional/Tactical**
Equity Market Neutral and Statistical Arbitrage	Merger Arbitrage	Long/Short Equity
Fixed Income Arbitrage	Distressed Securities	Managed Futures
Convertible Arbitrage	Special Situations	Macro

Very generally, the Arbitrage funds tend to have the most conservative overall profile because of their tendency to look for smaller, lower-risk opportunities. The LTCM blow-up from 1998 might cause investors to think that Directional/Tactical funds, specifically macro funds, are all taking large and unhedged positions. But not all macro funds "swing for the fences"; some produce regular and moderate returns year after year. Event-Driven funds can range from very aggressive to quite conservative. In keeping with these generalizations, we have already seen from some of the models and portfolio structures built earlier in this book that a market neutral portfolio (Arbitrage) will be less risky and offer less potential return than a long/short portfolio (Directional).

Another reason classifications suffer from a lack of utility is that hedge funds are creatures of their managers more than anything else. Each individual manager has a unique approach that is not typically institutionalized within the fund. Whatever distinctive "magic" the manager has does not belong to the fund itself so much as it belongs to the manager. There are many examples of hedge fund managers leaving and investors leaving with them because, if the manager was successful, the fund probably won't be able to repeat its past performance. Because of this culture, investors are often more interested in the manager than in the fund style.

About the only conclusion we can reach about hedge fund styles is that, by themselves, they don't tell us a whole lot. When S&P constructed the hedge fund index, they understandably wanted a broad cross section of funds represented. From that point of view, it made sense to create categories. But when drilling down to the level of individual funds, the fund's style should not necessarily dictate whether it is an attractive potential investment.

Anyone familiar with mutual funds has probably come across the ubiquitous "style box" that Morningstar so cleverly pioneered some years ago. Fans of the Morningstar style box have used it to take a first cut at what sort of mutual funds might be appropriate given an investor's financial goals and to make sure there is some fund diversification. Any hedge fund classification system is a bit like the style box—useful in a broad sense as a check on diversification but probably not the primary reason to choose a fund. In addition, there is a key difference between mutual fund and hedge fund styles: Mutual funds have fairly strict operational rules governing how they can invest. Hedge funds have comparatively fewer guidelines and may range further and wider than mutual funds in their opportunistic pursuit of positive returns.

Recent History

In the 1990s hedge funds really became a growth industry. Between 1990 and 2002, the number of funds grew almost fourfold (see Figure 12.2).

Several factors contributed to the increase in the number of funds. First, traditional institutional money managers began to leave their firms in order to establish hedge funds. These managers had an entrepreneurial streak that was rewarded with greater control and the opportunity to earn more money if they turned in a strong performance.

Second, even though some funds, such as LTCM, grew to enormous size, many other funds limited the amount of assets they would accept. Thus, instead of the same number of funds just getting larger, the 1990s saw more funds being created. Third, the 1990s saw an unprecedented amount of new wealth created by the bull market. Some of these newly affluent investors sought out hedge funds as a way to preserve their wealth.

As the graph in Figure 12.3 illustrates, investors in hedge funds were rewarded with good returns over those same years. While the S&P

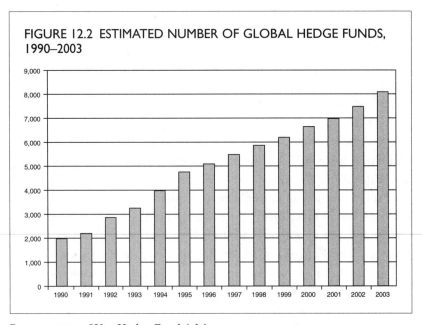

FIGURE 12.2 ESTIMATED NUMBER OF GLOBAL HEDGE FUNDS, 1990–2003

Data courtesy of Van Hedge Fund Advisors

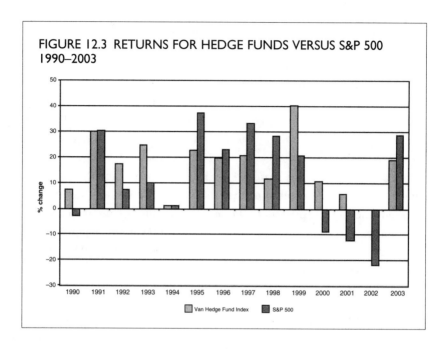

FIGURE 12.3 RETURNS FOR HEDGE FUNDS VERSUS S&P 500
1990–2003

500 achieved higher returns in some years, it is noteworthy that hedge funds as a group did not experience a negative year from 1990 to 2001 and then had a very slight decline in 2002. This once again illustrates a recurrent theme of this book: hedged portfolios have the capability and, indeed, the likelihood of generating positive returns in all market environments.

Looking at those returns in a slightly different way, we can see how an investment in a hedge fund index, such as that constructed by Van Hedge Fund Advisors, would have performed cumulatively from 1990 to 2003, when compared to the S&P 500. Figure 12.4 illustrates this performance remarkably well.

FIGURE 12.4 VAN HEDGE FUND INDEX VERSUS S&P 500
1990–2003

	Van Hedge Fund Index	S&P 500
Growth of $100,000 from 1990 to 2003	$809,386	$428,060

Fees and Rules

Because the results shown in Figure 12.4 reflect returns after management fees, it really is not fair to criticize the fee structure hedge funds typically use. As long as investors are enjoying outsized returns, even after paying all of the fees, no one is likely to complain. However, hedge funds do come with fees and restrictions that may raise eyebrows. At the very least investors need to understand them.

A fairly standard fee structure is the one and twenty arrangement. Hedge fund managers often charge 1 percent of the assets under management and then 20 percent of the profits generated. Thus, if an investor contributed $100,000 to a fund and then the fund gained 15 percent, the tab would amount to $1,000 as a management fee plus a $3,000 performance reward. At the end of the year the investor would have $111,000. It may be a small distinction, but the $3,000 tied to performance is not technically a fee, but rather an allocation of part of the profits.

But fee standards are not universal, by any means. Fund manager James Simons, who heads the Renaissance Technologies Medallion fund, charged a 5 percent management fee and received a 36 percent performance award in 2002. But even after fees, the fund was up a remarkable 26 percent. Apparently Simons is not too worried about price sensitivity because he raised the performance award to 44 percent for 2003, according to *Institutional Investor* magazine. Simons is reported to have earned $287 million for his efforts in 2002.

Aside from giving the hedge fund manager an opportunity to become extremely rich, the performance-based aspect of fees aligns the interests of the manager and the investors. There can be no question of whether the manager is going to give a 110 percent effort to achieving the highest possible return when so much potential income is at stake. Also, managers typically have a substantial amount of their own assets in the fund.

Most funds have a provision called a "high water mark." This is designed to prevent investors from having to keep paying out performance awards when a fund backtracks and then repeats gains from an earlier period. Suppose our hypothetical investor, who started with a $100,000 investment and now has $111,000, sees her fund lose money the next year. She will still pay the management fee but no performance award because there were no profits. Assuming the fund has a gain again the following year, the investor will not have to pay a performance award until her assets exceed the high water mark of $111,000.

The other side of the high water mark provision is that it can work against investors if a fund has a less than stellar couple of years. That's because if a fund gets too far underwater, with little prospect of the manager regaining the lost ground soon, the manager can close the fund's operations, return capital to the investors, and start a new fund.

Another provision sometimes found in the hedge fund partnership agreement is a "hurdle rate." Having it is advantageous to the investor because the *hurdle rate* states that before a performance fee becomes due, the fund manager must have attained some minimum benchmark return, usually between 0.5 percent and 5 percent. That means the investor only pays for performance that is superior. Interestingly, research conducted by Assistant Professor Bing Liang at Case Western Reserve found that hurdle rates were much less common than high water mark policies and did not appear to create as much of a positive incentive. In a paper published in the *Financial Analysts Journal* in May 2000, Professor Liang found a better correlation between exceptional returns and high water marks than he did between exceptional returns and hurdle rates.

A key question for hedge fund investors is how long money invested in the fund must remain committed to the fund. Hedge funds will certainly have some requirements, and they may vary from as little as one year to as long as three years. What's more, a notification period is required as well. Hedge fund managers require this because they do not want to be forced to liquidate positions suddenly in order to meet redemptions. You can bet that if mutual funds had evolved differently, they too would have lock-up periods rather than daily redemptions.

Finally, investors should be sure to find out the amount of leverage being used by a manager. Using leverage is fine, but the amount of leverage can provide some insight into how big the manager's bets tend to be. Most funds use some leverage but perhaps as many as one quarter do not. According to MAR/Hedge, an industry tracking group, of the funds that use leverage the majority do so at a less than 2:1 ratio. Recall that LTCM was leveraged at 25:1.

Some Not-So-Attractive Aspects of Hedge Funds

If the performance of hedge funds is what drives investors to their doors, there are a couple of not-so-attractive characteristics of hedge funds too. For example, because of the fee structure, managers have an inherent desire to gather more and more assets. Earning management fees and a percentage of profits on a bigger base is a powerful incentive for a hedge fund to get bigger. However, as funds get bigger, they sometimes lose the abilities that made them great, like moving quickly into and out of positions.

A 2001 research report by Undiscovered Managers, LLC, points out that increased size will have a more or less negative impact depending on the fund's strategy. They cite fixed income arbitrage and global macro as types of funds that can handle a large asset base. On the other hand, the researchers suggest that a distressed securities hedge fund will suffer from too many assets because the market is less liquid. Another size-related conundrum is that the most successful hedge funds with established track records are often closed to new money. That forces new investors to seek out new managers that have less experience.

What about dishonesty among hedge funds? The SEC has made noises recently that the incidence of fraud among hedge funds is on the rise. According to a 2003 Reuter's release, "SEC officials note a sharp rise in hedge fund fraud cases, saying the commission brought twelve cases in 2002, up from seven in 2001, six in 2000, and two in 1999." But others suggest that fraud among hedge funds is a relatively minor occurrence. Tanya Beder, Managing Director of Caxton Associates, said in an interview in *Financial Engineering News* that "if you actually look at the fraud rate, it's quite tiny relative to other types of financial institutions. It's significantly less than 1 percent."

As with any investment, caveat emptor applies. There have been, and will be, crooks in the hedge fund industry. For the truly cautious, HedgeWorld (http://www.hedgeworld.com) offers a service performing background checks on managers for about $1,000. We note that it does not appear that hedge funds are any more likely to engage in inappropriate practices than mutual funds, which have been charged with allowing some customers to engage in advantageous trades and levying incorrect fees.

How Much to Hedge?

It is easy for most investors to look at the above historical returns and see that hedge funds have performed very well. What is not so obvious is the way hedge funds have performed in terms of variability and expected returns, both independently and as part of a bigger asset allocation plan.

In the first place, the standard deviation, or volatility of hedge funds tends to be somewhere in between bonds and equities. While standard deviation is not the same as "risk," at least not as we defined it in Chapter 2, it does give us a statistical measure of how much variation we might expect to see in future returns: the more variation, the higher the standard deviation. It is a useful construct, particularly when it is applied to groups of stocks, rather than individual stocks. Modern portfolio theory (MPT) states that investors are best served if they get the maximum amount of expected return with the least amount of variability.

Even though hedge funds have a lower level of variability than an investment in a broad group of stocks, on average, they have had historically better returns. That combination is quite attractive. Relative to bonds, standard deviation among hedge funds is higher, but again, returns have been higher. That hedge funds are in this sort of "sweet spot" between bonds and equities makes them an excellent investment all by themselves. As the diagram in Figure 12.5 illustrates, hedge funds, as represented by the Van Hedge Fund Index, have a high historical return and a moderate historical standard deviation.

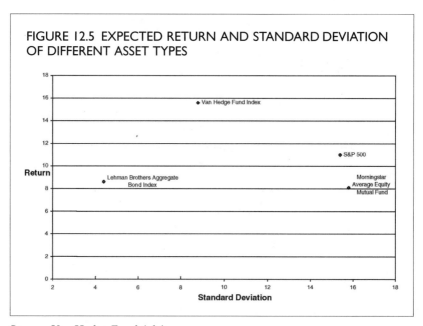

FIGURE 12.5 EXPECTED RETURN AND STANDARD DEVIATION OF DIFFERENT ASSET TYPES

Source: Van Hedge Fund Advisors

But as attractive as they may be by themselves, hedge funds in combination with other types of investments may be even better. The creator of MPT, Markowitz, theorized that groups of different types of investments could be combined in such a way that they were synergistic. That is, having a mix of bonds and equities, for example, was better than having either one separately.

Markowitz's idea was that by combining different asset classes, an investor could end up with a portfolio that was the most efficient in terms of the variability/return trade-off. He called this idealized mix the "efficient frontier." In an article that appeared in *Benefits Canada* in April 2002, Robert Parnell, of Tremont Investment Management, discussed the role that hedge funds can play in creating such an efficient portfolio. He concluded that an optimal division between bonds, stocks, and hedge funds would range from 50 percent bonds/25 percent stocks/25 percent hedge funds to 11 percent bonds/56 percent stocks/33 percent hedge funds. Moreover, Parnell suggests that including hedge funds in the mix creates a more efficient portfolio than just bonds and stocks together. The graph in Figure 12.6 illustrates the combinations that would lie along the efficient frontier.

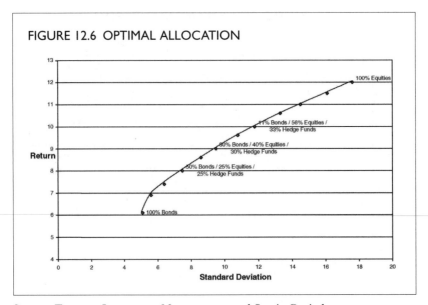

FIGURE 12.6 OPTIMAL ALLOCATION

Source: Tremont Investment Management and Scotia Capital

The assumptions about return and standard deviation that Parnell used in his work were very conservative, much more so than those in the earlier example using data from Van Hedge Fund Advisors. Even with reduced assumptions, his research suggested that having some hedge fund component was advantageous to investors.

Making Hedge Funds More Accessible

With the strong results demonstrated by hedge funds over the past decade, it should come as no surprise that there is an increasing amount of interest in them. The funds themselves have been working on ways to become more accessible to more investors. Aside from the proliferation of hedge funds and styles of hedge funds, the biggest development to impact the industry has been the advent of the fund of hedge funds (FOHF).

This innovation is analogous to mutual funds. Where mutual funds were developed to allow for diversification away from owning individual stocks, FOHFs were created so that investors could diversify their hedge fund holdings. The idea is for a professional money manager, with expertise in hedge funds, to pool money from a large number of individual investors and then place it in an assembled basket of different hedge funds. Like many aspects of the hedge fund business, A.W. Jones is credited with the idea. According to *Canadian Hedge Watch*, an industry newsletter, Jones changed his partnership agreement in 1984 so that his investors could participate in multiple funds.

FOHFs are still subject to the suitability requirements imposed by SEC; investors must still be accredited and meet the threshold for either high net worth or high income. The way FOHFs change the landscape is that they reduce the minimum investment and spread the investment across a range of different funds, making hedge funds a viable alternative for more people.

An unintended consequence of the current rules and the high minimum investment requirements for individual hedge funds is that they may put qualified investors more at risk than they should be. Moderately wealthy individuals who are qualified might still find themselves having to place an inordinately high percentage of assets into a hedge fund in order to meet the fund's minimum investment threshold. For example, someone with a net worth of $1.5 million is qualified, but what if half of that net worth is in the value of their home? Should that investor invest in a single hedge fund that requires a minimum initial investment of $250,000? Such an amount would represent one-third of "investable" assets, and it would not be prudent to place such a high percentage under a single manager. FOHFs help resolve this by requiring a lower minimum, more on the order of $25,000 to $100,000, as well as offering diversification.

The diversification element is very important, according to Rick Lake, of Lake Partners in Greenwich, Connecticut. His firm specializes in assembling funds for individuals and chooses multiple hedge fund managers who "represent different but complementary investment styles." Lake specializes not only in putting together groups of hedge funds, but he also puts together groups of mutual funds that use a market neutral or hedged approach.

Just as there is an optimal mix of different assets in a portfolio, Lake says that there is an optimal mix of different funds. The variability/return trade-off among different funds and managers can work in such a way that the composite results are better than any single fund. By blending managers that have a historically higher return and higher standard deviation with managers that have been lower on those same scales, investors can obtain a higher return and lower variability. That is one of the key added values of an FOHF. (See Figure 12.7.)

Another contribution FOHF managers make is conducting due diligence. For investors to take on this responsibility themselves is asking a lot, in part because there are so many funds and also because the information flow is poor. It would be like trying to pick a mutual fund without any of the analytic resources we now take for granted, such as Morningstar or Lipper. It would be even worse, because at least mutual fund prices are transparent, while hedge fund values are not. An FOHF manager has a store of knowledge and data that works to the investor's advantage. There is also a convenience factor. Investors in an FOHF receive a single statement that summarizes their returns and tax information no matter how many different hedge funds they are in.

What FOHF managers receive in return are, of course, fees. In addition to whatever costs are associated with the hedge funds themselves, FOHFs add another layer of fees, often a management fee of 1 percent and another performance-based charge that may equal another 10 percent of profits. All together, that can make FOHFs an expensive place to

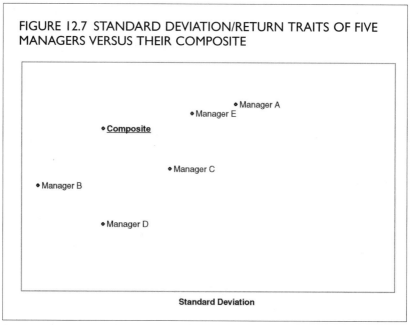

FIGURE 12.7 STANDARD DEVIATION/RETURN TRAITS OF FIVE
MANAGERS VERSUS THEIR COMPOSITE

Source: LakeVest Partners

put one's money. But for many investors who really want to take advantage of hedge funds, FOHFs may be the most realistic choice.

Imagine the following simple example: an investor puts $100,000 in an FOHF. Over the next year, the value of the investment grows by 30 percent, an outstanding return by any measure. At the end of the year, the gross total is $130,000. First, the hedge funds themselves take a management fee of 1 percent plus 20 percent of the profit, amounting to $1,000 plus $6,000 (20% × $30,000). Then the FOHF manager takes a 1 percent management fee plus 10 percent of the profit. That equals $1,000 plus $3,000 (10% × $30,000). All told the investor ends the year with $119,000. That is still $19,000 more than he had to begin with and a net 19 percent return, but the fees *are* high.

In choosing an FOHF manager, investors would be advised to inquire about whether the firm has been through an audit and ask to see the results. Just like hedge funds themselves, FOHFs will typically have an accounting firm audit their results, and investors will want to make sure the auditor's opinion is unqualified. More obviously, investors should be interested in the track record of the FOHF: what results have been achieved and over what period of time. Finally, what steps does the FOHF go through in performing due diligence on the hedge funds.

Summary

Hedge funds have changed considerably since the first one was formed in 1949. They no longer utilize just equities, and for that matter they no longer necessarily hedge. Increasingly sophisticated modeling has led fund managers into areas that A. W. Jones would not recognize today.

Because of their high returns, hedge funds have gotten away with establishing some fairly high fees and restrictive rules. Often, the more successful the fund, the higher the fees and more rigid the rules. The number of funds has blossomed in the past ten years until now there are over 8,000.

Funds of hedge funds have become a popular vehicle for many erstwhile direct hedge fund investors. They reduce the minimum investment required while adding diversity and impartial advice on what funds are best. They also add another layer of fees, but they remain the only practical entrée into hedge funds for many people.

13

CLOSING THOUGHTS

Individual investors and financial planners must give some consideration to an equity market neutral strategy. There are simply too many benefits to ignore. No one would advocate placing all equity assets into this type of a portfolio, but a market neutral approach has earned a seat at the investment table for many investors.

Most professionals agree that total financial assets should be allocated based on individual circumstances. Age, income, tax impact, level of risk tolerance, and lifestyle requirements are all part of the equation that should determine how much money should be in fixed income and how much in equities. Furthermore, those same factors help guide decisions about how much of the equity piece should be in overseas investments, dividend-paying stocks, growth stocks, etc.

Because it is such an individualized decision, no generic formula can effectively allocate funds across different asset classes. Often, older and/or more risk-averse individuals will tend to need a higher percentage of assets in fixed income securities, but there are many exceptions to that generality. At the extreme, a very risk-averse investor with a short time horizon might have 80 percent of assets in short-term bonds and 20 percent in long-term bonds.

At the other end of the spectrum are investors who are very risk tolerant and/or have a long time horizon. A typical allocation for this type of investor might be 80 percent equities and 20 percent bonds, with perhaps some real estate thrown into the mix. Of the 80 percent in equities, as much as one-fourth could be in international stocks with the rest typically divided between small-cap and large-cap domestic stocks.

How would a market neutral investment fit into any of these allocation schemes? As some of the data in Chapter 12 illustrated, hedge funds lie somewhere in between equities and fixed income but with historically higher returns. And because a good market neutral investment will not correlate closely with other equity investments or with bonds, it becomes an attractive component of a broader asset allocation mix. Because the whole idea of asset allocation is to diversify financial resources into types of investments that won't all rise or fall in value at the same time, a market neutral portfolio has a place in the blend.

Indeed, advocates of hedged portfolios usually point to this noncorrelation as a key reason to have a market neutral investment. Unfortunately, in yet another sign of its lack of popular acceptance, the allocation models commonly used by financial planners do not incorporate or address a market neutral asset class. Some financial planners have enough familiarity with market neutral investing to recommend it to clients, but most do not. Suffice it to say that placing some portion of assets into a market neutral style investment is appropriate for many investors.

What Form to Use?

Many forms of market neutral or long/short equity investing exist, and this book has spent a great deal of time on developing a do-it-yourself approach for carefully selecting undervalued and overvalued stocks on an individual basis. However, that will not be the best approach for every investor. Following is a series of questions an investor must answer in order to decide what might work best for his or her situation.

1. Should I Hire Someone to Do It for Me or Should I Do It Myself?

If an investor is accredited—that is, has an income of $200,000 per year ($300,000 for couples) and a net worth of at least $1,000,000—

there are thousands of hedge funds available. For financial planners, a client is considered "qualified" if he or she has a net worth of $1,500,000 or has assets under the planner's management of at least $750,000. A couple of resources for such accredited or qualified investors are: The Hennessee Group (http://www.hennesseegroup.com); Van Hedge Fund Advisors (http://www.hedgefund.com); or HedgeWorld (http://www.hedgeworld.com). These resources can assist in the process of choosing a hedge fund or a more diversified fund of hedge funds.

Or, as outlined in Chapter 10, there are a number of mutual funds that offer some form of a hedged portfolio, whether it is truly market neutral, long/short, or uses another variation. Morningstar (http://www.morningstar.com) is undoubtedly the definitive source of information on mutual funds for most investors.

Ultimately, the decision to pay someone else or not is largely a function of how much time and expertise an investor, or a financial planner, can bring to bear on developing their own portfolio. As should be fairly clear, the process can be time-intensive and requires a moderate amount of familiarity with the equity market.

2. If I Do It Myself, Which Structure Should I Implement?

Several structures of equity hedging can be effective. The first step is to conclude whether the best structure is market neutral, long/short, or hybrid. Recall the table that appeared at the end of Chapter 6 (see Figure 13.1).

FIGURE 13.1 RISK CHARACTERISTICS OF FOUR PORTFOLIO STRATEGIES

Portfolio Strategy	Market Risk	Industry Risk	Potential Returns
Market Neutral—Mechanical	Lower	Higher	Lower
Long/Short	Higher	Higher	Higher
Hybrid	Lower	Higher	Higher
Market Neutral—Handpicked	Lower	Lower	Lower

The more risk-tolerant investor may prefer a long/short approach, while the more conservative individual, a market neutral approach. It is worth noting that of the portfolios developed and tested in this book, the hybrid approach generally, albeit sometimes moderately, outperformed the others.

Another variation of the hybrid structure can be created by buying undervalued stocks and shares in an inverse index fund (see Chapter 8) at the same time. This "shortcut" version can be an effective way to hedge market risk but does not address industry risk at all. Because of this limitation, it is particularly important that the individual stocks on the long side are broadly diversified and do not represent a heavy concentration in one industry. For that matter, the stocks really ought to have very little correlation with each other; they should not all be in technology or heavy industry or energy, etc.

3. Aside from Portfolio Structure, If I Do It Myself, How Do I Select Potentially Undervalued and Overvalued Stocks?

In the models developed for this book, very different criteria were shown to work in the past. Of course, past performance doesn't say anything about what will happen in the future. The key point is that many different ideas will bear fruit, and the ideas don't have to be complicated. Some of the greatest opportunities may lie in the most tried and true axioms of investing. Valuation ideas first put forth by Graham and Dodd, for example, might be perfectly suited for a market neutral strategy. Adding short positions in stocks that Graham and Dodd would have considered classically overvalued adds a twist that reduces market risk. Alternatively, simple and commonly accepted technical indicators, such as moving averages, may lend themselves to identifying long and short candidates. What is most important is that investors developing their own methodology spend time testing ideas they come up with before committing real money to a portfolio.

In what is really a paradox, the stock selection method is the most important element of the strategy but in another sense the least important part of understanding market neutral investing. On the one hand, selecting undervalued and overvalued stocks correctly is paramount and will drive portfolio performance. On the other hand, the lesson of market neutral investing is that it should outperform any existing "long-only" stock selection system *on a risk-adjusted basis.*

The Best Little Investment Strategy
No One's Ever Heard Of

Market neutral investing is surrounded by some element of mystery and a certain level of ignorance. It is an extremely well-established investment strategy, having been used successfully for over 40 years. And yet, most individual investors and many financial professionals have never heard of it. Or, if they have heard of it, their understanding is hazy.

There are a number of what can be called "great ideas" in finance. Asset allocation, the efficient market hypothesis, Graham and Dodd's theories about valuing a company, diversification, various forms of technical analysis—these are all great ideas that have been generally accepted and are thought to have considerable merit. In contrast, market neutral investing is another great idea that has been accepted by a few, but not by the vast majority of individual investors or even by many personal finance experts.

Where market neutral investing *has* been well-received and implemented is among financial academics and, significantly, among a group of professionals managing funds for the wealthiest individuals in the world as well as for numerous endowments, trusts, and pension funds. The investment vehicle of choice for these groups is becoming the hedge fund, where the managers understand market neutral investing and put it to use. It is striking that some of the most affluent and sophisticated investors, through their use of hedge funds, employ a market neutral strategy, while millions of others are completely unaware that it exists.

The obvious question has to be "why?" and there is no clear answer. Do most investors, who are stock buyers, just not realize that they can also make money from selling short; i.e., betting *against* a particular stock or market? If so, that seems destined to change, as the level of financial sophistication among all investors increases each year. Or, perhaps the negative connotation surrounding short selling has acted as a drag.

Because market neutral investing requires some form of short sale, its lack of common acceptance may be due to the unpopularity of that strategy. For one thing, short sales have often been presented as risky, ergo, market neutral investing could be viewed as risky. As this book has tried to demonstrate, nothing could be further from the truth. Selling stocks short, as part of a broad and comprehensive portfolio strategy, actually reduces risk.

In addition, short-selling has traditionally been considered an almost disreputable practice because it creates profit from someone else's loss. Although it is an emotional reaction, short-sellers are often blamed for driving down markets. In fact, short-sellers help create liquidity in the market and, according to an article in *The Economist,* March 1, 2003, entitled "Don't Shoot the Messenger," "help to put a brake on irrational exuberance."

Another possible reason is the negative perception surrounding hedge funds, the most common practitioners of market neutral investing. Ever since the failure of Long Term Capital Management in 1998, hedge funds have been the investment vehicle most of the media love to wring their hands over. Even though hedge funds have generally been very successful, the investing public has heard much more about the occasional failure. If hedge funds carry a negative perception, then it may have spilled over to the market neutral style of investing.

A timing issue may also be at work. Throughout much of the 1990s, not many investors were interested in hearing about how they could hedge against market risk. The markets were going up. Who needed to hedge? In the last several years, as the markets have ceased to regularly rise, the idea of hedging has become more popular and will probably continue in that vein. In a way, this book is part of that movement.

Finally, there have been few champions for market neutral investing. Hedge funds are prohibited from advertising themselves to the general investment public. Only a handful of mutual funds use the strategy, not enough to gain much attention. Academics naturally tend to have a small audience. So no one has much incentive or a broad platform from which to discuss its merits.

The irony is that market neutral investing can be used by investors of all stripes, not just the wealthiest. Whether it is through a mutual fund or through a self-designed portfolio of undervalued and overvalued stocks, this investment style can offer a lower risk profile that is appropriate for many people. Indeed, as was pointed out in Chapter 1, it can be persuasively argued that market neutral investing is one of only two sensible ways to put money to work in the market. Either passive index-ing or market neutral investing seem to be the only truly logical choices.

How the Small Investor Got Left Behind

A number of observers have pointed out the irony of the current sit-uation. The smaller investor must either create his own market neutral portfolio, choose one of a few mutual funds, or be left behind. A proven and successful investment approach has been restricted, at least when it is practiced by hedge funds, to only the wealthiest individuals. Everyday investors who are worth less than $1,000,000 are prohibited by the gov-ernment from participating in an investment form that generally has *less risk* than many mainstream mutual funds.

How can that be? In a country that prides itself on free-market solu-tions, the U.S. regulatory authorities have stepped in to restrict most in-vestors from utilizing hedge funds. The roots of this situation stem from the fact that hedge funds are largely, although not completely, unregu-lated. The authorities, primarily the SEC, have been concerned that in-vestors participating in these unregulated investment pools need to be a pretty sophisticated lot in order to understand what they are buying into. But some of the laws governing hedge funds date back to the days before there *were* hedge funds. Rick Lake at Lake Investments believes that "regulations have not kept up with developments."

As for the suitability requirement, John Van, of Van Hedge Fund Ad-visors and an expert on the subject, explains it like this: "The SEC had to come up with some way of measuring investor sophistication. The best way they could think of was using an income or net worth test." In part, it served as a proxy for investment knowledge, but it also meant that those investors could better afford to sustain a loss. The goal of the agency is certainly an admirable one—to protect the small fry from get-ting in over their heads. But small investors could enjoy some protection from using a professional advisor, such as Van or Lake, who offer funds of hedge funds.

The other irony here is that the potential damage to an investor from investing in hedge funds is really no greater than it is with mutual funds or buying and selling individual stocks. Is it reasonable to allow small retail investors to put money into a mutual fund that goes on to *lose almost 50 percent of its value every year for three years in a row!,* as happened with the Munder NetNet fund from 2000 to 2002, and then prohibit those same investors from investing in hedge funds? Or would anyone argue that trading futures contracts, which is an investment vehicle open to most anyone, carries less inherent risk than owning a hedge fund? The bottom line is that there is the potential for loss with every investment, and investors must be smart about how they make decisions. Hedge funds, as a category, match up favorably on the basis of risk and return. As a point of comparison, Figure 13.2 shows the returns and standard deviation (a commonly used measure of volatility) for some key benchmarks over the past 15 years.

The SEC is reexamining its position on hedge funds in general, and it held public discussions on the subject in 2003. Regulators are focused on two related issues: (1) what they call the increasing "retail-ization" of hedge funds and (2) refining investor protections. Part of the reason for this is that the SEC is seeing how funds of hedge funds are finding their way into the marketplace and appealing to smaller, retail investors with much smaller minimum investments. If that trend continues, then the SEC believes a greater need exists for transparency and disclosure on the part of hedge funds.

In May 2003, SEC Chairman William Donaldson hinted that the commission might take steps to make hedge funds more open to small investors. And some in Congress have begun to ask questions. "Is this only a wealthy person's game?" asks Representative David Scott, a Democrat

FIGURE 13.2 RETURN AND STANDARD DEVIATIONS 1998–2003

Benchmark	Net Compound Annual Return January 1998–March 2003	Standard Deviation
Van Global Hedge Fund Index	15.6%	8.8%
S&P 500	11.0	15.4
Morningstar Average Equity Mutual Fund	8.1	15.8
Lehman Brothers Bond Index	8.6	4.4

Source: Van Hedge Fund Advisors

from Georgia. "Is there room for other players at various levels of the economic spectrum?"

One thing is certain. The state of regulation surrounding hedge funds is in flux. It remains to be seen what changes the SEC will recommend for the hedge fund industry, but changes do appear likely. The ideal solution would be some combination of increased transparency and disclosure along with greater opportunity for more investors to participate. Hedge funds, as a class of investment, have proven themselves to be successful in generating positive returns with less risk. The time has come to give *all* investors, not just a select few, a full range of investment options.

It's not that all investors should be invested in hedge funds; it's that all investors should have *the choice* to be invested in hedge funds.

As a group, hedge funds do have their problems. Some of them go out of business and take their investors' money with them. (The data provided by Van in Figure 13.2 may suffer from the same type of survivorship bias described in Chapter 10. It does not take into account hedge funds that have ceased reporting.) Hedge funds maintain a high fee structure. They are not very liquid investments because of restrictions on how often and when money can be withdrawn from accounts. But, with all that said, it is difficult to argue that hedge funds are more dangerous than other more commonly used investment vehicles.

And for those who don't choose to use a hedge fund vehicle, developing a market neutral strategy of one's own can be a powerful tool in building a portfolio. It's not as though putting some portion of assets into a do-it-yourself market neutral portfolio will suddenly make everyone's financial future brighter. It is not a panacea nor is it without risks. But successful investing is largely about improving the odds, and investors should look for every advantage they can.

Perhaps this book will have helped at least a few people overcome some trepidation. No doubt it is a slow process. A.W. Jones ran into some of the same skepticism over 50 years ago. He helped make the investment world a safer place, but, so far, only for a minority.

Summary

A number of good reasons exist to eschew market neutral or other forms of hedged investments. If an investor doesn't understand the concept and doesn't care to, that's a good reason to stay away. If an investor has very little in the way of investment capital, that's another good reason. If an investor wants guaranteed income with almost no risk, that's another good reason.

What is not a good reason for avoiding market neutral investing is being intimidated by, or afraid of, the idea. Writers in the financial press should be fined a nickel every time an article appears that points up the negatives surrounding hedging and hedge funds to the exclusion of the positives. We could use the resulting fund to educate investors and financial planners on both the pros and cons. There *are* pros and cons, but too often all we hear about are the cons.

TOOLS

For investors who wish to research and develop their own methodology for finding undervalued and overvalued stocks, they need look no further than the Internet. More investment information is available now than ever before, much of it for free. The single most important tool for most investors is a screening mechanism, and we will briefly review two different free screeners here, as well as some investment software available for purchase.

One popular screener, called "Deluxe Screener," is found at Microsoft's MoneyCentral site. In terms of ease of use, this product is the best because of its intuitive layout and pleasant graphic interface. It can be found at http://moneycentral.msn.com/investor/finder/customstocks .asp and from there the deluxe version can be downloaded at no charge.

As for content, it has some pluses and minuses. On the plus side, MoneyCentral incorporates some first-class research from an outfit called Camelback. Founded by finance professors, but with a very practical orientation, Camelback rates thousands of stocks on a numerical scale of 1 through 10. The lower the ratings, the more pessimistic Camelback is about the stock's prospects. MoneyCentral's screener allows users to search using this ranking as a criterion.

The Camelback rankings appear to be extensively back-tested. One of the contributors to MoneyCentral actually developed an experimental market neutral portfolio, using the highest and lowest ranked stocks in equal proportion. It performed very well.

Another plus is the system MoneyCentral uses to classify different industries. The classification scheme is provided by Media General and is much more narrowly defined than some other systems. This "granularity" is helpful when determining relative valuations. For example, Money-Central's fundamental database lists five different types of semiconductor company classifications: Broad Line, Memory Chips, Specialized, Integrated Circuits, and Equipment & Materials. Other databases will have only a single category of "Semiconductors."

If an investor wants a really accurate read on whether a particular semiconductor firm is priced too high or too low, it is better to compare it to other firms very much like it. There is no sense in comparing a semiconductor *equipment* company's ratios with the whole universe of semiconductor companies when it is possible to compare it to just other *equipment* firms.

Another minor but useful feature on MoneyCentral's screener is the "Display Only" option. This allows the user to select a criterion, say price-to-book ratios, but to tell the screener to display only those ratios, not to actually screen out companies based on them. Accordingly, when the results are generated, the price-to-book ratio will be shown, making for easy comparisons.

There are only a couple of minuses. One is the earnings forecast data, which is provided by a third party, Zacks Investment Research. Zacks earnings data, as it is found on MoneyCentral's site, is adequate but not as comprehensive as the data compiled by Thompson/First Call or Reuters on other sites.

Earnings estimates are compiled by surveying a number of research analysts and then summarizing their views about how much a company is going to earn. In a random sample of stocks on MoneyCentral, the Zacks data included surveys of fewer analysts in 80 percent of the cases. In the other 20 percent, the Zacks data had surveys from the same number of analysts. Thompson/First Call and Reuters were almost exactly equal in survey breadth. A smaller survey of analysts can, in turn, impact the consensus earnings estimate. The average number of analysts surveyed for a random selection of companies is listed below:

- Thompson/First Call—13
- Reuters—12.9
- MoneyCentral (Zacks)—10.7

More important is the difference this can create in the consensus estimates. Using the same sample, Thompson/First Call and Reuters/Multex had an exact match, to the penny, on current year earnings estimates 100 percent of the time. MoneyCentral, on the other hand, had a lower consensus estimate 80 percent of the time. Because earnings estimates can play a material role in calculating valuation, estimates that stray far from the rest of the market's expectations are to be avoided.

A very minor drawback with MoneyCentral is that the screener does not allow users to exclude a few characteristics. For example, when seeking companies that fit a particular profile, it is not possible to eliminate from consideration particular industry groups. Or, if we wanted to look only at stocks that are not part of the S&P 500 index, we cannot do that. Again, this is a fairly minor inconvenience that MoneyCentral might choose to improve in the future.

Yahoo! also offers two levels of screening tools, a simple one that is HTML-based and a more complex version using Java. Because the latter version was in beta mode when we examined it, there is little value in reviewing it here.

Another popular screening tool is one from Reuters, which can be reached through a redirect from Yahoo! A screening application called "Power Screener" can be found at http://yahoo.investor.reuters.com/StockEntry.aspx?target=/stocks. This service too is free and gives investors a great deal of flexibility in uncovering stocks that are undervalued and overvalued.

In terms of the data itself, one advantage Reuters offers over MoneyCentral is the earnings estimate figures because Reuters uses such comprehensive survey data. Also, the service provides a much more thorough description of a company's operations. The "Full Description" found under Company Profile is very in-depth, often listing specific operating units and competitors.

The Reuters screening interface is a bit clunky to use, and it has fewer fundamental criteria to select from. The industry classifications are also much less narrowly defined than on MoneyCentral. Despite these relatively minor flaws, Reuters has a very good product, and the company has a reputation for high-quality, clean data at the institutional level.

As a sort of simple test, we tried to reconstruct the models from Chapter 3 using the MoneyCentral and Reuters screeners. With MoneyCentral, we were able to find stocks that had the following characteristics:

- Priced below (for undervalued) or above (for overvalued) the average industry PS ratio
- Priced below (for undervalued) or above (for overvalued) the average industry PE ratio
- Carried a forward PE below (for undervalued) or above (for overvalued) the 2002 estimated earnings growth rate
- Had a relative strength index rating of greater than 50 (for undervalued) or less than 50 (for overvalued

What could not be done with the MoneyCentral screener was find stocks that had revenue growth higher than their industry average. There is no "industry average revenue growth" data available. But, except for this item, the screen was able to generate long and short candidates quite handily.

Reuters fared poorly on this particular test because it offered no industry average data. With Reuters we could only find stocks that carried a forward PE below (for undervalued) or above (for overvalued) the long-term estimated earnings growth rate.

Finally, there is another piece of fundamental data that is often helpful to investors but difficult to find. While earnings estimates are commonly found on many sites, revenue estimates are not. MoneyCentral does not carry them, nor does Reuters. However, a place on Yahoo! has both earnings and revenue estimates, provided by Thompson/First Call. From the basic quote page, a link, often labeled "Analyst Estimates," takes users to the Thompson/First Call data on earnings and revenues.

Beyond Free

If there is a shortcoming with these free screeners, it is one that probably is insurmountable for any Web browser-based tool. The fundamental data is not stored over time, and results cannot be back-tested. This flaw can probably be best illustrated with an example.

Suppose an investor has a brilliant idea regarding stock valuation. It occurs to him that undervalued stocks will tend to trade at less than one-half book value, and overvalued stocks will tend to trade at more than five times book value. With either of the screening tools just mentioned, he can go to the respective site and quickly identify all of the stocks trading at those particular price-to-book values. However, he cannot then back-test his idea to see how stocks with those characteristics have performed in the past! He can only watch those stocks and see how they perform in the future. It could take quite a long time to determine whether his idea has merit.

This example points out the difficulty in using any of the free browser-based screening tools. They are terrific at helping investors find particular stocks, but they do not lend themselves to back-testing. In order to have that capability, one needs to be able to store fundamental data and then subsequently return to it. That way, if an investor has a potentially good idea, he can go back two years (or longer), identify which stocks were then trading at one-half and five times book value, and see what happened to their prices. Having this capability almost certainly requires the purchase of some financial software. There are probably dozens of candidates, but we focus on one here that may offer the most bang for the buck.

The American Association of Individual Investors (AAII) offers a software product that is quite powerful and very reasonably priced. As part of the purchase price, which is currently $250, AAII provides weekly data updates. The advantage of this sort of arrangement is that, over time, the user develops a comprehensive database of stock fundamentals.

With this in place, an investor who comes up with a new idea that she wants to test can simply determine what stocks previously fit the criteria and then track what happened to those stocks' prices in the following months. Of course, the depth of the database develops over time. Historic fundamental data is available for purchase from AAII for those investors who want to immediately have access rather than develop it over months and years.

The most time-consuming element of this process is simply tracking the later price movement of stocks. Historic stock price data is also available from many sources, including Yahoo!, which makes it available at no charge. But back-testing by checking to see what subsequently happens to a stock's price remains a largely manual and tedious process.

The AAII software is very comprehensive. Indeed, it has an almost overwhelming assortment of fundamental data to work with. What's more, investors can create their own custom data elements by manipulating the existing numbers. For example, the AAII software calculates and displays PEG ratios (price-to-earnings ratio/earnings growth) using the five-year estimated earnings growth rate. If a user wants to instead calculate a shorter-term PEG ratio using next year's earnings growth, the software can easily accommodate that wish. This ability to create custom data points means that there are really an infinite number of indicators users can analyze.

Other Handy Resources

In Chapter 11, on alternative forms of hedging, reference was made to statistical arbitrage, which is a technique that looks for variances between two stocks' normal price relationship. Two sites that offer assistance, on a subscription basis, are ValuEngine and Pairs Trading.

ValuEngine (http://www.valuengine.com) really focuses on quantitative analysis of stocks. The statistical arbitrage element is almost incidental. Nevertheless, within the paid area of the site, the detailed analysis includes "Stocks That Move Like This." It is a simple list of stocks that have a strong price movement correlation with whatever symbol the user has input. However, it is only a starting point, where an investor can get some ideas about stocks that have correlated well in the past. In order to determine whether there is an arbitrage opportunity, an investor would need to run some basic statistical tests using historical price data (see below). ValuEngine covers over 5,000 stocks and costs $20 per month.

Pairs Trading (http://www.pairstrading.com) goes well beyond this simple application because the site is designed with arbitrage in mind. The site allows users to identify the 20 most correlated pairs of stocks in over 50-day, 100-day, or two-year time frames. In addition, correlated stocks in specific industries can be requested, and Pair Trading offers some technical indicators that serve as an overlay to the basic correlation study. None of this comes cheaply; a monthly subscription runs about $100.

For investors who wish to look for their own correlated pairs, a useful tool is the historical data available from Yahoo! For every stock symbol carried by Yahoo!, there is a tab called "Historical Prices." Users can download daily, weekly, or monthly historical price data into a spreadsheet format and then run any number of statistical measures (correlation, covariance, R^2, etc.) in order to determine how closely two stocks move together.

Finally, the author of this book is also the publisher of a newsletter on market neutral investing. With a model portfolio that is updated each week, *Market Neutral Strategy* (http://www.marketneutralstrategy.com) provides independent research on stocks that are undervalued and overvalued, then combines them in a portfolio designed to generate positive returns in any environment.